The Franklin Jasper Walls Lectures

Franklin Jasper Walls, who died in 1963, bequeathed his residuary estate to the Pierpont Morgan Library to establish a lecture series in the fine arts, iconography, and archaeology, with the provision that the lectures be ultimately published in book form.

Throughout his life, Mr Walls was interested in the fine arts and in the study of art history. When the Association of Fellows of the Pierpont Morgan Library was organized in 1949, he became one of the founding members. He was particularly concerned with the Library's lecture programme, and served on the Association's Lecture Committee. Without ever revealing his testamentary plans, he followed with keen attention the design and construction of the Library's new Lecture Hall, completed a few months before his death.

Dr Strong's lectures here printed in revised and expanded form are the third series of the Franklin Jasper Walls Lectures to be published.

ROY STRONG

And when did you last see your father?

The Victorian Painter and British History

with 186 illustrations, 13 in colour

Thames and Hudson

For Benjamin and Hilda
Sonnenberg

Photographs were supplied by the galleries or other owners mentioned in the captions, except in the following cases:

A.C.L., Brussels 119; Bibliothèque Nationale, Paris 102; British Library 39, 44, 45; British Museum 41; Bulloz, Paris 33, 98; Colour 061, Salford col. pl. XII; A. C. Cooper, London 158; Cooper-Bridgeman Library col. pl. VII; Courtauld Institute of Art, University of London 6, 9, 13, 66, 120, 129, 148, 149, 151, 162, 171; Department of the Environment (Crown Copyright) 131, 137, 163, 164, 165, 170, 174; John R. Freeman & Co. Ltd, London 18, 64; Giraudon, Paris 22, 109, 110; Lauros-Giraudon, Paris col. pl. XIII; Leger Galleries, London 128; Mas, Madrid 99; Paul Mellon Centre for Studies in British Art, London 8, 67; National Portrait Gallery, London 2, 11, 12, 15, 17, 27, 38, 62, 63, 78, 103, 125, 133, 135, 140, 143, 146, 147, 152, 153, 154; Radio Times Hulton Picture Library frontispiece; Rizzoli Editore, Milan 31; Royal Academy of Arts, London 136, 139; Tom Scott, Edinburgh col. pl. IX; Eileen Tweedy, London 132; Victoria & Albert Museum, London 10, 16, 36, 50–55, 58, 59, 68, 69, 71, 72, 74, 76, 79, 84, 112, 113, 114, 124, 126, 130, 167, 173; John Webb, London col. pls. I, II, III, IV, VIII.

The following are reproduced by gracious permission of Her Majesty the Queen: 3, 4, 5, 14, 85, 88, 89, 91, 92, 95, 97, 100, 101, 121, 138.

Filmset and printed in Great Britain by
BAS Printers Limited, Over Wallop, Hampshire

Contents

Colour Plates
PAGES 97–112

Part III : Themes and Obsessions

THE ANGLO-SAXONS
George Frederick Watts, *Alfred inciting the English to resist the Danes*, 1847
PAGE 114
THE PRINCES IN THE TOWER
Sir John Everett Millais, *The Princes in the Tower*, 1878
PAGE 119
LADY JANE GREY
Paul Delaroche, *The Execution of Lady Jane Grey*, 1834
PAGE 122
MARY QUEEN OF SCOTS
Sir William Allan, *The Murder of David Rizzio*, 1833
PAGE 128
CAVALIERS AND ROUNDHEADS
William Frederick Yeames, '*And When Did You Last See Your Father?*', 1878
PAGE 136
OLIVER CROMWELL
Ford Madox Brown, *St Ives, AD 1630. Cromwell on his Farm,* 1874
PAGE 146

Epilogue : The Victorian Image
PAGE 152

APPENDIX
*Subjects from British History from the Ancient Britons to the
Outbreak of the Napoleonic Wars exhibited at the Royal Academy, 1769–1904*
PAGE 155

NOTES
PAGE 169
INDEX
PAGE 174

Foreword

THE PICTURES reproduced in this book have always held a special fascination for me because they illustrated the history books of my childhood. Owing to the War, the books available remained unchanged, so that in the late 1940s one was still receiving a trickle of what had once been a mighty flood – the visual creation of the heroic British past. Unashamedly, I have always loved these visions. Many, I suppose, will regard them as bad art and as instances of a path of image-making that the artists of the Victorian age ought never to have trodden, but for me they still have that impact which produces a sense of wonder. When I was a child, they gave me the kind of visual excitement about the past which they must have communicated originally to visitors to the Royal Academy a century before. For them history was truly a glittering pageant, full of striking and romantic tableaux, peopled by their heroes and heroines. History as taught at the university, with its preoccupation with the administrative, economic and constitutional aspects, came as a terrible shock after this idyll of splendour.

The subject returned to my mind when I was asked to deliver the Walls Lectures at the Pierpont Morgan Library in 1974, and the research carried out for those lectures forms the basis of the present book. Although an enormous amount of work has been carried out on the art of the Victorian period, very little has been attempted in relation to its iconography. An approach through the latter indeed suggests that this may be a more fruitful way of penetrating the problem than the usual biographical one.

It is as always a pleasure to recall the help of so many people. Firstly I should like to thank Charles Ryskamp, Director of the Pierpont Morgan Library, the most patient and attentive of human beings. Others come to mind: John Sunderland and his staff at the Witt Library for allowing me to plough through innumerable boxes of photographs in search of lost works; Sarah Wimbush for many calls on her time at the National Portrait Gallery Reference Archive; T. W. Mason for loaning me a valuable collection of material on the theme of Cromwell in the nineteenth century; Claude Blair for help over armour sources; Valerie Cromwell for comments on several aspects; Leonée Ormond for help over Victorian concepts of womanhood; Allen Staley and Richard Ormond for reading and making many important suggestions about the book in typescript; Garth Hall for searching out engravings in the Victoria & Albert Museum; Nicholas Bird for feeding me with mounds of books and xeroxes; my own office staff, who always have to live patiently through each book as it happens. I owe much also to Nikos Stangos, Ian Mackenzie-Kerr and Frances Davis, not only because of their enthusiasm for the subject, but because of their pertinent suggestions as to the presentation of the material.

The book owes its present form also to the generosity of a grant from the Pierpont Morgan Library. Its dedicatees were the most endearing and perfect of hosts during the delivery of the initial lectures. To the eye of my wife, who knows more about recreating the past than any of the artists in this book, my debt is as always incalculable.

ROY STRONG
Victoria & Albert Museum
December 1977

Part I
The Century of History

To us, we will own, nothing is so interesting and delightful as to contemplate steps by which the England of Doomsday Book, the England of the Curfew and the Forest Laws, the England of the Crusaders, monks, schoolmen, astrologers, serfs, outlaws, became the England we know and love, the classic ground of liberty and philosophy, the school of all knowledge, the mart of all trade.

MACAULAY, 'Sir James Mackintosh', *Essays*

For the history of our country during the last hundred and sixty years is eminently the history of physical, of moral, and of intellectual improvement.

MACAULAY, *The History of England* (1848)

C. Cousens after J. Nash, *The Maypole*: nostalgia for the Merry England of Olden Time.

1 Sir John Everett Millais, *The Boyhood of Raleigh* (1870, Tate Gallery, London).

Introduction: The Victorian Vision

THE VICTORIAN VISION of the British past evokes a glorious panorama within the mind: Boadicea rallying the Ancient British against the autocratic forces of Rome, valiant Anglo-Saxons repelling Danish invaders from the shores of Britain, King John signing the Great Charter, the foundation of our liberties, innocent child Princes murdered in the Tower, beautiful tragic Queens making their way towards the scaffold, heroic Cavaliers on the battlefield, the Jacobites fighting for a lost cause. The figures we all know so well rise from our past: the Saxon hero-king Alfred, the valiant crusader Richard I, the wicked hunchback Richard III, bluff King Hal, magnificent Elizabeth, innocent Jane Grey, doomed Mary of Scotland, sad-faced Charles I and stern-countenanced Cromwell, the Merry Monarch and Bonnie Prince Charlie. They grip the imagination as history fuses with romance. In the old-fashioned way of teaching history, which still lingered a little when I was a child during the Second World War, history began with these heroes and heroines, stories and anecdotes. But it also began with pictures – not those dry-as-dust reproductions of old portraits and tombs, dead artefacts now in museums and ancient buildings, but something much more powerful, images which swung wide a window into the past, made it human, living and real. Millais's *Boyhood of Raleigh* (1870), in which the future poet and explorer listens to an old sailor telling of the voyages of his youth, made the Elizabethan age of discovery thrilling to me. Delaroche's picture (1830) of the young Edward V and his brother, the little Princes in the Tower, chilled the spine in anticipation of their imminent and horrible end. Frederick Goodall's *An Episode of the Happier Days of Charles I* (1853), in which the tragic King, his beautiful Queen and even more adorable children sail down-river on a summer's day, made me a Cavalier for life.

Until two generations ago, these pictures were part of the visual experience of every child brought up on British history. Now they have long been banished from school textbooks as inaccurate, misleading and unauthentic. The best-selling prints made after them that once adorned the walls of Victorian and Edwardian nurseries and schoolrooms have been taken down and relegated to the attic. Worst of all, art historians have come to regard these creations as dreadful aberrations which ought never to have happened,[1] and in public museums and galleries most surviving examples have been consigned to the stores, rolled up or even, in some instances, deliberately destroyed as worthless rubbish. An intensely creative part of British nineteenth-century painting has been dismissed as a dead end. But was it?

The studies which form the basis of this book began for me almost as a personal indulgence. I happen to like this sort of painting. On the lowest level, there is something incredible about an artist's ability to transport the onlooker back in time, give him glimpses of his heroes and heroines, recapture the modes and manners of distant ages. This may not, of course, be art, but it was something which obsessed the nineteenth-century painters and which they were extremely good at doing. Again, one wants to know why. What made them interested in some periods and not in others? What was the relationship between contemporary history painting and history writing? What was the impact of Sir Walter Scott and his successors as exponents of the historical novel? What was the connection between the rise of antiquarianism and the increasing pictorial accuracy of the painters of the past? What, overall, was the role of this national historic mythology in the make-up of the Victorian mind and imagination? These questions have to be answered before one can even understand, let alone pass judgment. Some readers may wonder why I choose to isolate this particular Victorian vision as against any other – their view of classical antiquity, for example, or of English literature, or even of events within living memory – but I believe that if we are ever to understand the motivation of art in the Victorian age we must concentrate on one aspect and analyse its iconography with a seriousness which until recently has been totally denied to it. This is what this book sets out to do: to tackle just one thread of image-making, but that perhaps the most nostalgic and potent thread of all, in British nineteenth-century painting.

The painting of Victorian England is for most of us unthinkable without the familiar milestones created by the art historians of the last generation, that generation which rediscovered the art of the nineteenth century. Guided by the Berensonian belief that art is really little more than the evolution of style, we now think in set terms of the Pre-Raphaelites, of Morris and his circle, of the resurrected personalities of Millais, Rossetti, Burne-Jones, Ford Madox Brown or Lord Leighton. These are the safe loadstones of the historian, and beyond them there exists a kind of condescension to the other figures of Victorian painting. We cultivate third-rate Pre-Raphaelite artists because we approve of their milieu – a world of images echoing the obsession of our own painters with private as against public mythologies – but we ignore the sheer quality and brilliance of C. W. Cope's or E. M. Ward's great historical set pieces in the Houses of Parliament. Indeed, I would go further and say that the technique of many of the figures we now place in the top rank of Victorian painting is often lax and feeble in comparison with that of several of the artists whose totally neglected works I shall go on to discuss.

The present pantheon of Victorian art has been created largely through literature. Like the Bloomsbury circle, which again has given prominence to third-rate painters, Rossetti and Morris are known to us as writers and even more as people who led romantic and often highly unconventional private lives. I believe this approach to Victorian painting, with its heavy bias towards the literary and biographical, to be a wrong one. Through it we have succeeded in creating a history of Victorian art as selective and biased as the Victorians' own attitudes towards their own past. We can no longer afford to accept this distortion. The serious consideration of the paintings dealt with in this book may not be a welcome innovation, particularly to those who still regard the subject-matter of Victorian painting as something for amusement but certainly not for analysis in depth. I feel, on the contrary, that these pictures should leave us with a sense of awe and wonder. There is something deeply moving and courageous about the confidence with which they evoke the visible past. It starts from a premise of self-possession and of security within the present, totally unknown to us, which enabled the painter's brush for a brief period to defy time as it moved triumphantly through it.

History Writing and History Painting

THE ROOTS of these childhood favourites lie, of course, in the eighteenth century. The initial desire to paint scenes from British history reflected not only a change in attitude to our national past, but also the alignment, in the second half of the century, of the aspirations of British artists with the rise of antiquarian studies. Paintings dealing with British history can be fairly conveniently categorized into three main groups which will give us a handy framework in which to move. The first I would define as 'Gothick Picturesque', by which I mean the earliest essays using noble and uplifting incidents from British history by artists such as Robert Edge Pine, John Hamilton Mortimer, Francis Wheatley or Angelica Kauffmann. As a phase it began after 1760, reached its apogee on the walls of the Royal Academy in the 1770s and 1780s, and came to a close in 1806 with the end of Robert Bowyer's Historic Gallery, which had been a major source of patronage in the 1790s through the commissioning of paintings for an illustrated edition of David Hume's *History of England*. Out of this sprang a second phase, 'Artist-Antiquarian'. This used the same mind-improving subject-matter from the past, but applied to it the discoveries of the antiquarians, thereby lifting its productions on to a new level of pictorial accuracy. Artist-Antiquarian had its beginnings in the achievements of Gavin Hamilton, Benjamin West and John Singleton Copley, reached a new level of historical veracity in France in the work of Paul Delaroche and found in Victorian England its prime exponents in artists such as E. M. Ward and C. W. Cope in the 1850s and 1860s. Eight years after the demise of the Bowyer Gallery came the publication of Sir Walter Scott's *Waverley*, an event which led directly to the development of a third format, 'Intimate Romantic' – that is, paintings which

take as their subject-matter personal, domestic glimpses of earlier ages, the great of the past caught informally or even, beyond this, the past painted purely for itself as an enchanted idyll. Through this the past was able to inspire the brushes not only of history painters but also of the exponents of genre.

Origins: British history, Vertue and Kent

The Gothick Picturesque phase was born of two movements in eighteenth-century England, the revival of history writing and the desire of British artists to fulfil academic theories on the primacy of history painting over any other genre. With regard to the first, it was not in fact until the third quarter of the century that the writing of history revived in England; when it did, it began to resemble history as we know it today rather than the chronicle or politico-religious polemic of the previous century.[1] 'History is philosophy teaching by examples,' wrote Bolingbroke, pioneering this new attitude in his *Letters on the Study and Use of History* (1735).[2] Through the study of history, and in particular of modern history from the fifteenth century onwards, man was able to gain not only ethical guidance but knowledge and judgment upon which he could act both immediately and in the future. This switch of emphasis was immensely important for shifting the focus of historical subject-matter away from classical antiquity. David Hume, William Robertson and Edward Gibbon represented the climax of history writing in eighteenth-century Britain; its masterpiece was Gibbon's *Decline and Fall of the Roman Empire* (1776). All three authors saw history as a search for truth, a pursuit of underlying political and philosophical motives. All three too shared an Augustan condescension to the past. History was fascinating for its lessons to the present, but never for itself alone. The subject-matter of Gibbon has no importance for our national saga. From the point of view of the development of scenes from British history, the two key books drawn upon by artists for subject-matter were the histories written by a Frenchman, Paul de Rapin-Thoyras, and by David Hume.

Rapin lived for a time in England, but wrote his history of the country after he had left and taken up residence in Germany and Holland. This was published in ten volumes between 1723 and 1727 and translated into English in 1726–31, and until superseded in 1754 by Hume's *History* was regarded as the standard narrative history of England from the remotest times. Rapin's central thesis was that the English monarchy had always been a limited one and that the liberty of the subject had only from time to time been violated by tyrannical kings. The most important edition of his work was that of 1743–7 illustrated by Charles Grignion, Hubert François Gravelot and the artist and antiquary George

2 George Vertue, imaginary scene of the abdication of Richard II. Detail of engraving from Paul de Rapin-Thoyras, *The History of England* (1726–31).

Vertue, who were commissioned to adorn the seven folio volumes with maps, genealogical tables and 'the Heads and Monuments of the Kings'. In these engravings, the renaissance in history writing joins hands with the revival of antiquarianism. As I will demonstrate in the next chapter, the rise of antiquarian studies in eighteenth-century England had a profound effect on history painting. Writers of history gave painters subjects to depict, but antiquarians gave them the means whereby to carry out such recreations. Vertue's portraits are thoroughly researched from tombs or 'antient pictures', even if in the process they are reinterpreted in a later stylistic idiom. Sometimes, too, if we examine his rococo borders we find he has inset scenes from the lives of the persons depicted. Beneath Richard II's portrait, for instance, based on the famous full-length in Westminster Abbey, he has drawn an imaginary scene of the King's abdication. In these insets Vertue, as a trained antiquary, shows a remarkable grasp of period reconstruction, far in advance of the history painters of the Gothick Picturesque. The main sections of Rapin's *History of England* are also preceded by small headpieces in which certain scenes from British history – seeds of the Victorian vision, destined to have a long and extraordinary life – made their artistic début: Rowena and Vortigern, for instance, the signing of Magna Carta or the trial of Queen Catherine.

If Vertue played a crucial role in translating history and antiquarianism into art, so also did William Kent.[3] With Kent's work we enter into the intellectual circle which centred on George II's Queen, Caroline, 'for Love of Arts and Piety Renown'd'. The Queen was primarily interested in religion, philosophy and letters, and the visual arts were used by her to give tangible form to her intellectual attitudes and cults. Kent was ideal for her because his genius lay in being able to translate into visual terms the philosophical and aesthetic ideas of others. For Caroline he executed three buildings in her garden at Richmond Palace, a thatched cottage called Merlin's Cave, a hermitage or grotto in the Gothick style and a third building which was to contain busts of all the kings of England since William I. The Queen's interest in the British

3 William Kent, *The Battle of Agincourt* (*c.* 1729–30, Royal Collection).

past found expression also in the decoration of her dressing-room at Kensington Palace. Here she framed and hung the celebrated Holbein drawings which she had rediscovered at the back of a bureau; here, too, were gathered together for the first time all the earliest portraits of monarchs in the royal collection. She even purchased such portraits.[4] To these she added a set of three pictures commissioned from Kent in 1729–30, depicting scenes in the life of Henry V: the Battle of Agincourt, the meeting of the victorious English King and the Queen of France and, finally, the King's marriage to the French Princess, Catherine.[5] Painted a year before Kent's first essay in the Gothick style, the rebuilt Clock Court Gatehouse at Hampton Court, they represent the first serious attempt to depict accurately scenes from medieval history.

His departure from the treatment of such themes by painters within the still vigorous baroque tradition of Verrio and Thornhill is so deliberate that, although feeble as pictures, they are manifestos as to the correct treatment of historical subjects. On a first glance it would, of course, be difficult to guess that this was what he was aiming at. In *The Battle of Agincourt* the landscape is reminiscent of Claude Lorrain and the combatants are arrayed in a hopeless confusion of inaccurate armour. In the middle we can identify Henry V only because he has the arms of England blazoned on his armour and he vanquishes an opponent, possibly meant for the Duke of Alençon, who wears the fleur-de-lis. Nor is there much advance in the canvas of the meeting of Henry with the Queen of France. Once more we have an odd assortment of

4, 5 The start of historical research: detail of Kent's *Meeting between Henry V and the Queen of France* (*c.* 1729–30). The likeness of the King was based by the artist on an authentic portrait *(below)*. (Both Royal Collection.) See also colour plate 1.

armour, the ladies attired in nondescript robes and the action backed by exotic tents. But, in spite of these vagaries, the King's head is based on one of the two portraits we know Caroline owned.[6] This in itself is significant. The urge to research the subject and integrate such discoveries into the composition was there. And this was new. Kent was aware that the Middle Ages were different, but he had not as yet the means to put together just how different. Crude and wooden though these canvases are, they foretell all that was to come for almost the next two hundred years.

Gothick Picturesque

Vertue and Kent were central figures in the propagation of the idea of the British past as heroic. They were also artists turned antiquaries; they knew that the past has to be researched before it can be reproduced. In the case of the mainstream of painters I would categorize as exponents of the Gothick Picturesque, this approach to the British past was purely incidental. And it is to these and to the proliferation of historical subjects that we must now turn our attention.

Late-eighteenth-century painters were primarily drawn to the British past because it provided a whole new range of subjects – national rather than classical – fit for those aspiring to the genre of history. Inheriting the primacy of history painting in the hierarchy of genres from the French Academy of the previous century, all theorists from Richardson down to Opie, Barry and Haydon adhered to this fundamental tenet. In heroic action and perfect physical form man could see his own ethical and corporeal potential. Such an art called for scenes of bravery, self-sacrifice, noble love and triumphant faith. The principles which led to this search for a new, meaningful nationalistic iconography are admirably summed up in a letter written by Benjamin West to Charles Willson Peale in 1809:

. . . the art of painting has powers to dignify man, by transmitting to posterity his noble actions, and his mental powers, to be viewed in those invaluable

6 F. Aliamet after Robert Edge Pine, *The Surrender of Calais to Edward III* (1760, engraved 1762).

lessons of religion, love of country, and morality; such subjects are worthy of the pencil, they are worthy of being placed in view as the most instructive records to a rising generation.[7]

Such a theoretical position was to dominate British art and artists for a century and provide the aesthetic basis for their recreations of the past. Its culmination was the mid-Victorian cult of High Art – the idea that the greatest art could only be expressed in the form of monumental commissions – which reached fruition in the competitions for the decoration of the new Houses of Parliament.

History painting really began in 1760 with the first exhibition of the Society of Artists, an annual event which led to the creation of the Royal Academy in 1768. Both gave British artists for the first time the opportunity of exhibiting in public, and the importance attached to history painting was emphasized by the two premiums, one of a hundred guineas and one of fifty, offered by the Society each year for subjects taken from English history. In 1760 the first premium was won by Robert Edge Pine for his canvas *The Surrender of Calais to Edward III*. Pine won the prize again three years later for his *Canute reproving his Courtiers for their Impious Flattery* (unlocated, engraved Aliamet), which Walpole described as 'much the best'.[8] Both were on the subject of monarchy, the first celebrating the King's mercy on the intercession by his Queen, Philippa, for the lives of the burghers of Calais, the second Canute's reproof to his courtiers for

7 Robert Edge Pine, *Earl Warren making Reply to the Writ commonly called 'Quo Warranto' in the Reign of Edward I, 1278* (1771, National Trust, Sudbury Hall).

their flattery, asserting that the essence of monarchy lay in the attribute of humility. John Sunderland has pointed out Pine's sympathy with anti-monarchical currents in sixties' politics, and suggested that the subjects were chosen to draw a political moral against reassertions of the royal prerogative.[9] This may certainly be true, but they could as easily be read the other way, as commemorations of royal virtues. The ambiguity of interpretation was no doubt deliberate. If, for instance, the subject of the burghers of Calais was generally considered to be anti-monarchical, it would hardly have been included by the Tory-oriented West in the series on the wars of Edward III painted in the eighties for George III's Audience Chamber.

The *Canute* painting was exhibited again by Pine in 1768, and in 1771 came his last picture drawn from British history, an unfinished canvas drawn from an incident in Rapin, *Earl Warren making Reply to the Writ commonly called 'Quo Warranto' in the Reign of Edward I, 1278*. By that year Pine was deeply engaged in the cause of John Wilkes, so the choice of a subject which dealt with the infringement of civil liberties in late-thirteenth-century England was clearly

intended as an outspoken criticism of royal pretensions. Edward I had commissioned an inquiry into all encroachments on the royal demesnes, but his commissioners went too far and began to question titles of estates which had passed from father to son for several generations. Earl Warren, asked to show his titles, drew a rusty sword from its scabbard and said: 'This is the instrument by which my Ancestors gained their Estate, and by this I will keep it as long as I live.'[10] This being reported to Edward I, he prudently annulled the commission. Pine has grandly conceived the composition in terms of a Judgment of Solomon, Esther before Ahasuerus or Christ before Pilate, but it cannot be said to have much merit as a painting. Pine did not return to history again, but turned to illustrating Shakespeare, again without success, and finally left England to seek his fortunes in the newly formed republic of the United States.[11]

The second prize in 1763 went to Pine's pupil, John Hamilton Mortimer, then aged twenty-two and notorious for his passion for bizarre subject-matter. The picture was *Edward the Confessor stripping his Mother of her Effects* (unlocated).[12] 'Edward's Figure', Walpole wrote, 'strong and bold, but not characteristic and too large in proportion to the rest, most of which is bad.'[13] The allusions are obscure, but again, as in the case of Pine's *Quo Warranto*, the general theme seems to be British liberties, the accession of the saintly Edward the Confessor being billed as the return of the freedom-loving Anglo-Saxon monarchy in place of the hegemony of the Danes. Edward's mother, Emma, was Norman by birth and had married successively Ethelred the Unready and the Danish Canute. She, therefore, with her preference for her second husband and her children by him, represents the Danish interest, whereas Edward, her son by her first marriage, stands for the Anglo-Saxon.[14]

The year after, Mortimer took the first prize with his *St Paul preaching to the Britons* (1764, Town Hall, High Wycombe), an excursion into the mythology of the Church of England. Mortimer did not return for another thirteen years to British history, and then, at the age of thirty-six, he painted three pictures: *King John delivering Magna Carta to the Barons* (c. 1776),

Vortigern and Rowena (*c.* 1776) and *The Battle of Agincourt* (*c.* 1776, private collection). The last, a heroic battle scene, needs no explanation. Magna Carta, of course, symbolizes the birth of representative government, a reassertion of Anglo-Saxon liberties against the bondage and slavery of feudalism: 'And thus', wrote Hume, 'the establishment of the great charter . . . became a kind of epoch in the constitution.'[15] From whatever political stance it was viewed, it was a moment to be celebrated, and the pictorial apotheosis of the British Constitution, which reached its climax a century later, began in earnest with this canvas by Mortimer.

Vortigern and Rowena, however, take us on a more exotic voyage into the past. This was a subject essayed by Henry Fuseli in 1769 (Kunsthaus, Zürich) and by Angelica Kauffmann the year after (engraved Ryder, 1803).[16] Mortimer's picture, like those of Pine, was a monarchical morality. Vortigern was the British Prince who had invited the Saxons, headed by Hengist and Horsa, into the country in order to defend the Britons against the ravages of the Picts and Scots. Subsequently, however, Hengist used the charms of his niece Rowena to further his ambitions, and this is the scene Mortimer depicts. At a great entertainment given by

8 John Hamilton Mortimer, *King John delivering Magna Carta to the Barons* (*c.* 1776, private collection).

9 John Hamilton Mortimer, *Vortigern and Rowena* (*c.* 1776, unlocated).

Hengist, Rowena was bidden by him to take their royal guest a cup of wine. Vortigern was so overcome by her loveliness that he refused to drink from the cup until Rowena had touched it with her lips. This she did, after which he drank and kissed her passionately. Although already married, Vortigern divorced his wife and married Rowena, ceding Kent to Hengist in return. So he began on the downward path which led to his deposition and banishment to a life of solitude as an object of contempt.[17]

Pine and Mortimer had set a pattern, choosing subjects which were to be repeated time without number in the next hundred years. That they were influenced by scenes depicted in Rapin's *History* and other illustrated histories cannot be doubted. From about 1770 onwards there appeared a whole succession of histories which,

however wildly inaccurate and feeble their illustrations, must have done much to accustom the public to the idea of 'seeing' the past.[18] To those essaying the Grand Manner in painting, the subject-matter thus disseminated must indeed have given material for thought: 'King Edmund the First assassinated by Leolf the Robber, while celebrating the Feast of St Augustine in the Church of Puckle, Gloucestershire' or 'Judge Jefferies in the disguise of a sailor seized at Wapping' evoke the ambience of the penny dreadful rather than the ennobling pages of our national history. Scenes from British history, therefore, proliferated greatly during the last thirty years of the eighteenth century in the work of Mather Brown, Richard Westall, Thomas Stothard, John Downman, James Northcote and John Opie, who systematically excavated the past for scenes of heroism and patriotic self-sacrifice.

The painting of such canvases was encouraged in the final years of the century by two major schemes of patronage, the first Alderman Boydell's Shakespeare Gallery, inaugurated in 1785 with the explicit purpose of aiding the formation of a British school of history painting, and the second, much less well known or investigated, Robert Bowyer's Historic Gallery in Pall Mall, a collection of paintings of scenes from British history commissioned for a large folio edition of Hume issued between 1793 and 1806. The Boydell scheme, which belongs to another iconographic stream, that of illustrations to literature, has been studied in some detail by T. S. R. Boase, W. Moelwyn Merchant and Winifred Friedman.[19] Bowyer, however, remains to be examined in depth. More than a hundred pictures were painted for him by artists who included Gavin Hamilton, Henry Fuseli, James Northcote, Robert Smirke, Benjamin West, Henry Tresham, Richard Westall, Francis Wheatley, John Francis Rigaud, Henry Singleton, Philippe de Loutherbourg and Maria Cosway. Bowyer's work was designed 'to raise the passions, to fire the mind with emulation of heroic deeds, or to inspire it with detestation of criminal deeds'. Although influenced in its subject-matter by Rapin, the book in its turn contained a repertory of scenes decisive for the canon of the Victorian vision: Queen Margaret of Anjou and the robber, Lady Elizabeth Grey entreating Edward IV to protect her children, Lady Jane Grey's reluctance to accept the crown and her execution, Mary Queen of Scots' escape from Lochleven and execution, and Lord William Russell's farewell to his wife, were to recur again and again on the walls of the Royal Academy.[20] As a group, they were definitive for what I have categorized as the Gothick Picturesque view of the British past. They reveal in addition the ambitions of artists whom we now think of in quite another context. Who would ever, for instance, associate Francis Wheatley, immortalized by his sentimental prints of the 'Cries of London', with canvases on the subjects of *Alfred in the House of the Neatherd* (1792, private collection) and *The Death of Richard II*

10 A. Smith after Francis Wheatley, *The Death of Richard II* (1795).

(1795)? It is irresistible to quote a contemporary reaction to the latter: 'If Mr Wheatley ever prays, we hope he will repeat in the words of the Litany "to be defended from all privy conspiracy and rebellion, from battle and murder, and from sudden death" '.[21]

An analysis of subjects from both Bowyer's Historic Gallery and the Royal Academy reflects an overwhelming preoccupation with the Middle Ages; scenes from Tudor and Stuart history run neck and neck in second place, while incursions into remoter antiquity in the form of Boadicea and Caractacus are fewer and represent little more than an attempt to find purely classical Roman scenes from British history. The choice and the repetitious nature of the subject-matter are not without interest. Three incidents in British history positively obsessed the late-

11-13 The Gothick Picturesque approach to history. *Top left,* John Francis Rigaud, *Lady Elizabeth Grey petitioning King Edward IV for her Husband's Lands* (1796, unlocated). *Top right,* John Downman, *Edward IV on a Visit to the Duchess of Bedford, is enamoured of Lady Elizabeth Grey* (1797, unlocated). *Below,* after John Opie, *Lady Elizabeth Grey entreating Edward IV to protect her Children* (1798).

eighteenth-century artist: King Edward IV's encounter with Lady Elizabeth Grey, incidents connected with the story and the eventual death of the Princes in the Tower, Edward V and his brother the Duke of York (also, of course, relevant for those whose approach to history was through literature), and finally scenes from the life and, more particularly, the death of Mary Queen of Scots. Samuel Wale (1760 and 1763), Angelica Kauffmann (1776), John Francis Rigaud (1796), John Downman (1797) and John Opie (1798) all depicted the encounter of the Yorkist King Edward IV and the widow of Sir John Grey. David Allen (1791), Gavin Hamilton (1776), John Howes (1786), John Opie (1787), Richard Westall (1789 and 1791), John Francis Rigaud (1791 and 1792), John Graham (1787, 1788 and 1792), Samuel Medley (1793) and Mather Brown (1788) tackled moments in the life of Mary Queen of Scots, and Joseph Highmore (1769), Samuel Wale (1769 and 1775), James Northcote (1786) and Henry Singleton (1797) depicted incidents leading up to and including the murder of the Princes in the Tower. In addition, the celebrated intercession of Edward III's Queen, Philippa, for the lives of the burghers of Calais was painted by Robert Edge Pine (1760), Benjamin West (1788) and Richard Westall (1790).

Even if the quality of these paintings, where they are still traceable, is in the main depressing, the explosion in subject-matter was extraordinary. Within a wider context, it was paralleled from 1760 onwards by similar developments in other fields: the discovery of new literary sources for art (Milton, Shakespeare, Spenser, Dante, medieval legends and romances); a more intensive study of the phenomena of nature, whether expressed in Stubbs's analytical drawings of the horse or William Hodges' records of Cook's voyages; new emphases within religious imagery on the Old Testament and the Apocalypse; a realization of the actuality of the world of classical antiquity as a result of the archaeological finds of Herculaneum and Pompeii; a curiosity regarding every aspect of the present, whether in the form of great events or humble occupations; and over all, animating this furore of originality, a release of the emotions, made possible by the empirical philosophy of Locke and his successors, leading to an examination of every facet of the human psychology. The national past is just one idiosyncratic thread in this pattern of ideas and obsessions which led up to the romantic movement.[22]

It would not add greatly to our understanding of this phenomenon as it affected subject-matter from British history if we examined each of the main themes in detail; I propose simply to take one as an instance of the method and approach of the Gothick Picturesque School as a whole. Edward IV's encounter with Lady Elizabeth Grey is a particularly well documented example because so many of the pictures are still identifiable. Incorporated into the standard narrative histories of both Rapin and Hume is the story of the Yorkist King Edward IV's passion for Elizabeth Woodville, the widow of Sir John Grey, a lady 'remarkable for the grace and beauty of her person, as well as for other amiable accomplishments'. Here is an abridgement of Hume's account of their meeting:

The king came accidentally to the house after a hunting party ... and as the occasion seemed favourable for obtaining some grace from this gallant monarch, the young widow flung herself at his feet, and with many tears entreated him to take pity on her impoverished and distressed children. The sight of so much beauty in affliction strongly affected the amorous Edward; love stole insensibly into his heart under the guise of compassion ... He raised her from the ground with assurances of favour ... and he was soon reduced, in his turn, to the posture and style of a supplicant at the feet of Elizabeth.[23]

The widow, of course, honourably resisted his advances, so that the King finally asked her to marry him. It was a perfect subject for the close of the eighteenth century, combining a scene fit for a romance by Mrs Radcliffe with visual spectacle akin to the family of Darius imploring mercy of Alexander.

John Francis Rigaud, in 1796, set the scene in a Strawberry Hill Gothick hall, with Lady Elizabeth and her children flinging themselves at the feet of Edward IV – a dramatic tableau conceived almost wholly in terms of decoration. A year later John Downman, heavily influenced by Rigaud, delineated exactly the same type of interior: within it the King clutches his heart, while Lady Elizabeth, on her knees, gestures frantically both towards him and to her children, who literally hold up her petition for the restoration of her husband's lands. Anything less like life in England in the last quarter of the fifteenth century would be difficult to compile. These pictures are the essence of the Gothick Picturesque. There is no attempt at correct historical research on portraiture, dress or architectural setting. A portrait of Edward was available in the illustrated Rapin, but no one bothered to look. Any feeling for the Middle Ages demonstrated here belongs firmly to the world of Strawberry Hill and the vagaries of historical dress as introduced by David Garrick to the stage. When the scene reappeared on the walls of the Royal Academy a year later in John Opie's version (1798) for Bowyer's Historic Gallery, a chiaroscuro treatment heavily indebted to the Bolognese School, there was no development in approach.[24] This may be a better picture, but Elizabeth could literally be any aristocratic lady of the 1790s in a state of distress. Indeed, she looks more like Marie Antoinette than Elizabeth Woodville. Nor, over a decade later, did that prolific illustrator of the British past, Robert Smirke, show any advance. He drew little more than a fancy-dress tableau suitable for any Gothick novel of the day. The important point is this: if any of these four artists had wanted to recreate the past more accurately, he could easily have done so. Benjamin West and John Singleton Copley alone pursued the incipient antiquarianism of Vertue and Kent in the late eighteenth century, and it was from them that a new style, which I shall call Artist-Antiquarian, flowed down into the Victorian age. Exponents of the Gothick Picturesque ignored the antiquarian implications of their subject-matter, and cheerfully indulged in a repertory of pasteboard architecture across which they swagged draperies to conceal their lack of knowledge of the structure of the historical styles. They had no clue as to accuracy in dress, which rarely rises above an orgy of ecclesiastical vestments, slashed doublets, plumed hats, frills, ruffs and armour thrown together to serve for virtually any period from the Anglo-Saxons down to Elizabeth Tudor. This Gothick Picturesque evocation of the British past was as charming and as insubstantial as a gazebo by Batty Langley. By the close of the Napoleonic Wars it had vanished, vanquished by the dual forces of the serious antiquarian standards being introduced to history painting and the ethos of romanticism epitomized by Scott and the historical novel.

The creators of the Artist-Antiquarian: Hamilton, West and Copley

If the subject-matter of the Gothick Picturesque artists was a vivid reflection of one aspect of the revolutionary currents in British eighteenth-century painting, the application to these subjects of standards of antiquarian accuracy represented another. This search belonged to a wider canvas, of which scenes from British history formed only a part. The investigation and reconstruction of the past was one facet of the movement, stemming from the Enlightenment, which animated the whole realm of knowledge and experience in late-eighteenth-century Brit-

ain. And it is crucial to grasp that those artists who were pioneers in incorporating the latest archaeological discoveries into their paintings of the classical world were the very same who pioneered historical accuracy in their evocations of the medieval, post-medieval and modern periods.

First amongst these was Gavin Hamilton, whose six illustrations to Homer, begun about 1761, were seminal not only for the neoclassical style as such but also for the use of the most recent archaeological evidence.[25] In *Priam pleading with Achilles for the Body of Hector* (c. 1761–5, Tate Gallery), for example, as Dora Wiebenson has pointed out, he made extensive use of ancient representations of the subject, the composition almost certainly being based on the relief sculpture in the Villa Borghese.[26] Hamilton is therefore a key figure, the more so because he did make one solitary expedition into British history, *Mary Queen of Scots resigning her Crown*, which was commissioned in 1765 by James Boswell, painted in Italy and exhibited at the Royal Academy in 1776. Not only was this the first major visual manifestation of the romantic cult of the Scottish Queen – a Victorian obsession – but in it Hamilton attempted to recreate sixteenth-century Scotland with the same thoroughness that he bestowed on the worlds of ancient Greece and Rome. The figure of Mary is taken from an engraving of a portrait then thought to be of her in the famous collection of Dr Richard Meade, while the hirsute man in the background is based on the traditional figure of a wild Scotsman as found in any of a number of manuals of costumes of the nations issued during the second half of the sixteenth century.[27]

Such an attitude towards accuracy was enormously extended in the work of Benjamin West, not only in the sphere of the national past but also when dealing with the events of the present. *The Death of General Wolfe* (RA 1771, versions in the National Gallery, Ottawa and the Royal Collection) accorded to a contemporary general the kind of apotheosis normally reserved for the heroes of antiquity, but the artist reinforced the potency of the image by clothing the characters in contemporary dress.[28] At the time this was cause for comment, and provoked

152

14–16 Artist–Antiquarian versus Gothick Picturesque.
Above, Benjamin West, *Edward III and the Burghers of Calais* (1789, Royal Collection). *Below left,* John Hall after Edward Edwards, *The Surrender of Calais to King Edward III* (1776); *below right,* A. Smith after Robert Smirke, *The Surrender of Calais* (1796).

the famous intervention by Reynolds to stop such an innovation, to which West is supposed to have retorted that the event had taken place in the eighteenth century and 'at a period of time when no such nations [i.e. Greece and Rome], nor heroes in their costumes, any longer existed'.[29] The sensational success of this picture led to the proliferation of scenes from contemporary history, executed always, of course, according to the idealizing tenets of the history painter, but with the setting and dress of the present.

In doing this, West was only extending the principle which both he and Hamilton had applied earlier to scenes from antiquity. West had initially established his reputation in England as a prime exponent of neoclassicism in the vein of Hamilton seven years before with his picture *The Landing of Agripinna at Brundisium with the Ashes of Germanicus* (1766, Yale University Art Gallery). The cavalcade here seems to have been based on the *Ara Pacis Augustae*, fragments of which were then in the Uffizi, and is set against an architectural background derived from the harbour façade of Diocletian's Palace at Split as it appeared in Robert Adam's *The Ruins of the Palace of the Emperor Diocletian, at Spalato* (1764).[30] West was concerned not only with the spirit but, where he was able, with the actuality of the past as revealed by the latest archaeological research.

These instances of his accuracy in contemporary and classical scenes went hand in hand with its application to the British past in a thoroughgoing manner unequalled by any other artist until the Victorian period. From 1778 until his death in 1820, West covered virtually every period of British history. In 1778 he exhibited a scene of mind-boggling obscurity from the Anglo-Saxon period, derived from a passage in the *Itinerary* of the Tudor antiquary John Leland: *William de Albanac presents his three Daughters (naked) to Alfred, the third King of Mercia* (unlocated). The following year he painted *Alfred the Great divides his Loaf with a Pilgrim* (RA 1779, Stationers' Company), in 1780 he moved on to the thirteenth century in *Alexander, the third King of Scotland rescued from the Fury of a Stag by the Intrepidity of Colin Fitzgerald* (unlocated), and at about the same time to the

Civil War period in *Oliver Cromwell ordering the Mace to be taken away* (1783). From 1787 onwards he was working on his most significant series, on the French wars of Edward III, commissioned by George III for the Audience Chamber at Windsor Castle. His other historical pictures included two for Bowyer's Historic Gallery – *The Citizens of London presenting the Crown to William* (1808, Walker Art Gallery, Liverpool) and *Prince John's Submission to Richard I* (unlocated) – and a group on late Stuart England, *The Landing of Charles II* (unlocated), *The Battle of the Boyne* (RA 1780, unlocated) and *The Destruction of the French Fleet at La Hogue* (RA 1780, National Gallery, Washington D.C.).[31]

As in the cases of *Wolfe* and *Agripinna*, there is a new level of pictorial accuracy here which can be illustrated by the artist's approach to a single scene from his Edward III series, that depicting *Edward III and the Burghers of Calais* (1789). A comparison with versions by Edward Edwards or Robert Smirke of the same scene demonstrates immediately West's enormous advance in archaeological accuracy. As I will show in Part II, he had consulted the works of the antiquarian Joseph Strutt for information on fourteenth-century dress, weapons and armour. A contemporary records that West's historical research sometimes led him 'to depart from the first plans, as he obtained new historical facts, particularly in the armorial bearings'.[32]

In 1794, to take another instance, West exhibited *Queen Elizabeth going in Procession to St Paul's Cathedral after the Destruction of the Spanish Armada*. The Queen is very carefully depicted, both likeness and dress being the results of a study of contemporary portraits and engravings. Lord Burghley, who bows reverently to her, wears a skullcap and bonnet and leans on his Lord Treasurer's white wand of office. In this case West has succeeded in turning almost full circle the well-known portrait of Burghley as a white-haired Garter Knight. A comparison with Richard Westall's *The Earl of Essex's first Interview with Queen Elizabeth after his Return from Ireland* (1789) reveals the vast difference in approach and intent between the Gothick Picturesque and the Artist-Antiquarian treatments of the Elizabethan age.

17-20 Benjamin West's *Queen Elizabeth going in Procession to St Paul's Cathedral after the Destruction of the Spanish Armada* (1794, unlocated) reveals the study of contemporary sources: *below left*, Francis Delaram's engraving after Nicholas Hilliard's portrait of Queen Elizabeth I (*c.* 1617–19, British Museum; detail), and *below centre*, the portrait of William Cecil, Lord Burghley attributed to Marcus Gheeraerts (after 1585, National Portrait Gallery, London; detail). By comparison, Richard Westall's *The Earl of Essex's first Interview with Queen Elizabeth after his return from Ireland* (1789, Laing Art Gallery and Museum, Newcastle-upon-Tyne) is a purely imaginary scene.

John Singleton Copley, even more than West, established himself as a leading exponent of heroic scenes from contemporary British political and military life. *Watson and the Shark* (1778, Detroit Institute of Arts), *The Death of the Earl of Chatham* (1779–81, Tate Gallery), *The Death of Major Peirson* (begun 1782, Tate Gallery) and *The Siege of Gibraltar* (1783–91, Guildhall Art Gallery) are all detailed recreations of current events with elaborate topographical, portrait and costume research.[33] Like West, Copley also painted religious subjects and episodes from British history. In the last category, his three great contributions were *Charles I demanding in the House of Commons the Five Impeached Members* (1782–95), first exhibited to the public in May 1795, *Monmouth before James II refusing to give the Names of his Accomplices* (Fogg Art Museum, Harvard University), painted at about the same time, and *The Offer of the Crown to Lady Jane Grey* (1806–7).

144

It is only necessary to take one of these – the first – to realize the important part which Copley played in the change of approach to history painting. Jules Prown has traced stage by stage the compilation of this picture, from Alderman Boydell's initial approach in 1781 to its completion fourteen years later.[34] The subject was chosen as being the most significant of the many confrontations between the King and the opposition which led up to the outbreak of the Civil War in 1642. Charles I had sent a message demanding the five Members of Parliament who had openly defied him, only to receive an evasive reply, so that he himself went down to the House to demand their arrest. The King asked the Speaker, Sir John Lenthall, whether any of the accused was present. This is the pregnant moment Copley depicts, just before the Speaker's famous reply: 'I have, Sir, neither eyes to see, nor tongue to speak, in this place, but as the house is pleased to direct me, whose servant I am here.'

In tackling this composition Copley's first move was to write to Edward Malone, Shakespearian scholar and historian, who, in a long letter dated 4 January 1782, provided him with a mass of historical data. The picture contains no less than fifty-eight portraits, thirty-six of which

were listed by Malone with references as to where Copley could find authentic likenesses in paintings, engravings and medals. Malone, who may actually have suggested the subject to Copley, stated that the best moment to depict would be when Lenthall, kneeling before the King, was about to reply. He even went on to explain where certain of the characters would have been in the House at the time.

With Copley, as with West, we are suddenly in a very different world. The artist has become an antiquarian, seeking the advice of scholars for historical information and correct visual detail.[35] As a result, it was to take over a decade for Copley to put this extraordinary picture together. Periods prior to the eighteenth century were a great deal more troublesome to recreate than were classical or contemporary scenes. The painter inevitably came up against terrible difficulties. Copley's daughter remembered vividly the visits made to old manor houses so that her father could sketch and study particular portraits. What was worse, no portrait actually portrayed the sitter in the year 1642, so that each had to be aged or rejuvenated accordingly. Mercifully, in 1793 there appeared John Thane's *Autography*, an antiquarian biographical history combining portraits of worthies with specimens of their handwriting. Copley clearly had access to this before publication, and he also made extensive use of the 1717 illustrated edition of Clarendon's *History of the Great Rebellion*.

A couple of instances will suffice to show the enormous advance he had made in comparison with the Gothick Picturesque School. Charles I is clearly derived from the celebrated portrait in the Louvre showing him *à la chasse*, but altered to the reverse. Sir Ralph Hopton, who is to the left behind the Speaker's chair, is based on a version of the portrait now in the National Portrait Gallery. One could multiply this research to cover all fifty-eight figures across the picture's surface. In 1795 this was a remarkable achievement, even if as a work of art we now regard the picture as little more than tedious.

It is crucial to grasp the originality of Hamilton, West and Copley within a European context. Everyone now accepts that the British contribution in the 1760s directly inspired a new, more serious preoccupation with classical antiquity throughout the Continent; it is less commonly realized that British artists also led the field in exploring the medieval and post-medieval past. But between this revolutionary achievement and that of their Victorian successors stands a twofold dividing line. On the one hand, the Napoleonic Wars profoundly affected people's attitude to the past and precipitated a renaissance in history writing. More significantly still, a new art form was born which accelerated and transformed everyone's response to the past and gave rise to the third style of painting which I have categorized as Intimate Romantic. This was the historical novel.

21-3 John Singleton Copley spent over a decade collecting portrait material for *Charles I demanding in the House of Commons the Five Impeached Members* (1782–95, Public Library, Boston, Mass.). Two examples illustrate his method: details of *(top left)* a portrait after an unknown artist of Sir Ralph Hopton (National Portrait Gallery, London) and *(top right)* Van Dyck's *Charles I* (1635, Louvre).

The historical novel: Scott and others

Although the historical novel has roots stretching back to Bishop Percy's *Reliques* (1765), Horace Walpole's *Castle of Otranto* (1764) and the whole school of Gothick novelists, for our purposes it began as an art form with the publication of Sir Walter Scott's *Waverley* in 1814. Fleishman in his important study of Scott states that the author 'conceived history from the outset as a past that allowed itself to be made present without losing its double character'.[36] The novels are set in the past, yet they speak in the language of the present. They are no longer the masquerades and mummeries of Walpole, Monk Lewis or Mrs Radcliffe; each is set within a definite historical period and is the product not only of brilliant creative writing and a sustained view of the past but also of real historical research. On the whole Scott is very good on what in theatre would be called his scenery, costumes and props. Although he frequently derides antiquarianism, the strength of his books lies in their basically keen observation of correct period detail.

The historical novel as conceived by Scott viewed the past with sensibility and moral commitment. It placed man, with his complex emotions and reactions, in the web of history, tracing his personal, private response to its great moments. And, as in the case of the new wave of history writing in the post-Napoleonic period, the historical novel stemmed from the powerful new forces of nationalism, industrialization and revolution. No age was more intensely nationalistic than the nineteenth century, in which the myth of the historic destiny of the British was inexorably tied up with the whole saga of their history. Britain was the earliest industrialized society in Europe. Its rapid urbanization saw country migrate to town and the dank dreariness of factory life become a fact, leading to nostalgia for an Arcadian golden age vision of Merry England in Olden Time. In the same way, the Napoleonic Wars created a gulf in time when it seemed that all which had gone before belonged to a world that was lost. The nineteenth century

as a result felt infinitely more distant from the eighteenth than had the eighteenth from either of the two previous centuries. The historical novel drew on all these threads to create its stories and sustain its readership.

The relationship of Scott to the antiquarians is a significant one, and I will have more to say about it in the next chapter. One instance will suffice to show the importance Scott attached to obtaining correct antiquarian information wherever he could, thereby giving his novels a reality and a power beyond anything achieved by his forerunners in the Gothick style. The novel *Kenilworth* (1821) culminates in 'the Princely Pleasures of Kenilworth', the spectacular entertainments presented by Elizabeth I's favourite, Robert Dudley, Earl of Leicester, in the summer of 1575. For these Scott drew freely on the account by Robert Laneham which had been published by John Nichols in his *Progresses of Queen Elizabeth* in the 1820s, but in a subsequent edition he revised his account of Kenilworth Castle in the light of a newly discovered inventory of the household effects sent to him by an antiquarian friend, William Hamper. This single example of factual accuracy foreshadows the techniques shortly to be adopted by painters confronted with the same problems of composition.

As a footnote to the impact of Scott, it is important to bear in mind the influence of the various illustrated editions of the Waverley novels. Scott himself supervised the first series of illustrations, which involved the same principle as did the novels themselves: the integration of actual historical characters and locations with imaginary ones. Illustrations to Scott are therefore of ordinary mortals caught up in the fabric of British history. Hundreds of such illustrations were produced from the 1820s onwards, and all were based on this idea. Scenes from Scott are romantic, dramatic, heroic and yet often extremely domestic, and they extended the grand moral, heroic and patriotic repertory of the Gothick Picturesque School immensely by bringing the past right down to earth in terms of everyday people and events. History became human.

Scott had an enormous impact on the development of history painting – his novels provided subjects for artists as diverse in stature as Delacroix[37] and Yeames – and, in broader terms, on people's attitude to the past. Carlyle summed it up when he wrote: 'These historical novels have taught all men this truth, which looks like a truism, yet was unknown to writers of history and others, till so taught: that the bygone ages of the world were actually filled with living men, not by protocols, state papers, controversies and abstractions of men.'[38] This obvious fact flung wide the door of the past, giving painters unlimited material for their canvases and substituting subjects more human, domestic and anecdotal – and often more trivial – for the heroic scenes seized upon by the eighteenth-century artists. History was no longer the province solely of High Art; it had been opened up to the genre painters, who now abandoned classical Arcadia in favour of May Day in the reign of Elizabeth Tudor or the arrival of the Yule log. And practically no period of the British past went uncovered by the pen of Scott, who dealt with Richard I in *The Talisman* (1825) and *Ivanhoe* (1819), Richard III in *The Fair Maid of Perth* (1828), Mary Queen of Scots in *The Monastery* (1820), Elizabeth I in *Kenilworth* (1821), the Commonwealth in *Woodstock* (1826), Charles II in *Peveril of the Peak* (1823), George I in *Rob Roy* (1817), George II in *Waverley* (1814) and George III in *Redgauntlet* (1824).

Up until about 1850, the historical novel followed the Scott tradition with slight variants.[39] Its prime best-selling exponents were G. P. R. James, Harrison Ainsworth and Edward Bulwer Lytton. James wrote almost a hundred novels based for the most part on French or British history.[40] The first appeared in 1829. He covered the Tudor period in *Darnley; or, the Field of the Cloth of Gold* (1830), *Arabella Stuart* (1844) and *Rizzio* (1849), and the Stuart period, in particular the Civil War, in *Henry Masterton; young Cavalier* (1832), its sequel *The Life and Adventures of John Marston Hall* (1834) and *Bernard Marsh* (1864); several titles dealt with the eighteenth century. He churned out three books a year, and claimed that his recreations of distant eras were aimed 'to improve and elevate the human mind and to purify and ennoble the

24 E. Smith after J. Nash, *Wayland, Amy Robsart and Janet* in a scene from Scott's *Kenilworth* engraved in 1834.

heart'. On a higher level came Harrison Ainsworth's still eminently readable novels of the forties, *The Tower of London* (1840), *Old St Paul's* (1841) and *Windsor Castle* (1843). Ainsworth hit upon a neat formula. Each novel takes an existing historical location which is then filled with events and peopled with characters actually connected with the place. On to these is grafted a whole company from the stock grotesquerie of Gothick romance. More serious than either James or Ainsworth was Bulwer Lytton, who designed his elaborate reconstructions of the past as vehicles for moral and ethical lessons for the present.[41] Although his most famous novel, *The Last Days of Pompeii* (1834), was written on a non-British theme, he nevertheless tackled the Wars of the Roses and the Norman Conquest in *The Last of the Barons* (1843) and *Harold* (1848) respectively. In the former he saw mirrored the contemporary struggle of Whig, Tory and

Radical, in the latter the defeat of a helpless democratic system by efficient organized despotism.

By the fifties the historical novel had passed its zenith in fashionable esteem. Writers began to delve into the past not so much for the sake of antiquarian pyrotechnics, or to recreate the great moments of history as reflected in their effects on ordinary people, but rather in order to focus attention on a single individual and his voyage through time in search of his own identity. *Romola* (1862–3), *John Inglesant* (1876) and *The Cloister and the Hearth* (1861) led into a new path, away from the mainstream which had earlier had such an impact on painterly visions of the British past. But through the novel even those who did not read history had been drawn into its web, and writers and painters alike could use the past as a vehicle for contemporary comment.

The triumph of history and history painting

The years of the Napoleonic Wars were quite unproductive as far as the writing of history was concerned. This is reflected in Bowyer's ambitious project to illustrate an edition of Hume, still the standard narrative history of England though already almost half a century old. Then, more or less coincidentally with the advent of the historical novel in 1814, came a new phase in history writing.[42] Two books introduced this era: Henry Hallam's *View of the State of Europe during the Middle Ages*, published in 1818, a remarkable advance in the serious study of the medieval period, and Lingard's *History of England*, which appeared the year after and replaced Hume as the standard narrative history throughout the first half of the nineteenth century. These were the years of history as best-selling literature, a period which closed with the death, in 1859, of its presiding genius, Thomas Babington Macaulay. Thomas Carlyle's *French Revolution* (1837) – another subject that obsessed Victorian painters – and Macaulay's *History of England* (1849–61) sold by the thousand, and the middle classes of Victorian England devoured history with the same kind of hunger as they had

for the historical novel. Indeed, for a brief period Macaulay rivalled the fiction writers; Thackeray responded to his success with *Henry Esmond* (1852), an effort to win the captured audience back to the novel. As a result, there was a profound change in the make-up of the educated person which enabled him to read the iconography of British history on the walls of the Royal Academy each year with eyes of comprehension.

The first half of the nineteenth century throughout Europe witnessed a deliberate attempt to create national mythologies strong enough to hold the minds of the masses who now made up and were necessary to the working of the modern state. In the years immediately following the close of the Napoleonic Wars, conscious historicism reached a peak. There was a longing for the vanished past as unsuccessful efforts were made to put the clock back to the world of the *ancien régime*, and history, seen by the philosophers of the Enlightenment as a triumph of reason over the ignorant feudal absolutism of the past, was now cast as the bearer and realizer of human progress. This was reinforced by the continued belief, inherited from the previous century, that history revealed laws for the proper conduct of affairs. History to the Victorians was practical wisdom. It was presented in nationalistic terms as the evolution of a people and their culture; the past was seen as a purely national affair directly connected with the present state of the country. In Britain this development was prefaced by Sharon Turner's *History of the Anglo-Saxons* (1799–1805) with its eulogy of its subjects as a freedom-loving people from whom stemmed the unique 'liberties' which had saved Britain from the horrors of a revolution of the type which had engulfed and continued to engulf the countries of the mainland of Europe. Such stability made British history of special interest to foreign historians, who saw the country's past as a unique progression to constitutional government, made possible by the struggles of the seventeenth century which, they believed, had averted any equivalent to the French Revolution. This view was enshrined above all in the works of Lord Macaulay, whose *History* went through so many editions during the fifties and sixties. His particular blend of Whig

historiography cast the enlightened ruling classes of England, who had defeated royal absolutism in the seventeenth century, avoided
radicalism in the eighteenth and allied themselves with the middle classes by conceding
parliamentary reform in the nineteenth, into a
role with almost sanctimonious overtones.
History of this kind reinforced the ideology of
the 'establishment' and restored confidence in its
right to rule.

The Victorian age saw the spread of history to
the middle and working classes. At the opening
of the century, history was essential for men who
aspired to a career in politics or administration.
After the Reform Bill of 1832, educational
reform in the public and in some grammar
schools introduced history in order to make the
children of the newly enfranchised classes fit for
government and political responsibility. It was
not until after the 1870 Education Act, however,
when history painting was already going into
eclipse, that the working class entered into
consideration, and the mythology they were to be
brought up on was late Victorian and Edwardian
imperialism (another fruitful subject for iconographical analysis).

For the mid-Victorian age the received view
of history was overwhelmingly Whig, with its
exaltation of the political freedom of the Anglo-
Saxons, its celebration of Magna Carta, its
interest in the development of Parliament, its
belief that the Civil War had reprieved ancient
liberties, its fear of revolution and its nurtured
complacency. And it was always presented as a
story of virtue and vice with morals to be
drawn.[43]

'Our annals', wrote Lingard, the great Catholic historian, in the fifth edition (1849) of his
History of England, 'are fraught with animating
scenes of national glory, with bright examples of
piety, honour, and resolution, and with the most
impressive and instructive lessons to princes,
statesmen, and people.'[44] The idea of national
history as a quarry for *exempla* for contemporary
society is crucial to an understanding of the
subject-matter of British nineteenth-century art.
The novel was, of course, the greater Victorian
art form; painting and sculpture offered no real
substitute as vehicles for the ideas and aspi-

rations of the age. The novel had all the
advantages: it could unfold and develop both
characters and environment, moving through
historic time and the motions of the mind. The
nineteenth-century painter had also learnt to
move through time, but he could only capture a
split second within the frame of his picture.[45]
The images he produced presupposed an audience far differently educated and read from that
of the previous century. They implied a literate
public with a common set of facts, if not uniform
attitudes to the past, which enabled them to read
these images in a way totally lost to us a century
later.

The history of Britain was therefore worthy of
celebration by the whole nation, including its
painters. History served as a collective genealogy
of the new literate middle classes. Moving into the
heyday of Victorian England, the public became
saturated with history.[46] This development was
accelerated by a number of other parallel
phenomena: by the Gothic revival in architecture, the Pre-Raphaelite dream-world, Disraeli's
Young England group in politics and the
Oxford Movement in religion. It was sustained
and nourished by the publication of historical
memoirs and diaries and the printing of sources,
above all the state papers in the Public Record
Office, and supported by the proliferation of
learned societies – Roxburghe, Shakespeare,
Philological, Aelfric, Caxton, Hakluyt, Early
English Text, Chaucer, Ballad, English Dialect
and Scottish Text. The poets of the Victorian
era, as well as its deplorable playwrights, also
lived a great deal in the past: Tennyson's *Harold,
Becket* and *Queen Mary*, Browning's *Strafford* or
Swinburne's Mary Stuart trilogy are all evidence
of this. And cheap printing and the spread of
literacy made the heroic past part of the stock-in-
trade of the educated, literate Victorian.

An important development on the visual side
was the invention of lithography, which led to
the mass-production of cheap illustrated histories of Britain. Charles Knight (1790–1873)
was the hero of this popularizing tendency.
Three of his publications are of immense
importance. Around 1844 he wrote *Old England:
A Pictorial Museum of Regal, Ecclesiastical, Mun-
icipal, Baronial and Popular Antiquities*, a work

25, 26 Popular festivals illustrated by Charles Knight in *Old England . . .* (1844): *above*, 'Maypole before St Andrew Undershaft'; *below*, 'Playing at bucklers, and maids dancing for garlands'.

produced cheaply and addressed, as were all his subsequent works, to 'the People'. From 1837 onwards, over a period of seven years, Knight published in monthly instalments George Craik and Charles MacFarlane's *Pictorial History of England*, followed from 1850 on by *The Popular History of England*. The latter was designed, as the author stated at the beginning of the book, to tell the masses 'to trace through our annals the essential connection between our political history and our social, to enable people to learn their own history – how they have grown out of slavery, out of feudal wrong, out of regal despotism – into constitutional liberty, and the position of the greatest estate of the realm'. It was completed by 1862, went into an abridged *School History* version in 1865 and was republished for the same use in 1870 as the *Crown History*. These were the books which formulated the concepts of history in the minds of the teeming populace of mid-nineteenth-century Britain – the people who went to the Royal Academy exhibitions or purchased prints after the great history paintings with which to adorn their suburban villas. And into these books, along with prints of old buildings, portraits, views and redrawings from authentic sources, went those very history paintings, for all the world as though there were no difference between the actual past and its contemporary recreation.[47]

If cheap illustrated books played a large part in popularizing history, so too did museums and galleries. In the past art, both aesthetic and historical, had been in the possession of the aristocracy. Now, through the foundation of public collections, art became part of the visual experience of the middle and lower middle classes. The British Museum, the principal institution exhibiting antiquities in the eighteenth century, was joined in 1824 by the National Gallery and in the 1850s by the Victoria & Albert Museum. By 1900 the National Gallery possessed no less than twenty-three paintings by British artists of scenes from national history.

Whereas the subject-matter of the Gothick Picturesque painters must have come as a recondite surprise to visitors to the Royal Academy in the 1780s and 1790s, by the 1840s

27 Exhibition of cartoon drawings in Westminster Hall, from *Illustrated London News,* 8 July 1843.

and 1850s a generation had grown up to whom the heroes and heroines of British history were infinitely better known and far more comprehensible than the myths of classical antiquity. Painters could now give free expression on canvas to national historic mythologies, assured of immediate understanding from their history-hungry audience. This was an ideal background for the mid-Victorian belief in High Art as the most suitable vehicle to demonstrate the powers of artists of the British School; the desire to excel in history painting inherited from the previous century was now reinforced by the whole thought-context of nineteenth-century Britain. It was a current which was to reach its climax in the commissions for the decoration of Sir Charles Barry's Houses of Parliament.[48] In 1842 the first of a series of competitions was organized for cartoon drawings illustrating subjects from British history or from the works of Spenser, Shakespeare and Milton. The projects – a hundred and forty of them – were unveiled in Westminster Hall in the summer of 1843. To

28 Furniture of the sixteenth century, from George Craik and Charles MacFarlane, *Pictorial History of England* (1837–44).

35

29 Richard Parkes Bonington, *Meditation* (1826, Wallace Collection, London).

begin with, 1,800 people a day paid to see the cartoons; later the exhibition was made free and the public came in droves, with no less than 4,000 visitors recorded on the final day, 4 September. The winners of the competition were Edward Armitage's *Caesar's Invasion of Britain*, G. F. Watts's *Caractacus led in Triumph through the Streets of Rome* and C. W. Cope's *The First Trial by Jury*. In many ways the competition was a fusion of the Boydell and Bowyer projects, and its products on the whole were equally depressing. But for artist and public alike it represented the climax of nearly a century of struggling to revive history painting in Britain.

It was around this time, too, that the number of history paintings in the Royal Academy annual exhibitions reached its highest level. The statistics on this are not uninteresting, although of course it is difficult to be absolutely exact.[49] Roughly speaking, the Academy exhibited about half a dozen historical subjects a year in the 1820s, up to ten in the thirties, up to or just over twenty in the forties, between ten and twenty in the fifties, fifteen to twenty in the sixties and five to fifteen in the seventies, tailing off in the eighties to half a dozen again. In other words, the heyday of the historical painting was coincidental with the apogee of history writing as literature. As history itself became an academic discipline, strictly for professors and dons, at the close of the century, so the painting of scenes from the British past went into decline.

None the less, the achievement at its best is not to be despised, and its supreme High Art expression remains more or less intact to this day in the monumental historical paintings which adorn the Houses of Parliament. But these monstrously under-appreciated masterpieces by Dyce, Cope and Ward demand yet another approach, for in order to understand them we must explain the recreation of the past as it occurred on the other side of the Channel.

Intimate Romantic: Bonington, Ingres and the 'style troubadour'

Intimate Romantic is a genre which could be presented almost as an interlude from the main stream, and yet it will take us into the interrelationship of France and Britain during the renaissance of romantic antiquarianism in art. As we mentioned earlier, the impact of Scott and the historical novelists was all-important in opening up a range of subject-matter to the nineteenth-century artist which was more domestic, more intimate: glimpses of the private lives of the great recorded as though we looked not through an archway into the past, but through a keyhole. The first British painter to open up this genre was Richard Parkes Bonington. All his life he was obsessed with history, 'which from the moment our infant artist was capable of thought became his favourite study and research', accord-

30 Richard Parkes Bonington, *Henry III and the English Ambassador* (1827, Wallace Collection, London).

ing to his obituary in the *Gentleman's Magazine* when he died at the age of twenty-five.[50]

Following in the wake of Copley and West, Bonington was antiquarian-minded. Sheet after sheet of his sketchbooks is filled with studies of costume, armour, furniture and architectural detail which he put down as he studied the contents of a great house, an armour collection or a medieval manuscript. And Bonington's career was played out entirely in France. He studied in Paris, first at the Louvre and later at the Ecole des Beaux-Arts. After the Salon of 1824 he journeyed to England, one of the reasons being to study the armour in the famous collection of Sir Samuel Rush Meyrick. It seems to have been here that he first met and befriended the young Delacroix. On his return to France, Bonington began a series of scenes from French and English history on this theme of the intimate glimpse, the painter turned writer or diarist. These included *The Earl of Surrey and the Fair Geraldine* (1825–6), *Henry IV and the Spanish Ambassador* (1827–8), *Leicester and Amy Robsart* (1827, Ashmolean Museum, Oxford) from Scott's *Kenilworth* and *Henry III and the English Ambassador* (1827). The last of these was exhibited at the 1828 Academy. None of them is a heroic scene momentous for the future of the nation. Only Scott's works could have inspired such recreations: poet and mistress; a great king *en famille*, his children riding on his back; Queen Elizabeth I's favourite indulging in an illicit

104, v
96

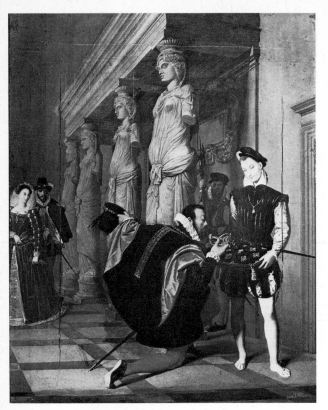

31 Jean-Auguste-Dominique Ingres, *Don Pedro de Toledo kissing Henry IV's Sword* (1820 version, private collection, Oslo).

amour; and the shock of the English ambassador on seeing Henry III, the last Valois, decadent and effeminate, attended by a minion and carrying a woman's feather fan in his hand. Of the last, it was significantly written in the *Literary Gazette*: 'As a graphic illustration of the character and habits of the French monarch it may be ranked with some of the well-described scenes by Scott in *Quentin Durward* or any other of his historical novels.'[51]

As a footnote, it is significant that Bonington took his passion for the past a stage further. Inspired by Gerard Dou, Vermeer and other Dutch painters of domestic life, he painted the past entirely for itself. *A Child at Prayer* (1825, 29 Wallace Collection), *Meditation* (1826) or *The Declaration* (1827, Collection M. René Longa) are straight historical pastiche, the fount down to our day for hundreds of imitators who depict a never-never land of the past inhabited by models in costume. This aspect of Bonington's work was the source of all the sentimental and anecdotal glimpses of the past which were to pepper the walls of the Royal Academy for the next century.

Meanwhile, across the Channel there had been an even more compulsive preoccupation with the past, intensified by the convulsions of the French Revolution and the career of Napoleon.

Bonington's unique role was as a bridgehead whereby the French *style troubadour* was introduced into England. This style, which was such a feature of painting under the Empire and was patronized by the Empress Josephine, began among the pupils of David during the revolutionary period.[52] Painters explored the Gothick world, choosing subject-matter of familial or amorous drama in which they aimed to combine 'historical interest' and 'ideal beauty' with a renewed feeling for colour based on a study of Dutch painting. Aligned to this was a rigid antiquarianism in reconstruction directly in the tradition of West and Copley. And it is in the work in the *style troubadour* of Ingres that we find the vital source which inspired Bonington and through him the whole tradition of Intimate Romantic iconography. From 1813 onwards Ingres painted a whole series of minutely researched reconstructions of the past – *genre historique*, as they were called – including scenes from the lives of Raphael, Pietro Aretino, Henry IV and Louis XIV.[53] In the 1824 Salon he exhibited his *Henry IV surprised by the Spanish Ambassador while playing with his Children* (painted in 1817), a work which must have directly inspired Bonington's composition. Ten years before, in 1814, Ingres had painted one of four versions of *Don Pedro de Toledo kissing Henry IV's Sword* (original version unlocated), again a recreation not of a grand scene but of an intimate one on the level of an incident recorded in a diary or memoir. Preoccupation with the domestic virtues of Henry IV, always regarded as the ideal healing King of France in the aftermath of war, was natural in a period of return to monarchy

98

32 Edward Matthew Ward, *Interview between Charles II and Nell Gwynne, as witnessed by Evelyn* (1854, Victoria & Albert Museum, London).

which demanded a search into the past for heroic prototypes.

Naturalized into England through Bonington, the Intimate Romantic style was to bear rich fruit above all in the work of William Powell Frith and Augustus Egg. Such artists suddenly found their subject-matter extended so that they could now apply all the standards of historical accuracy needed for the Artist-Antiquarian style to subjects they chose in the Intimate Romantic vein. Thus the Victorian iconography of the British past could include such classic idylls as Goodall's *An Episode of the Happier Days of Charles I* (1853) and E. M. Ward's witty evocation of Charles II's encounter with Nell Gwyn (1854), both subjects which would have been condemned by the high priests of academic theory in the eighteenth century. History had become the province not only of the history painter but also of the exponents of genre.

XII

32

Delaroche and British history

If Ingres and Bonington, along with Scott, were central to the establishment of the Intimate Romantic view of the past for the genre painter, the influence in England of Paul Delaroche (1797–1856) was crucial for the climax of the Artist-Antiquarian tradition for the history painter.[54] Delaroche in the 1820s and 1830s recreated the past with a degree of accuracy far in advance of that of his English contemporaries. Although now his work has gone into almost total eclipse, in his day he enjoyed a reputation European in its extent for his grand historical scenes. Through mass-produced prints, Delaroche's set pieces had an enormous influence, and throughout the decade of his greatest success (1825–35) he returned again and again to scenes from British history. His pictures, indeed, would have been more relevant to the walls of the Royal Academy than to those of the Paris Salon. Anglomania was at its height in France in the 1820s and the 1830s, and the obsession with British history went beyond the cult of Sir Walter Scott to include the production of works of serious historical import such as

Guizot's *History of the English Revolution* (1826–7) and Victor Hugo's *Cromwell* (1826). Interest in British history, and above all the Civil War period (to which we shall return in greater detail later), was stimulated by post-mortem studies of the French Revolution and the meteoric career of Napoleon. In the English Civil War Frenchmen saw a foreshadowing of 1789, in Cromwell a precursor of Napoleon, in Charles I a forerunner of Louis XVI. In the spectacular and melodramatic ends of British monarchs they were able tactfully to allude to their own rapid changes of dynasty, to the fall of Louis XVI and Marie Antoinette, of Napoleon, Louis XVIII or Louis Philippe.

Through engraving, Delaroche's huge set pieces must have established new standards of historical accuracy to be emulated by the artists who decorated the Houses of Parliament. His antiquarianism was allied to a startling illusion of reality and a genius for choosing moments in which drama intertwined with sentiment. His first scene from British history was on a Jacobite theme, *Flora Macdonald succouring the Young Pretender* (c. 1825, unlocated), exhibited in the Salon of 1827. Thanks to Scott's novels, the cult of the Jacobites and the fate of Bonnie Prince Charlie were to obsess painters until the close of the century. Delaroche followed this up with his dramatic *Death of Queen Elizabeth* (1828, Louvre), which placed on canvas a total reversal in attitude to the great English Queen, recording her as a pathetic grovelling hag. In 1830 came *The Children of Edward IV*, a theme already familiar from the previous century but now painted with a new degree of accuracy and psychological penetration, and in 1831 his macabre *Cromwell gazing at the body of Charles I*, which was exhibited also at the Royal Academy in 1850. In 1834 he showed *The Execution of Lady Jane Grey*, in 1837 *Strafford on his Way to Execution* (unlocated, formerly Duke of Sutherland) and *The Mocking of Charles I*. All these paintings, which were seminal for attitudes to the British past, will be discussed in Part III. Delaroche's only omission was a scene from the life of Mary Queen of Scots; otherwise, he covered all those themes most compelling to the Victorians from their heroic past.

172

XII

142

162

33 Paul Delaroche, *The Death of Queen Elizabeth* (1828, Louvre).

34 David Wilkie, *The Preaching of John Knox before the Lords of the Congregation, June 10th, 1559* (1822–32, Tate Gallery, London).

The painters of the past

From 1830 onwards, the language of the past was part of the iconographic make-up of every artist of any importance. For some artists it went beyond this to become a major obsession and the most potent vehicle for their ideas. Roughly speaking, the painters who inhabited the past fall into three groups stretching from the post-Napoleonic period to the close of the century. The first contains the earliest essays of the 1820s and 1830s by artists whose main work lay in other genres. They were succeeded during the period 1840–70 by the generation for whom the past was a major ingredient in their intellectual background and in that of their public. By the close of the century, the tide had ebbed, and activity was confined to an ever-shrinking group of Academy painters who attempted to continue a tradition from which the vitality had already gone.

The most distinguished pioneers of the twenties and thirties were C. R. Leslie and Sir David Wilkie. Wilkie's contribution consisted of three pictures, *Alfred in the Neatherd's Cottage* (1806, Commander A. F. Armitage), *The Preaching of John Knox before the Lords of the Congregation, June 10th, 1559* (1822–32), and *The Escape of Mary Queen of Scots from Lochleven Castle* (1837,

unlocated). They form a minor stream in his work, but the last two were major commissions which reveal him as a brilliant recreator of the past. We know that he was deeply interested in history from the fact that he designed and supervised *tableaux vivants* from Scott novels, enacted at Hatfield for the Marchioness of Salisbury.[55]

C. R. Leslie's career was made in 1818 with his picture *Sir Roger de Coverley going to Church* (unlocated), and in 1821 he exhibited *May Day Revels in the Time of Queen Elizabeth*, a picture twice viewed by Sir Walter Scott, who invited Leslie to Abbotsford and subsequently asked him to contribute illustrations to the Waverley novels.[56] His *Lady Jane Grey prevailed upon to accept the Crown* (1827) contributed greatly to the hagiography of that Queen, but in the main Leslie stuck to subjects from literature, from Shakespeare, Cervantes, Goldsmith and Molière.

Turner should be included almost as an interloper, for although he made use of the past in his landscape vision during the thirties, his only overtly antiquarian picture was that of 1831, *Lucy, Countess of Carlisle and Dorothy Percy's Visit to their Father, Lord Percy, when under Attainder upon the Supposition of his being concerned in the Gunpowder Plot* (Tate Gallery).[57] His use of Van Dyck portraits (actually far too late in date for the event he depicts) in this, his only expedition into British history devoid of landscape, speaks for itself.

The period 1840–70 was the great age of history painting. Its prime exponents were E. M. Ward, Sir Edwin Landseer, Daniel Maclise, Charles Lucy, John Calcott Horsley, Frederick Goodall, Charles Landseer, W. P. Frith, Augustus Egg, John Faed, Eyre Crowe and C. W. Cope. The work of some, such as Egg, Frith and Ward, has already begun to be resurrected, but on the whole a heavy cloud of disapproval hangs over these images of the past. Our attitude to them is still coloured by the verdict, for example, of Graham Reynolds: 'These historical subjects were not felt sufficiently for the artists to enter into them. But they could enter with a sense of participation into those aspects of the world around them which attracted most attention.'[58]

145

35 William Dyce, *George Herbert at Bemerton* (1861, Guildhall Art Gallery, London).

This prejudice has led to the exaltation of the painters of scenes of contemporary life and the condemnation of painters of history. It has meant, in the case of Frith, to take the most obvious instance, that his historical works have been ignored and his achievement assessed almost solely in the light of his contemporary genre compositions. How Frith would have hated it! It was not the artists who did not feel sufficiently; it is we, the twentieth-century onlookers. Only when we try to relive their excitement as they recaptured the past, as they relived it, as they used it to point a moral and give hope to a mass audience, can we begin to see these creations in a different light. We have to shed our Bloomsbury prejudice and condescension.

It would be pointless to embark on biographi-cal notices of all these artists. It is not the purpose of this book to review the historical works of each Victorian painter, but rather to recapture an idea. Their works are represented among the illustrations and must speak for themselves. To my eye they are often maligned and underestimated as works of art in their own right. The monumental history paintings of Ward and Cope in the Houses of Parliament are triumphs, not failures. So too are their genre equivalents. W. P. Frith's *Coming of Age in the Olden Time* (1849) and *Claude Duval* (1859) are bravura pieces of genre painting quite as delightful as *Ramsgate Sands* (1854) or *The Railway Station* (1862). Frederick Goodall's *An Episode of the Happier Days of Charles I* (1853) is just as good as, if not better than, his evocations

III, VI
127

XII

of life in harems. And the work of painters who made only occasional sallies into the British past has given us some of the most haunting pictures of the age: William Dyce's *George Herbert at Bemerton* (1861, Guildhall Art Gallery), William Shakespeare Burton's *A Wounded Cavalier* (1856), Ford Madox Brown's *Chaucer at the Court of Edward III* (1856–68) or Millais's *Boyhood of Raleigh* (1870).

These artists were the great ones, and theirs was the true achievement. After 1870 the driving force had gone and it was left to a small group of establishment artists to take the theme into the present century – Philip Hermogenes Calderon, Sir John Gilbert, Frank Stone, David Wilkie Wynfield, John Seymour Lucas, John Pettie, A. C. Gow and Ernest Crofts. The century of history had reached its close.

Past into present

But what was it they painted, and why? Statistically, of course, landscape and portraiture far exceeded these historical scenes, but they did not compare in impact on the public. The study of the complex subject-matter of Victorian art is still in its initial exploratory stages, but it is already clear that the themes cannot be so easily disentangled as they can, for example, in France.[59] There the developments in historic subject-matter can be readily followed: scenes of stoic heroism during the Revolution, followed by the creation of the Napoleonic myth and finally the use of history to buttress the restored Bourbon monarchy. The contrast with England is very marked. History as expressed in scenes of heroic endeavour made very little appearance here during the long years of the Napoleonic Wars, and, as for the monarchy, never was it to sink so low in public esteem as it did in the years after 1815. Neither art nor history was called upon to create any new mythology of monarchy, and there was no real reflection of the ideals of the Crown until the advent of Victoria and Albert in the 1840s. Then Queen and Consort appeared as Anglo-Saxons, as guardians of ancient British liberties, or the family of Charles I was evoked to mirror the domestic bliss of the present royal family. In the iconography of

Victoria and Albert the allusions to the past, to *ancien régime* autocracy, were deliberately muted, in contrast to the assertive presentation of George IV. It would, however, take us too far from our path to investigate the subtle idealization of the royal family as it took shape in the forties and fifties. Its central theme would be the use of motifs from Van Dyck to suggest a refinement of bourgeois ideals of family life – a radical distortion of what the portraits of Charles I and his court were really about. Victoria and Albert were presented as knight and lady living out a romance in a chivalrous Victorian dream-world which drew for its imagery on the Caroline. And, like Charles I, they were also seen as ideal parents of an ideal family, a pattern for emulation by their subjects. This mood of chaste romance and domestic virtue drew strength from mirror images in the British past.

On the whole, though, the scenes from history are preoccupied with the vanishing and transitory nature of monarchy. Imprisonments, executions, the sad fate of exile and defeat in battle are recounted again and again in the persons of Mary Queen of Scots, Lady Jane Grey, Henrietta Maria, Charles I, Charles II, James II and Bonnie Prince Charlie. Perhaps through these figures, comfortably far distant in time, it was possible to meditate on the kind of disaster which was still happening on the mainland of Europe. Also relevant in this respect is the Victorian obsession with the more recent fate of Louis XVI and Marie Antoinette. The miseries of this ill-fated pair harrowed the hearts of visitors to the Royal Academy with as relentless a regularity as did those of the Queen of Scots.

Politically, the subjects from British history focus not on the Crown but on the central issue for the whole period, the reform of elected government by the gradual extension of the franchise. The crucial development in England in the period after 1815 was the resolution of a series of crises in such a way that the old establishment was able to open its doors to the new pillars of power, the industrial cities and the burgeoning middle classes who created and sustained the economic boom of mid-Victorian England. Everyone, regardless of political persuasion, extolled the Anglo-Saxons as the forerunners of later liberties – which 'liberties', of course, were interpreted quite differently according to one's political stance. Alfred the Great was seen as the ideal philosopher-king, Harold as a monarch still to be mourned because with his death at the Battle of Hastings Anglo-Saxon liberty gave way to Norman tyranny and bondage.

This concept of conflict between the old establishment and the new classes found its ideal expression in the Civil War. In the person of Charles I, reinterpreted in the romantic Scott tradition, was discovered the perfect symbol of the *ancien régime* at its best – aristocratic, paternal and pious – as well as an exponent of the virtues of family life. In Cromwell the Chartists and other reformers saw their historic sanction for the new self-made man; they presented him as the hero of the common people, a man of deep Christian morality, a man of resolution, courage and decision, even if it meant the destruction of the *ancien régime*. The patterns of passionate and contradictory loyalties at every level were seen in microcosm in the events and personalities of the Civil War. Out of this struggle had been born that most prized possession of British people, the Constitution, monarchic yet democratic, the envy of the rest of Europe. The greatest single visual celebration of this idea survives in the programme of decorations for the Houses of Parliament.

But there are other threads. In an age of renewed evangelical piety and religious revival, patterns of the virtuous life needed reinforcing by example, and although Britain as a Protestant country could not turn to the cult of saints, it could make use of its historic mythology. Kings and queens, poets and writers, statesmen and men of action, as they became known through the spread of literacy and the popular reading of national history, took on roles within a pantheon of virtue and vice. The National Portrait Gallery was founded at the close of the 1850s with precisely this in mind. So history was reduced to a parade of heroes and heroines, which of course could all too easily become trivialized. Sir Thomas More and his family were celebrated as examples of the domestic virtues, while Cardinal Wolsey represented pride before the fall. Loyalty

to lost causes animated scene after scene focusing on the Stuarts, on Mary Queen of Scots, on Charles I and Bonnie Prince Charlie. Passionate and romantic loyalty to the losing side is a characteristic of the subject-matter of vast numbers of history pictures. Perhaps, through self-identification, those who suffered reversals at the hands of the forces of change were able to find compensation by surrounding themselves with a haze of romantic, doomed righteousness.

In no other area was history a more useful quarry than in supplying Victorian society with models of ideal womanhood. Perhaps the most revealing of all transmutations was their casting of Mary Queen of Scots, Lady Jane Grey and Henrietta Maria as examples of the perfect Victorian gentlewoman. Nothing could have been further from historic truth, but the artists remained undeterred by the facts staring them in the face.

History for the Victorians was a vehicle for a wide variety of political, moral and religious ideas. The events of the British past as reflected in the art of the age were conditioned by a middle-class gloss. These scenes and their heroes were selected to inspire calm, even complacency, with regard to the present. They gave expression and substance to the all-pervasive Whig interpretation of history as progress, with ancient liberties guarded and restored. They were aimed at kindling patriotic pride and moral virtue in the minds of the onlookers, and a fear of revolution. In short, they were history as cast in the mental mould of the post-Reform-Bill electorate. In looking at any nineteenth-century presentation of the past, we should always remember Thomas Buckle's revealing statement in his best-selling *History of Civilisation in England* (1856–61): 'There must always be a connexion between the way in which men contemplate the past, and the way in which they contemplate the present; both views being in fact different forms of the same habits of thought, and therefore presenting in each age, a certain sympathy and correspondence with each other.'[60] This sentence provides the Ariadne's thread for anyone who wishes to unravel the inner meaning of any Victorian vision of the British past.

Pl. 9

1   2   3   4

5   6   7   8

9   10   11   12

13   14   15   16

Pub. March 1. 1785   Hamilton Sc

The Recreation of the Past

IT IS NOT EASY actually to recreate the past in the eye of the present. Indeed, it is not altogether possible. We now know that such reconstructions, however brilliant, can never be entirely accurate. Norma Shearer as Marie Antoinette remains entirely a product of her environment, Hollywood in the 1930s, and even that most careful of cinematic evocations, *La Kermesse Héroïque*, which brings to life scenes from Flemish genre painting, ultimately fails in many of its details. A century and a half ago there were no such feelings or failure. Artist and antiquary stood on the brink of a new and startling adventure: they could make the past live again. Through the discoveries of the antiquarian, the artist acquired the almost magical power to waft the onlooker back in a time machine to witness the fall of Clarendon or watch Mary Queen of Scots make her way to the scaffold. The artist seemed to possess superhuman abilities, as though he alone could make time stand still. Although capturing only a single moment, the artist could do something the writer could not: he could actually bring the public face to face with the living reality of their own past. One can understand the obsession of the challenge, one can begin to comprehend the emotions aroused by some of the canvases as visitors to the Royal Academy jostled to see them, one can see how the line between actuality of historical artefact and recreation in modern painting seemed at times barely to exist. In the early stages it must have been immensely exhilarating.

In order to recreate the past an artist needed to adopt the role of researcher. There was nothing particularly new in this in the sense that ever since the Renaissance there had been a continuous tradition of applying higher standards of pictorial accuracy to painting in respect of classical antiquity. Poussin is an obvious instance, and in eighteenth-century England the impact of the discoveries at Pompeii and Herculaneum was evident in the work of Gavin Hamilton, Josiah Wedgwood and Robert Adam. What was new was the application of this technique to modern periods by artists such as Kent, Hamilton, West and Copley. They began the crusade for the painter to clothe his characters correctly and to place them within an accurate historical environment. Cope's *Charles I erecting his Standard at Nottingham, 1642* (1861) or Brown's *Chaucer at the Court of Edward III* (1856–68) posed problems not only of composition but also of historical research. What was a mid-fourteenth-century lectern like, how did members of the court of Edward III dress, what portrait sources were available for the poet, the King, the Queen and the Prince of Wales? What, in the case of Cope, was armour like in 1642, and who was present at Nottingham when the standard was raised? A hundred such details had to be resolved before the artist could even start. From 1820 onwards such points were studied hard by critics, to the extent that by the middle of the century writers considered any anachronism in a historical composition to be little short of a crime against art itself.

Antiquarianism and the arts

All this was the consequence of the modest and praiseworthy birth of antiquarianism in the modern sense in England. The importance of the rise of antiquarian studies, and its impact on the whole range of the visual arts during the period

164
60, III, IV

36 A selection of helmets recorded by the Antiquarian Francis Grose in his *Treatise on Ancient Armour and Weapons* (1786).

37 Historic dress arrives in the theatre: William Hogarth, *David Garrick as Richard III* (*c.* 1745, Walker Art Gallery, Liverpool).

1750–1850, seems to me never to have been fully grasped. This, I think, can be very easily explained. Antiquarianism can so quickly become the pedestrian, dry-as-dust recording of artefacts from the past that it seems to be quite cut off from the mainstream of creativity in the arts. This may be the case now, but it most certainly was not in the eighteenth century.

Although there had been a Society of Antiquaries in the Elizabethan age, it was not until the close of the second decade of the eighteenth century that it was re-established.[1] The leading light in this revival was William Stukeley, who believed that 'without drawing and designing the study of Antiquitys or any other Science is lame and imperfect'. The Articles of Association included provision for the examination of the 'Relicks of former Ages', including the Roman: of all types of building, sculpture, artefacts, costume, portraits and manuscripts. From the very beginning the new Society commissioned one of its most gifted Fellows, George Vertue, to draw and engrave historical portraits. In its early years the Society was medieval and Tudor in its antiquarian preoccupations, but the classical upsurge of the thirties reached a crescendo in the fifties when Robert Adam, Richard Wilson,

James 'Athenian' Stuart, Francesco Bartolozzi and Giovanni Battista Cipriani were Fellows. By the seventies, medieval studies had reasserted themselves. Moving into the new century, a list of Fellows includes several of importance for the recreation of the past in architecture, interior decoration and painting: Benjamin West (elected 1792), Francis Chantrey, the sculptor, and Charles Alfred Stothard, the artist and antiquary (both 1819), Edward Blore, architect of Scott's Abbotsford and Meyrick's Goodrich (1823) and Anthony Salvin and John Nash, architects.

In other words, the Society of Antiquaries in the eighteenth and early nineteenth centuries was not merely a closed world of antiquarians, but actually numbered among its members many of the most influential creators of the age. Particularly important was their steady production of engravings of the visual sources of the past, the series of prints bound up as *Vetusta Monumenta* (1747 onwards) and *Archaeologia* (1770 onwards), their illustrated journal of learned communication. These were available for use even by those who ridiculed the antiquarian – an attitude succinctly caught by Horace Walpole in a letter to Cole in September 1778:

The antiquaries will be as ridiculous as they used to be; and since it is impossible to infuse taste into them, they will be as dry and dull as their predecessors. One may revive what perished, but it will perish again, if more life is not breathed into it than it enjoyed originally. Facts, dates and names will never please the multitude, unless there is some style and manner to recommend them, and unless some novelty is struck out from their appearance. The best merit of the Society lies in their prints; for their volumes, no mortal will ever touch them but an antiquary.[2]

The work of the antiquarians in the field of architecture has long been recognized as significant by architectural historians, for it gave rise to the revivalist styles of the eighteenth and nineteenth centuries. By comparison, the lesser paths of costume, armour, portraiture or antique furniture – all crucial for piecing together the past – remain little explored. And yet the work carried out by scholars and antiquarians at the close of the eighteenth century and into the nineteenth century had a profound effect not only on the advance of scholarship, but also on theatrical production, interior decoration, furniture design and, of course, on painters, giving them the material they needed, in an age before museums, to paint their visions of the Britain of other ages. In the explosion of antiquarian activity that characterized the first half of the nineteenth century, the discoveries of the previous century were extended and popularized. These were now codified for artist and public alike in book after book on historical architecture, furniture, portraiture, costume, armour and weapons. And these are the handbooks which made the vision possible, and which we must now turn to study.

Historic dress: Strutt, Planché, Fairholt and others

The documentation of historic dress was included amongst other objectives listed by Humphrey Wanley in his draft for the foundation of a society of antiquaries about 1708.[3] This was to cover not only clothes of every rank and class in society, but also armour and weapons. Seventy years, however, were to elapse before this subject of antiquarian research was in fact taken up. For most of the eighteenth century ideas as to correct historical costume were extremely vague. There were no English books on the subject, and indeed very little published material apart from the volumes depicting costumes of the nations which had been produced in Italy and Flanders in the second half of the sixteenth century. These included standard works such as Cesare Vecellio's *Habiti Antichi e Moderni* (1590) and Boissard's *Habitus Variarum Orbis Gentium* (1581). Such books, illustrated with engravings of hundreds of costumes, became part of the reference library of any painter, much as the manuals by Cartari and Ripa were essential for the attributes of the classical gods and goddesses.

The first stirrings of an awareness of historical dress can be traced to the 1730s, and more particularly to the stage. In 1737 a tragedy on the life of Charles I was staged 'Dressed after the Manner of the Time',[4] but it was not until

38 Gothick Picturesque in historic costume: after Francis Wheatley, *Baptista's House* (1795).

Garrick's reforms of stage costume in the 1740s that any serious attempt was made at correct dress. Even then, its effect was parallel to that of the clothes which appeared in the Gothick Picturesque phase of history painting; this phase lasted just as long on the stage, ending in 1824 when Planché supervised Kemble's production of *King John*. Hogarth's famous portrait of Garrick as Richard III (*c.* 1745) illustrates the Gothick theatrical style, in which the actor has abandoned contemporary dress for a costume reminiscent of the Tudor period. Little advance was made on this for over half a century, as a glance at any of the paintings commissioned by Alderman Boydell for his Shakespeare Gallery in the 1780s will prove. Francis Wheatley's *Baptista's House* (1795), painted over forty years after Hogarth's portrait, shows the same mélange typical of the Gothick Picturesque: plumed bonnets, slashed doublets and vaguely Cavalier costume derived from portraits by Van Dyck. That high priest of the academic tradition, Reynolds, objected to scenes in medieval or modern dress because, he said, 'the effect . . . will always be mean and vulgar'; yet he also felt that 'to depart from the Costume is as bad on the other side',[5] which effectively ruled out this kind of subject-matter altogether. The controversy was still alive during the 1840s, when it affected

39, 40 The quest for accuracy in dress begins: plate XXXVIII *(above)* from Joseph Strutt, *The Regal and Ecclesiastical Antiquities of England* (1773) is based on an illustration *(top)* from Royal MS. 18 E.II depicting the coronation of Henry IV.

the choice of subjects in the competitions for the decoration of the Houses of Parliament.[6]

It was to take almost half a century for the researches of one man to have an effect both on painting and stage production. The most important single figure in the investigation of the costume of the past was Joseph Strutt.[7] Born in 1749, the son of a wealthy miller, he received a grammar school education, after which he was apprenticed to an engraver. In 1770 he entered the Royal Academy Schools, and the year after became a student in the British Museum Reading

Room. Strutt's first, extraordinary book, *The Regal and Ecclesiastical Antiquities of England*, appeared in 1773, when he was twenty-four. It was an amazing and original contribution to antiquarian studies from someone who had virtually been self-taught. He was to follow this over a period of thirty years with a whole series of profusely illustrated and elaborately re-searched books, all basically of the same type, publishing the visual sources for English social and domestic history: three volumes entitled *Honda Angel-cynnan or, A compleat View of the Manners, Customs, Arms, Habits, etc. of the Inhabitants of England . . .* (1774–6), two volumes out of a projected six of *The Chronicle of England* (1777–8) and, finally, two books which were as seminal as his first – *A Complete View of the Dress and Habits of the People of England* (1796–9) and *Sports and Pastimes of the People of England* (1801). Burrowing, as no one else had ever done, through a morass of visual and written evidence, together with early printed source material, he pieced together for the very first time a picture of everyday life in England from the Anglo-Saxons down to the Tudor age. The consequences were revolutionary for the art of historical recon-struction, and it was Strutt more than any other person who gave the painters of the new Artist-Antiquarian phase the sources that they so desperately needed.

A full-length book on Strutt is a desideratum, as he emerges as an influential but totally neglected figure in the history of art in Britain. His guiding star and inspiration was the great French antiquarian Montfaucon. We need only consider two of Strutt's works, which will show his method in action. *Regal and Ecclesiastical Antiquities*, which ran into a second edition in 1793 and a third, edited by Planché, in 1842, is made up of a series of engravings of the monarchs of England from Edward the Con-fessor to Henry VIII, together with other notabilities. Each, Strutt states, is 'correctly copied from the ORIGINALS, which particularly expressed the DRESS and CUSTOMS of the Time, to which each Piece respectively relates'.[8] Plate XXXVIII, for instance, is taken from British Museum Royal MS. 18 E.II and depicts the coronation of Henry IV at Westminster by the

Archbishops of Canterbury and York. There is a long footnote by Strutt as to the exact colour of the robes in the illumination.[9] The book contains sixty plates of this type in all, and Strutt states that he produced it not only for the benefit of those to whom he alludes as 'the curious', but more particularly for artists, so that 'those that have occasion to represent scenes from the ancient English history, may find the dress and character'. 'Hitherto', he continues, 'our artists have been extremely deficient in their delineations of the early history – the Saxons are drawn in the habit of the figures on the Trajan and Antonine columns; and the Normans are put into the dresses and armour worn in Edward the Fourth's time, and indeed, are often made still more modern.'[10] What a manifesto from a young man of twenty-four! It was the death knell of the fancy dress masquerades of Wheatley or Downman. None the less, Strutt charitably defends these artists of the Gothick Picturesque School, because until the publication of his book the sources were not available to them, so that they had been prevented from achieving 'the truth of antiquity'.

The impact of Strutt's *Regal and Ecclesiastical Antiquities* was minimal in comparison with the enormous influence exerted by his *Complete View of the Dress and Habits of the People of England*. Here, as in the earlier book, Strutt had produced something entirely original – the first systematic documented history of dress from the earliest times down to the close of the fifteenth century. He chose to end at the point where source material in the form of portraits and engravings became more plentiful. Strutt was acutely aware of the originality of his production:

The Engravings, which form the most material part of this publication, are taken from drawings in Manuscripts coeval with the times that they are intended to illustrate, or other monuments of antiquity equally authentic; and they are faithfully copied from the originals, without additional folds being made to the draperies or the least deviation from the form of the garments.[11]

Strutt's *Dress and Habits* became a fundamental source book for all painters, not only in its own right but also because it was ruthlessly plag-iarized by the two great costume historians of the nineteenth century, Planché and Fairholt. Through them the costume figures of Strutt reached a far wider audience, and continue to have a life in histories of costume, unbelievably, down to the present day.

Strutt's own publication is a monument to the antiquarian standards of its period. He used the evidence of archaeology for the earliest ages, but in the main he relied on manuscript illuminations in the British Museum Royal, Harleian and Sloane collections, with occasional items drawn from the Bodleian Library in Oxford. Each illustration is carefully documented, revealing the wide range of original historical material consulted: chronicles, legal documents in the form of sumptuary legislation, manuscripts plus literary sources of every kind. But it is the illustrations above all which are the most important, for Strutt opened up, for the very first time, a window into the English Middle Ages, carefully selecting illustrations to depict all levels of society – rustics, noblemen, lawyers, merchants, officers of state, ecclesiastics – and all types of costume: travelling dress, masquerade attire, dresses for young ladies and for matrons, hunting costume, soldiers' gear, monastic habits. We need only look at two illustrations to demonstrate his method. Plate IX represents 'Dresses of the Anglo-Saxon Women of the Eighth Century' and is a selection of figures copied from Cotton MS. Claudius B.IV, a Saxon Book of Genesis. Plate XCIII, 'Ladies of High Rank of the 14th Century', is typical of many plates which amalgamate single figures from more than one source. The figures on the left and right are taken from Royal MS. 15 D.III, while the centre figure is from Royal MS. 16 G.V, *Gestes des Roi de France*, a manuscript which had belonged to Humphrey, Duke of Gloucester. The latter Strutt drew upon for no less than ten other costume figures.

Inevitably, redrawing leads to inaccuracy, but Strutt's fidelity is remarkable for his period, and his technique of rearranging costume figures from various original sources in tableaux evocative of life in a distant age is richly suggestive of the possibilities of such historical reconstruction. One can see how Strutt's mind moved

41, 42 'Dresses of the Anglo-Saxon Women of the Eighth Century' *(above)*, plate IX from Strutt's *Complete View of the Dress and Habits of the People of England* (1796–9), uses various details from a page of Cotton MS. Claudius B.IV *(top)*.

on to another, irresistible stage. He had recreated the past; all that remained for him to do was to animate it, to breathe into it life and speech, action and plot. The figures would then move, the robes flow, the plumes nod, the veils flutter, the burghers and nobility would exchange words, the arms of the knights would once more resound, the horsemen would gallop. From *The Dress and Habits* to an antiquarian historical novel must have seemed a short step, and Strutt took it. After his other important book, *The Sports and Pastimes of the People of England* (essential to the Victorian myth of Merry England in Olden Time), he embarked on a novel entitled *Queenhoo-Hall*, a romance set in fifteenth-century England to illustrate its manners, customs and habits. Strutt died in October 1802 leaving it unfinished. John Murray, the publisher, passed it on to Scott, who completed it rather badly. A few years later, however, it inspired Scott to write *Waverley*, so we can understand the significance of Strutt from every point of view. It is possible to grasp also the integral links which existed between antiquarians, writers and artists as the doorway to the past was opened. We are able to share their excitement as they began to make the figures of history move and speak once more upon the stage of the British past.

Strutt towers above every other figure in the history of dress in England. Planché and Fairholt, in contrast, were essentially popularizers. James Planché (1796–1880) combined a somewhat unlikely career as a highly successful writer of burlesques and harlequinades with that of an antiquary and scholar of heraldry and costume, something which led him eventually to be appointed to the College of Arms. Such activities were not mutually exclusive, and in 1824 Planché supervised a landmark in theatrical production, Charles Kemble's revival of Shakespeare's *King John* at Drury Lane, the first occasion on which a Shakespearian production was staged with correct historical costume. Planché acknowledges, however, that Kemble had earlier consulted Douce, the antiquarian, on the staging of the Roman plays, which emphasizes the fact that accuracy in the archaeological detail of the ancient world went hand in hand with accuracy in respect of the post-classical eras. Planché's designs for *King John* were subsequently published in three volumes, but his most important book was the *History of British Costume*, written with the encouragement of Douce and Meyrick and published in 1834. This ran into two more editions, in 1847 and 1874, and was designed from the outset to preserve artists from committing grave errors in their representation of the costume of the past. Planché says that the painter is now expected to depict the past accurately, and if he fails to do so he abuses 'the faith accorded to him' by the public as 'an illustrator of habits and manners'.[12] He praises the genius and learning of Sir Walter

43–6 Strutt, in plate xciii of *The Dress and Habits (above)*, combined figures from Royal MS. 15 D.iii *(top centre)* and Royal MS. 16 G.v *(top right)*. Frederick William Fairholt, in *Costume in England* (1846), used the former unchanged *(top left)*.

Female costume, reign of Henry VI.
Figs. *a* and *b*, from Harleian MS. 2278; *c*, from the blade of a miséricorde, in the Meyrick collection; the rest from Royal MS. 15, E. 6, fol. 450.

47–9 James Planché, illustrating 'Female costume, reign of Henry VI' *(above)* in his *History of British Costume* (1834), made use of Strutt's plates CXVIII *(top left)* and CXIX *(top right)* from *The Dress and Habits.*

Scott, although even he in *Ivanhoe* describes armour more suitable to the sixteenth than the twelfth century. 'Antiquities', Planché roundly declares, 'are now considered valuable only in proportion to their illustration of history or their importance to art.'[13] His book is largely derived from Strutt, but it is an immense improvement in arrangement in that the material is now presented chronologically, reign by reign; what is more, he carries the story beyond the early Tudors and on to the close of the reign of George III. The quality of the illustrations is frankly deplorable compared with those of Strutt, and in spite of his numerous references to the original manuscript sources it would be surprising if Planché ever looked at the majority of them. One illustration is sufficient to show his method. A group of fifteenth-century ladies is a combination of figures from two separate plates in *The Dress and Habits*, for which Strutt had already combined more than one source in the first place![14]

The second popularizer, Frederick William Fairholt (1814–1866), like Strutt and Planché, was a self-taught antiquary. He came of extremely humble origins and made his reputation as a prolific engraver of historical subjects, immensely in demand because of his antiquarian knowledge and fidelity as a draughtsman. He illustrated Hall's *Mansions of England* (1843–5), Halliwell's *Life of William Shakespeare* (1848) and the proceedings of the major antiquarian societies of the day. In 1846 he produced his *Costume in England*, which went into a second edition fourteen years later. The preface to the 1860 edition, written at the high point of the art of the artist-antiquarian, is worth quoting for its categorical statement on the role of historical accuracy in art, much more stringent than Planché's a generation before:

As no historian could venture to give wrong dates designedly, so no painter should falsify history by delineating the character on his canvas in habits not known until many years after their death, or holding implements that were not at the time invented. Whatever talent may be displayed in the drawing, grouping, and colouring of such pictures they are but 'painted lies' and cannot be excused any more than history that falsifies fact and dates would be, although clothed in all the flowers of rhetoric.[15]

By 1860 inaccuracy had become a crime against art, and art had been led hard along the sterile path of pedantic historical reconstruction. Here again there is a rifling of Strutt's sources,[16] but Fairholt, unlike Planché, seems to have consulted the originals. A fifteenth-century couple, for instance, come directly from Royal MS. 15 D.III and are not split up as they are by Strutt.[17] Fairholt too continues the story down to the reign of George III, ending with a few feeble cuts after Heideloff's *Gallery of English Fashion*.

Planché and Fairholt also assimilated into their works three other major contributions to the rediscovery of the dress of the past, Charles Alfred Stothard's *The Monumental Effigies of Great Britain* (1811–33), Francis Grose's *A Treatise on Ancient Armour and Weapons* (1786) and Sir Samuel Rush Meyrick's *A Critical Inquiry into Antient Armour, as it existed in Europe, but particularly in England, from the Norman Conquest to the Reign of King Charles II* (1824). Stothard (1786–1821), who was historical draughtsman to the Society of Antiquaries, embarked in 1811 on his vast work on effigies, a subject already opened up at the end of the previous century by

50 The past lives again: the frontispiece to Charles Alfred Stothard, *The Monumental Effigies of Great Britain* (1811–33).

Richard Gough, whose *Sepulchral Monuments of Great Britain* appeared between 1786 and 1799. Stothard unfortunately died before he was able to complete his work by falling off a ladder while copying figures from a stained glass window in a remote Devonshire church. His prime motivation had been the service that 'these Monumental effigies would render the Historical Painter', the straight historian and biographer and the theatrical costumier. The frontispiece to this massive work, in which the tomb effigies of the famous in British history rise to life from the grave, captures beautifully the ambience of early-nineteenth-century antiquarianism. 'By these means,' Stothard wrote, 'we live in other ages than our own . . . In some measure we arrest the fleeting steps of Time, and again review those things his arm has passed over, and subdued, but not destroyed.'[18] The book is made up of

51, 52 *Top*, Stothard's details of the effigy of Sir Thomas Cawne in Ightham church, Kent; *above*, as copied by Fairholt for use in *Costume in England*.

hundreds of plates rich in information on English medieval costume and portraiture. And it was, as I indicated, shamelessly plagiarized by Planché and Fairholt. Stothard had a continuous stream of successors throughout the Victorian period and right down to the present day.

Armour and the weapons of war were subjects first essayed by Francis Grose (1731–91), also an Antiquary, whose contributions included *Military Antiquities respecting a History of the English Army from the Conquest to the Present Time* (1786–8), which went into further editions in 1801 and 1812, and *The Antiquarian Repertory* (1775). But it was his *Treatise on Ancient Armour and Weapons* (1786) which was aimed specifically at the painters of history as well as antiquarians and those bent on a study of the curious. Grose hoped that it might 'be useful to sculptors, painters, and designers, and enable them to avoid those anachronisms and violations of the *coustume*, which we too often meet with in works otherwise excellently performed'.[19] Forty-two plates illustrate whole suits of armour and pieces, weapons and horse furniture. As an instance of antiquarian research it is far inferior to Strutt. Edward III, for example, is shown in armour of the Tudor rather than the Plantagenet period.

Sir Samuel Rush Meyrick (1783–1848) was likewise an Antiquary and took an active part in the affairs of the Society. Later he assisted in the formation of the British Archaeological Association. His earliest publication was on British costume down to the sixth century,[20] but his fame and influence rested on the critical study of ancient armour and weapons. As we have seen, Bonington and Delacroix met while studying and drawing examples of armour from the remarkable collection he had assembled first in London and later at Goodrich Court, the Gothic fantasy which he built himself in Herefordshire. Writing in the preface to the 1824 edition of his work, Meyrick stated that his main aim had been to establish a chronology of armour, which until then had been imperfectly understood by writers, painters and dramatists. The barons of the reign of King John, for example, would be made to wear armour of the period of Edward I. Recent research on the history of dress 'had not only given a general stimulus to the arts, but

53–5 Antiquarian research into armour and weaponry: *right*, a knight from Grose's *Treatise on Ancient Armour and Weapons; above and below,* two of the compositions from Sir Samuel Rush Meyrick, *A Critical Inquiry into Antient Armour . . .* (1824).

introduced into paintings and scenic representations of all kinds an historical correctness with which our ancestors were unacquainted'. He ridiculed artists, West among them, who used the Tower Armouries as their only quarry when these did not contain a single suit dating from before the reign of Henry VIII.[21] In the tradition of Strutt, this is an immensely erudite work, profusely if melodramatically illustrated with coloured engravings of knights of every period. The book is a tremendous leap forward from Grose, but the illustrations are tableaux from the medieval novels of Meyrick's friend, Sir Walter Scott.[22]

What was the influence of all these manuals? The first artist to 'come at the truth of antiquity' by means of Strutt was Benjamin West. *Regal and Ecclesiastical Antiquities* appeared in time to be used by West for his monumental series of paintings for George III on the French wars of Edward III. Moving on in time, we can see such instances increasing in number as antiquarianism came to preoccupy the painters. Thomas Stothard, father of the compiler of the *Monumental Effigies* and a prolific artist mainly in the Gothick Picturesque manner, used Strutt for the dresses of the medieval pilgrims in his most famous picture, *The Pilgrimage to Canterbury* (1806–7). Twenty years later, Bonington used Strutt even more directly for his picture of *Anne Page and Slender* (1826). Ford Madox Brown's *Chaucer at the Court of Edward III*, painted during the period 1856–68, again made use of Strutt for the ladies' headdresses, and the artist went on to use the Westminster tomb effigy of the King and the Canterbury Cathedral tomb effigy of the Prince, both drawn almost certainly from Stothard's *Monumental Effigies*. The result is slightly odd, as the Black Prince stands in full battle armour at an informal social gathering! In addition, Brown made use of the colourful illustrations in a French costume book, Camille Bonnard's *Costume Historique* (1829–30).[23] These few examples could be multiplied as we move into the High Victorian period, where every item on the surface of a historical canvas had to have its correct source.

By then, of course, artists were busy making costumes or hiring them from theatrical cos-

56, 57 The influence of Strutt's 'Travelling Dresses of the 14th Century' *(above)*, from *The Dress and Habits*, can be clearly seen *(top)* in Thomas Stothard, *The Pilgrimage to Canterbury* (1806–7, Tate Gallery, London). See also colour plate II.

58–61 Ford Madox Brown's *Chaucer at the Court of Edward III* (1856–68, Tate Gallery, London), together with some of the source material: *above left and centre*, tomb effigies of the Black Prince and Edward from Stothard's *Monumental Effigies; left,* 'Ladies' Head Dresses of the 14th Century', from Strutt's *Dress and Habits*. See also colour plates III and IV.

tumiers, but the sources were the same. Rossetti's visions of medieval romance are arrayed in clothes of the reign of Edward III which he had made up for him. We catch glimpses of this in letters written in the early seventies, when the artist was trying to locate what can only be described as his 'studio wardrobe' of medieval costume. 'Neither can I guess at all', Rossetti wrote, 'what has become of all the mediaeval costumes I used to have. For instance, I remember distinctly one woman's dress – cote-hardie, open up sides and kirtle to go under it – of white velvet quartered with yellow. This is not in your list and there were a number of men's dresses I know, not one of which seems to be extant.'[24]

Thackeray's amusing reviews of Royal Academy exhibitions in the 1840s, when accuracy in dress became a major preoccupation, are revealing on the attitude of both critics and public. Condemning Alfred Elmore's representation of Thomas à Becket with a 'black cassock beneath his canonicals', he writes: 'A painter should be as careful about his costumes as an historian about his dates.'[25] A bouquet is then handed to Charles Landseer for accuracy but, alas, 'the gentlemen and ladies do not look as though they were accustomed to their dresses, for all their correctness, and had put them on for the first time'[26] – which they probably had! Four years later, in 1844, he wrote of John Herbert's *The Trial of the Seven Bishops* (unlocated): 'In his attention to dress, Mr Herbert's picture is very praiseworthy; the men are quite at home in their quaint coats and periwigs of James the Second's time; the ladies in their stiff, long-waisted gowns, their fans, and their queer caps and patches.'[27] In these critical comments, which can be endlessly duplicated from other reviews of the Academy exhibitions, we witness the triumph of the costume historian.

In the small world of early- to mid-Victorian art and letters, the costume historians also acted directly as consultants on dress. Planché's *Recollections and Reflections* (1872) vividly recount the part he played in advising the history painters of the day. He was, for example, summoned to correct Wilkie on historical detail in his celebrated picture of John Knox preaching, although his information was promptly ignored.[28] He also helped Benjamin Robert Haydon over details in a vast canvas depicting the Black Prince thanking Lord Audley for his valour at the Battle of Poitiers.[29] Haydon wrote to Planché stating his belief in the artist's role as purveyor of historical truth.[30] Maclise sent the following request when he was about to start on his painting *An Interview between Charles I and Oliver Cromwell* in January 1836:

161, XI

Boldly then I would beg of you, if it were in your power, to put me in the way of getting a dress of Charles I., by borrowing or begging, or even if I knew

the address of a stage tailor I would give him an order and some black silk. I am about to paint a picture of Charles and Cromwell and Ireton, &c., and the dresses must be faithfully rendered. The picture being life-size we are forced to have the materials to paint from.[31]

Planché goes on to remember how his 'good friend and master', Sir Samuel Rush Meyrick, advised Abraham Cooper on his *Bosworth Field* (1825, unlocated), and explains how his own reputation as an authority on historic dress brought within his orbit most of the art establishment: Henry Perronet Briggs, William Etty, Charles and Edwin Landseer, George Cattermole, Bonington, Sir Charles Eastlake, Alfred and John Chalon.[32] Even at the age of eighty-two, he was approached by Millais for information on how to clothe the two boys for his picture of *The Princes in the Tower*. As a footnote, we know that Fairholt did the same thing, for William Powell Frith records his help in connection with the picture of *Claude Duval* (1859).

13

12

One final point which should perhaps be briefly mentioned is the simultaneous movement towards period accuracy in scenery and costume in the theatre. Like so many other facets of the relationship of antiquarianism to the arts in the nineteenth century, this really deserves a book on its own. As established by Planché in his famous production of *King John* in 1824, the theatre was one of the greatest vehicles whereby the present could indulge in recreations of times past. And Planché was a crucial pace-setter in the field; in 1834, for instance, he placed on stage the 'Hampton Court Beauties', based on the famous series of portraits by Sir Peter Lely. There was, in fact, a constant interplay between historical subject-matter on the stage and its manifestation in the visual arts.[33] Beyond even this, Planché leads us to a final, almost trivial nuance: the vogue for the costume ball. The three great costume balls given by Queen Victoria and the Prince Consort in the late forties and early fifties all had Planché as their consultant. Through them, past was assimilated to present for a night as the upper classes played the parts of their ancestors from the courts of Edward III, George II and Charles II.

The faces of the past: Vertue to Lodge

Ford Madox Brown's *Chaucer* is not only concerned with correct costume; it shows portrait likenesses based on tomb effigies. As in the case of dress, the Society of Antiquaries from its inception was greatly involved with the engraving and publication of portraits from the past. For this purpose George Vertue was employed as official draughtsman. In 1718, for example, he was asked to engrave for them the full-length portrait of Richard II in Westminster Abbey.[34] The year after, he was sent to Kensington Palace to inspect Remy van Leemput's copy of Holbein's destroyed wall-painting depicting the family of Henry VII, which he also subsequently engraved. At the same time the Society, like Queen Caroline, began to collect historical portraits.[35] As we saw in the last chapter, Vertue's greatest contribution was the portraits of kings and queens in the illustrated edition of Rapin, but he also went on to engrave a hundred portraits for Thomas Birch's *Heads of Illustrious Persons* (1747–52), which went into a second edition in 1813.

This portrait mania was intensified by James Granger's *Biographical History of England* (1769–74), a huge compilation of biographies and anecdotes combined with a list of all known engraved likenesses designed as 'a help to the knowledge of portraiture'. This led to the creation of extra-illustrated editions into which were inserted as many of the engravings he listed as possible, with a consequent terrifying defacement of early printed books. Later came the publication of books of engraved historical portraits designed specifically to illustrate Granger: *Richardson's Collection* (1792–1812), *Woodburn's Gallery of Rare Portraits* (1816) and *A Collection of Portraits to illustrate Granger's Biographical History* (1820–22). In addition to this, the pioneering work of Vertue was taken up again by John Thane, whose *Autography* (1776) combined portraits with specimens of handwriting.

Most of this passed by unnoticed as far as the painters in the Gothick Picturesque manner were concerned. It was not until the 1820s that

62, 63 The faces of the past: *left*, an engraving by Vertue of Lord Burghley, from Thomas Birch, *Heads of Illustrious Persons* (1747–52); *right*, the portrait of Anne Boleyn included by Edmund Lodge in his *Portraits of Illustrious Personages of Great Britain* (1821–34).

historical portraiture became definite in its reference, and this movement is epitomized by one book, Edmund Lodge's *Portraits of Illustrious Personages of Great Britain*. Like Planché, Lodge was a herald, and his interest in portraiture began with biography. He undertook, for instance, the biographies for John Chamberlaine's *Imitations of Original Drawings by Hans Holbein* (1792–1812), in which the famous portrait drawings were published for the first time. As a handbook for artists, *Portraits of Illustrious Personages* occupied a place comparable to that of Planché and Fairholt. In 1850 the *Art Journal* wrote of it as 'a valuable authority for costume and identical impersonation'.[36] No artist who wished to people his canvases with the great of the past could afford to be without this vade-mecum, in which portraits appeared side by side with a series of pleasantly written biographical and historical memoirs. The walls of the great houses of England – Hatfield, Petworth, Knowsley, Cassiobury, Penshurst, Wilton and Woburn – had been scoured for true likenesses of these famous characters. The work was initially published in forty parts from 1814 onwards. A collected edition was issued in four mammoth volumes between 1821 and 1834, and a second in twelve volumes in 1835, and finally it was made available to a mass public in an eight-volume edition issued in 1849–50 by Bohn's Illustrated Library.

64, 65 An engraving after Sir William Allan's *Lord Lindsay compelling Mary to abdicate* (1824), and *(below)* the 'Oudry Portrait' of Mary on which Allan's likeness is based (National Portrait Gallery, London).

Once again we sense the influence of Sir Walter Scott, whose letter printed in the 1821 edition sums up the tremendous appeal of this book to those who wished to voyage into the past: 'It is impossible for me to conceive a work more interesting to the present age than that which exhibits before our eyes our "fathers as they lived", to compare their persons and countenances with their sentiments and actions.'[37]

The heyday of Lodge's *Portraits* takes us right up to the era of the mass popularization of antiquities through cheap engravings and lithography. A decade after the Bohn edition of Lodge, the National Portrait Gallery opened in Great

George Street, Westminster. Behind its creation lay a formidable array of intellects, and above all the apostles of the role of the great man in the saga of a nation's history: Prince Albert, Lord Stanhope, Carlyle and Macaulay. For three years also, beginning in 1866, a great annual exhibition of historical portraits was held at the South Kensington Museum under the direction of the Portrait Gallery's first director, Sir George Scharf. The exhibitions covered the whole span of time from the fifteenth century down to the reign of Victoria, and for the first time the portraits were photographed. Many of these negatives still exist in the Victoria & Albert Museum. By 1870, the faces of the past could no longer be interpreted according to the whim of the present. The science of portrait iconography had been born.

When we turn to historical painting, it is during the 1820s, simultaneously with the publication of Lodge, that we find a definite effort by artists at correct historical likeness and genuine portrait research. In 1824 Sir William Allan painted his dramatic portrayal of the abdication of Mary Queen of Scots (unlocated), carefully basing his portrait of her on a version of the celebrated 'Oudry Portrait'. Bonington, for his picture of Surrey and his mistress, the fair Geraldine, painted in 1825–6, must have drawn on the engraving of the full-length portrait at Hampton Court believed to be of the poet Earl. In 1827 C. R. Leslie undertook careful research for his *Lady Jane Grey prevailed upon to accept the Crown*. The figure of Jane's unpleasant mother is derived from Vertue's engraving of the famous Hans Eworth double portrait then believed to show the Duchess of Suffolk and her last husband, Adrian Stokes. Leslie was also regarded as a major pioneer of accuracy in costume during the twenties: Richard Redgrave, Surveyor of the Queen's Pictures, recorded that 'his dresses at least have the air of truth', and when asked how he achieved this, Leslie replied that he 'made them up from old prints and pictures'.[38] By the thirties and forties the mania was being carried to extremes by artists such as William Fisk, whose trials of Strafford and Charles I boasted about a hundred authentic portraits between them – a phenomenon paralleled by the

14

66, 67 *Above*, Augustus Leopold Egg, *Queen Elizabeth discovers she is no longer Young* (1848, unlocated); *below*, a detail from William Larkin's portrait of Anne Clifford, Countess of Dorset (*c*. 1610, The Lord Sackville, Knole).

vast groups in George Hayter's *The Reformed House of Commons* (1833–43, National Portrait Gallery) and Maclise's *Meeting of Wellington and Blucher* (*c*. 1858–9, Houses of Parliament). By then artists were moving around and studying independently the portraits on the walls of the great houses of England. An instance of this is Augustus Egg's *Queen Elizabeth discovers she is no longer Young* (1848), a scene set in James I's state bedroom at Knole where the lady-in-waiting to the extreme left has stepped down from a canvas by Larkin of Anne Clifford, Countess of Dorset, now in the Knole ballroom. Of the travails attendant upon portrait research we obtain a glimpse in C. W. Cope's letter of 5 August 1861 to Redgrave, asking for permission to make a sketch of the head of Charles I from a picture at Hampton Court. 'I am told that you are the man who can help me,' writes Cope, and he goes on to inquire whether it would be possible to 'procure a scaffold there to get near the face'.[39] Here speaks the true descendant of Benjamin West and John Singleton Copley!

68, 69 A fifteenth-century canopied chair *(left)*
and a chair from Knole House *(right)* illustrated by
Henry Shaw in *Specimens of Ancient Furniture drawn
from existing authorities* (1836).

Historic furniture:
Henry Shaw

Costume and portraiture are two ingredients of
the visible past; interior decoration is another.
Terrible difficulties beset the artist as he attempted, before the advent of museums, to create the
mise en scène of an earlier age. Many of them
dodged the issue altogether by concentrating on
architecture, placing their characters in a landscape or resorting to a massive use of draperies.
By the 1830s, however, concern about accuracy
in furnishings had become as great as concern
over historic dress. Until then, as in the case of
dress, Strutt had been the pioneer source. His
*Manners, Customs, Arms, Habits, etc. of the
Inhabitants of England* did include an enormous
amount of information on furniture and interiors, which seems to have been used by West,
but no handy book of reference devoted entirely
to antique furniture appeared until 1836, when
the Antiquary Henry Shaw's *Specimens of Ancient
Furniture drawn from existing authorities* was
published.

This book was a milestone, and the learned
introduction written for it by Sir Samuel Rush
Meyrick reveals that, like the other manuals, it
was specifically designed for use by artists:

From the want of such a collection, artists of the
highest repute have sometimes produced pictures, of
which the details are so full of incongruities and
anachronisms, as materially detract from the general
merit of the piece. In an historical composition,
correctness of the auxiliaries is scarcely less important
than in the more prominent parts ... Extreme
accuracy, even in the minutest detail, can alone
produce that illusion which is requisite for the perfect
success of a work of art; everything must be
consistent to be complete, and an anachronism in an
historical picture is as offensive to the eye of taste as is
an imperfect metaphor or a defective verse to the ear.[40]

Thus Meyrick enunciates the gospel of the artist-
antiquarian. The book, which, it is stated, was
designed to complement Planché's work on
costume, consists of seventy-four plates cover-
ing tables, chairs, sideboards, mirrors, chan-
deliers, beds, lecterns, firedogs and other impe-
dimenta of bygone households. One plate, for
instance, illustrates a chair from Knole House
which is actually mid-seventeenth-century in
date, although included by Shaw as Jacobean.

Seven years later, Shaw followed this with his
Dresses and Decorations of the Middle Ages (1843),
an extremely lavish expedition into 'the varying
changes in dress and fashion' in which coloured
engravings of actual artefacts, illuminations
from manuscripts, portraits and other sources
are welded together to give a highly spectacular
impression of medieval life.

Whether or not artists actually used these
books is almost beside the point. What Shaw's
books did was to lay down that, here also,
accuracy was to reign supreme. By the 1850s the
South Kensington Museum collections were
becoming available for study as a source for
domestic utensils, and there were also the
hundreds of manor houses the length and
breadth of England which were believed to have
survived 'unchanged', encapsulating the ethos of
other eras. It is difficult to find specific instances
in which Shaw was definitely used, because the
material could have been obtained from other

70–72 *Above*, Ford Madox Brown, *John Wycliffe reading his Translation of the Bible to John of Gaunt* (*c.* 1847, Bradford Art Galleries and Museums), details of which were undoubtedly inspired by a study of Shaw. *Below*, Shaw's plates of the reading desks in Detling and Ramsay churches.

sources. One picture which probably draws on Shaw is Ford Madox Brown's *John Wycliffe reading his Translation of the Bible to John of Gaunt* (*c.* 1847). The lectern could be a combination of the reading desk from Detling church in Kent with the one from Ramsay church in Huntingdonshire. The Gothic canopied chair to the right could have been inspired by the plate of chairs, stools and beds of the fifteenth century, derived by Shaw from various manuscripts. With Shaw's books on furniture we have suddenly arrived in the modern world of 'antiques', and they had an immediate influence on contemporary furniture design.

Research for authentic furnishings, therefore, became a major preoccupation for artists engaged on historical compositions. The progress of Daniel Maclise's reconstruction of Edward IV's visit to William Caxton at Westminster can be followed in a letter he wrote to his friend John Forster in 1851:

Caxton's monograms, copied from original all seen pasted against a pillar – a facsimile of a hand bill – preserved in the Bodleian Library at Oxford . . . I was fortunate in getting an old press – which had been in the possession of Jeremy Bentham & worked by him – differing in no respect from the oldest representation in the woodcuts and exactly agreeing with the one in the title-page of a book printed in 1498 by a famous printer, Iodocus Badius Ascensianus.[41]

Maclise's approach to the England of Edward IV makes a dramatic contrast to that of Downman or Opie, sixty years earlier, when they depicted the amorous Edward encountering Elizabeth Woodville.

Historic architecture: Batty Langley to Hunt

Parallel with these developments ran the discovery of the architecture of the past. We do not need to linger long over this because it has been the most fully documented of all our fields of study owing to its very real relationship with revivalism in building. Kenneth Clark pioneered the subject in 1928 in his first book, *The Gothic Revival*, but he and the others who have followed have been primarily concerned with re-assessing the achievement of Victorian revivalist architects. In other words, the work of the early investigators has been looked at vertically, in terms of its influence on later generations, but never horizontally, in the broad context of its overall relationship to the rediscovery of the past. The pattern it follows is well plotted and reflects exactly that already seen in other fields. A Gothick Picturesque phase, typified by Batty Langley's *Gothick Architecture Improved* of 1742, was followed by an antiquarian phase represented by John Carter's *Ancient Architecture of England* (1795–1814) and John Britton's *Archit-*

ectural Antiquities of Great Britain (1805–26) and his *Cathedral Antiquities* series (1814–35). Then came the serious work of the twenties: Pugin's *Specimens of Gothic Architecture* (1820) and Joseph Nash's *A Series of Views Illustrative of Pugin's Examples of Gothic Architecture* (1830). These covered the Middle Ages, with detailed measured drawings, while Tudor and Stuart architecture was soon opened up in T. F. Hunt's *Exemplars of Tudor Architecture* (1830) and similar works by T. H. Clarke and C. T. Richardson.

Of these figures, John Carter (1748–1814) will serve to enlarge our understanding of the impact of antiquarianism on the visual arts in eighteenth- and early-nineteenth-century England. Carter received a grounding in architectural drawing, and at the age of thirty-two was employed as a draughtsman by the Society of Antiquaries. In 1795 he became a Fellow, and his first important work was *Specimens of Ancient Sculpture and Painting* (1780–94), the first volume of which was dedicated to Horace Walpole. Henceforth his preoccupation was to be the exact archaeological recording of Gothic, but a watercolour he executed in 1790, entitled *The Entry of Prince Frederick into the Castle of Otranto*, demonstrates a talent for accurate recreation of the past far greater than any displayed by the history painters of the Gothick Picturesque in the Academy. Into an amalgamation of real and imaginary Gothic architecture he has inserted a throng of people in medieval dress. The general feeling is that of the late fifteenth century; a king and queen stand to the right, knights in armour with plumes fluttering enter through a castellated gateway to the left, and trumpeters and musicians are grouped in the foreground.[42] In this composition, significantly, the antiquarian draughtsman has crossed the bridge of the imagination and become an artist.

73 An antiquarian recreates the Middle Ages. John Carter, *The Entry of Prince Frederick into the Castle of Otranto* (1790, Mr W. S. Lewis, Farmington, Connecticut).

74, 75 *Top*, the hall at Penshurst, Kent, as depicted by Joseph Nash in *The Mansions of England in the Olden Time* (1839–49); *above*, Strutt's 'Ladies of Rank of the 15th and 16th Centuries', from *The Dress and Habits*.

Antiquarian into artist: Nash and Cattermole

Useful though all these works of reference were to the painter – as indeed were the actual buildings themselves – one book more than any other had a potent influence on how people wished to see the England of the past. This was Joseph Nash's (1809–78) *The Mansions of England in the Olden Time*, published between 1839 and 1849. It had an enormous success, and ran into several subsequent editions in the course of the century. Through its picturesque recreation of life within a great house, inspired by the Intimate Romantic tradition of Bonington, it cast a powerful spell. The formula which Nash hit upon was a simple one: into not particularly accurate views of medieval, Tudor and Stuart houses he inserted scenes and figures appropriate to the period of the architecture.[43] Perhaps it is no coincidence that this book appeared around the same time as Harrison Ainsworth's *Tower of London* (1840), which employs exactly the same technique in the novel.

The great hall at Penshurst Place is evoked by Nash in its splendour as of old. We are asked to witness the arrival of the Yuletide log (a happening derived from Strutt's *Sports and Pastimes* and symptomatic of Merry England), and the hall is filled with revellers; the huge log is presided over by a man dressed as a medieval wildman; guests lean down from the minstrels' gallery while elegant figures parade in the foreground, ladies in elaborate fifteenth-century trailing gowns and fantastic headdresses attended by gentlemen in equally rich attire. If the figures look a trifle familiar, it is hardly surprising, for they are lifted straight out of Strutt. Nash, of course, states that all his costumes and activities are derived from authentic sources.

76–8 *Top*, the Gallery at Hatfield House as Nash saw it. *Above left*, Strutt's portrait of Anne of Denmark, from *The Dress and Habits*; *above right*, Marcus Gheeraerts, *Anne Pope, Lady Wentworth, later Countess of Downe, and her Children* (1596, unlocated).

76 In the Long Gallery at Hatfield House, James I and his Queen, Anne of Denmark, stand

77 graciously receiving. Queen Anne is again from Strutt, but the lady and her little boy to the right are taken from a portrait then at Wroxton Abbey

78 of the Countess of Downe and her children. The formula is so brilliant and persuasive that one almost misses the fact that the costumes represented in this animated group stretch over a period of twenty-five years, from 1595 to 1620, and that the chair on the left is definitely not Jacobean. Down the celebrated staircase at Hardwick Hall sweeps a lady wearing a dress of about 1610, based on the portrait that Egg was later to use of the Countess of Dorset at Knole. It would be easy not to notice that she is walking downstairs past tapestries woven many years after her death.

George Cattermole (1800–1868) indulged in similar antiquarian reveries in his works. He was in fact trained by the antiquary John Britton, who encouraged Planché, and contributed to his *Cathedral Antiquities*. A watercolourist and illustrator, he has been categorized as 'the greatest representative, if not the founder, in England of the art that sought its motives in the restoration of bygone times, with their manners and customs, their architecture and costumes, their chivalrous and religious sentiment, complete'.[44] Simultaneously with Nash, he hit on the formula of inserting costume figures, often based on portraits, into carefully reconstructed architectural settings of previous periods. Nothing was to touch Nash's *Mansions*, but Cattermole's *The Great Civil War of Charles I and the Parliament* (two volumes, 1841 and 1845) and *Evenings at Haddon Hall* (1846) contributed greatly in their own way to this visual voyage into times past.

79 The staircase at Hardwick, from *The Mansions of England*.

And, as in the case of Nash, his debt to Dutch
genre painting is patently obvious; *Goring
Carousing*, for example, is a straight adaptation of a
Netherlandish tavern scene. In *Republican Preaching* he inserts Roundhead soldiers into a compilation of ecclesiastical architecture which could
only have been conceived by someone trained as
an antiquarian draughtsman.

The last point is important. The background
and training of both these artists were utterly
different from those of the painters who went
through the Academy Schools. Nash was trained
by the elder Pugin, and assisted him in his exact
drawings of Gothic architecture. Cattermole
owed his career to the architectural and topographical antiquary Britton. In other words, one
of the strongest forces in the movement to
recreate the past came from antiquarian
draughtsmen turned artist-illustrators. They had
a grounding in the accurate recording of the
background to history which could not be
paralleled in the training of an academic painter.

80, 81 George Cattermole, *Republican Preaching* and
Goring Carousing from *The Great Civil War of
Charles I and the Parliament* (1841 and 1845).

71

Artist into antiquarian

Cattermole and Joseph Nash were antiquarian draughtsmen turned artist, but of course the process worked both ways. In response to the demand from scholars and public alike that paintings should be an accurate record of time past, the artist himself was progressively forced to become an antiquarian. We only have to look at pictures or photographs of the interiors of artists' studios in the Victorian period to realize that a revolution had taken place. Instead of being filled with plaster casts after the antique, they are often piled high with old furniture, armour and clothes. Models were dressed up in reproductions of medieval costume. A glance at any of the figure studies, for instance, for Ford Madox Brown's *Chaucer at the Court of Edward III* reveals that it was standard practice in the forties to clothe models in costumes made up according to the illustrations in Strutt, Planché or Fairholt.

A letter from Brown to Lowes Dickinson written during the painting of the earlier version of this picture reads like a shopping list:

I have been out this evening to procure divers little articles which still remain to be painted in, and have procured a hood of chain mail from Cross, who returned last night from Devonshire, also some feathers to make a fan, and some cloth of gold. Some flowers, a dog, and some white velvet will complete the nasty list of little things to be run after.[45]

Sketchbooks were now constantly filled with drawings of useful antiquarian matter; they became a painter's visual repository for accurate period detail of his own selection. The contents of both studio and sketchbook were fundamental for the methodology of recreating the past.

As accuracy of this kind came within reach through the forties and fifties, it became more and more meaningless and more and more crippling. What had begun as a thrilling adventure, an artistic time machine, had by the third quarter of the nineteenth century become paralysing. A door had been flung open into the past, the artist had entered and had found himself not emancipated but imprisoned. To the generation coming up in the eighties and nineties, it was anathema.

By 1865, the demand on the artist for authenticity of detail was such as to be almost suffocating. In that year Ford Madox Brown looked back over the previous two decades and wrote the critical epitaph on the artist as antiquarian:

... twenty years ago, extreme exactness in matters external and archaeological was less in vogue than it is now ... With me in those days, the dramatic interest in a subject outweighed every other consideration, such was the example set by Delacroix in France ... set, though not followed.[46]

These views were to be re-echoed even more strongly eight years later by Frederick Leighton as he deliberately abandoned medievalism to pursue classicism:

... my growing love for Form made me intolerant of the restraint and exigencies of costume, and led me more and more, and finally, to a class of subjects, or, more accurately, to a set of conditions, in which supreme scope is left to pure artistic qualities, in which no form is imposed upon the artist by the tailor, but in which every form is made obedient to the conception of the design he has in hand.[47]

These words herald the end of that brief brilliant alliance of the artist and the antiquarian, a relationship which was to be relegated by the end of the century to the world of the illustrator and the theatre designer – and, in our own century, the movie spectacular. At its best it had created some of the most stirring and astounding tableaux of our national history, so strong that a hundred years later we are still unable to visualize them in any other way.

82 Ford Madox Brown, pencil study for *Chaucer at the Court of Edward III* (1847, by courtesy of Birmingham Museums and Art Gallery).

Conclusion: Decline and Eclipse

THE HEYDAY was suddenly over, and history was in retreat. How could this vast and exciting expansion in visual imagery have become, within a generation, almost meaningless? The re-creation of the British past in painting belongs to that age when history was still literature for a mass audience, when historians espoused causes with fervour, inviting their readers to take sides, to make moral judgments and to follow the emergence of their nation to its present glory. The climax of this belief might be said to be J. R. Green's best-selling *A Short History of the English People*, published in 1874. This was virtually the last time that serious history was also popular literature.

By 1895, when Acton was appointed Regius Professor of History at Cambridge, everything had changed. Although the scientific study of history had developed earlier on the Continent, and above all in Germany, the home of Niebuhr, Ranke and Burkhardt, it did not reach Britain until the last quarter of the century. Gradually, history became the province of professors and dons and no longer that of men of letters, artists and poets. The educated public came to regard history as a field for scientific inquiry. Historians buried themselves in the critical study of their sources and reacted to the discoveries of Darwin and Spencer. And as this happened, history progressively ceased to be a vehicle of any substance or meaning for the visual arts.

Not only this, but the whole iconography of Victorian painting came under attack. One of the objects of the artists who belonged to the New English Art Club, founded in 1886, was a change of attitude to subject-matter in painting. The late-nineteenth-century rebels, Sickert, Whistler, Sargent, Steer and the rest of them, wanted a reassertion of purely pictorial values in painting and a rejection of the illustrative and anecdotal.

In other words, their stylistic statement implied a radically revised iconography in which the Victorian vision of the British past could no longer have any validity or meaning.

More important still than these raps at the door of the establishment was the canker within. We can trace this vividly in G. A. Storey's *Sketches from Memory* (1899), where the artist's sudden realization that he is doing little more than producing meaningless, bogus costume masquerades is vividly recounted. Storey was a member of the St John's Wood Clique, the group foremost in the sixties in promoting these scenes from the past. Here is what he writes about his efforts to compose a picture on the subject of the Lady Arabella Stuart, a favourite doomed heroine of the mid-Victorian age:

But what did I know about Arabella Stuart and James I., except what Miss Lucy Aikin had told me in her two volumes, and what I could pick up from prints of the period? I got up my accessories just as a stage manager would do for a new piece, borrowed costumes from Nathan & Co. [the theatrical costumiers], and dressed up my model like a pantaloon, to signify the canny King of Scots . . . I tried to imagine William Seymour as a sentimental lover, and to make Arabella pretty, despite her bald forehead and her dreadful farthingale.[1]

This sudden disillusionment was born of a visit to Madrid and a study of Velasquez's *Las Meninas* (1656, Prado) and *The Surrender of Breda* (1634, Prado), and here followed the crucial confession:

In the work of Velasquez I knew that not only were the costumes correct, but the actual men of the time were there before me, the period stamped, not only on the dress, but on every face, in the very attitudes even of the figures; the whole belonging so completely to its own day, even as the hand that wrought it, that I felt I had a true page of history before me, and not a theatrical make-up of a scene dimly realised in the pages of some book written many years after the event.[2]

This passage sounds the death knell of such reconstructions, because in it the artist has finally acknowledged failure. More and more contact with the art of the past, which by 1899 was being made easy by the advent of the half-tone block, must have accentuated the shortcomings of these recreations and confirmed the total impossibility of their aim. The great adventure had reached its end.

But for almost a century, the adventure had attracted the most brilliant in the world of the arts, and the vision of the British past had been strong and effectual. It is now lost to us, because our eye still tends to be offended by these evocations, which seem on first encounter so shallow and artificial and apparently reduce the painter to the level of a trivial illustrator. But that is where modern critical judgment is wrong. The study of the iconography of Victorian painters is in its infancy. Their historical mythology is just as rich in comment and allusion as their genre paintings of contemporary life, but it requires reading, and we have lost the art. In order to recapture it, we have to take a different path in our pursuit of the Victorian vision of the British past. We have to face up to the irony that the past was only reconstructed in order to speak about the present. And the only way to show this is to unravel the pictures themselves, to study the recreators and their recreations, to trace their themes and obsessions through the history of Britain, revealing the truth of Buckle's tenet that there is always 'a connexion between the way in which men contemplate the past, and the way in which they contemplate the present; both views being in fact different forms of the same habits of thought'.[3]

83 'Milkmaids' Dance, with pile of plate, on May Day', from Charles Knight, *Old England* (1844).

Part II
Recreators and Recreations

Historical subjects require a very great deal of thought and research, which, perhaps, accounts for their having almost disappeared in the present days. I have always considered that the art that can conjure up past events and make them a living reality is something of an achievement, well worth all the pains bestowed upon it.

MRS. E. M. WARD
Memories of Ninety Years (1924)

84 Plate VI from Strutt, *Honda Angel-cynnan* . . . (1774–6).

85   *The Institution of the Order of the Garter.*

Benjamin West
Edward III series, 1787–9

The Institution of the Order of the Garter
1787
Oil on canvas, 113 × 176½ in. (287 × 448.3 cm)
On loan to the Palace of Westminster

Edward, the Black Prince, receiving King John of France after the Battle of Poitiers
1788
Oil on canvas, 113 × 177 in. (287 × 449.6 cm)
On loan to the Palace of Westminster

Edward III with the Black Prince after the Battle of Crécy 1788
Oil on canvas, 113 × 176 in. (287 × 447 cm)
On loan to the Palace of Westminster

Edward III entertaining his Prisoners 1788
Oil on canvas, 39⅜ × 60⅛ in. (100 × 152.7 cm)
Kensington Palace

Edward III crossing the Somme 1788
Oil on canvas, 54 × 59 in. (137.2 × 149.9 cm)
Kensington Palace

Queen Philippa at the Battle of Nevill's Cross 1789
Oil on canvas, 38¾ × 59¾ in. (98.4 × 151.8 cm)
Kensington Palace

Edward III and the Burghers of Calais 1789
Oil on canvas, 39⅜ × 60⅜ in. (100 × 153.4 cm)
Kensington Palace

Royal Collection

86, 87 *Top*, the various officers of the Order of the Garter, as recorded by Elias Ashmole in his book of the same name (1672); *right*, the Earl of Shrewsbury in garter-embroidered mantle, from *Regal and Ecclesiastical Antiquities*.

88 *Edward, the Black Prince, receiving King John after the Battle of Poitiers.*

BENJAMIN WEST (1728–1820)[1] was born in Pennsylvania. He went to Italy in 1760, where he met Cardinal Albani and Anton Raphael Mengs, and arrived in England in 1763. Through the Archbishop of York he gained the patronage of George III and was appointed Historical Painter to the King in 1772. A founder member of the Royal Academy, he succeeded Reynolds as President in 1792. Throughout the eighties he was high in royal favour, embarking on a series of thirty-five canvases illustrating the history of revealed religion for the royal chapel at Windsor Castle. By 1811 royal patronage, which had been declining for some time, ceased altogether.

West initially established his reputation with canvases on classical subjects, such as *The Landing of Agripinna at Brundisium with the Ashes of Germanicus* (1766), which incorporated the latest archaeological evidence in the manner of Mengs and Gavin Hamilton. With his most famous painting, *The Death of General Wolfe* (1771), he caused a revolution in history painting by applying the same principles to the reconstruction of the recent past as he used for the recreation of scenes from classical antiquity or the Middle Ages, besides apotheosizing a contemporary hero without the apparatus of allegory. His work remains to be studied and evaluated in depth.

West's series of canvases for the King's Audience Room at Windsor Castle were painted between 1787 and 1789.[2] Their theme was appropriate to Windsor, home of the Order of the Garter, for they celebrate the victories of Edward III and the Black Prince during the Hundred Years War and the foundation of the Order. In their original setting they centred on a picture of St George slaying the dragon, also painted by West, which hung over the fireplace. Their subject-matter was derived from Hume, although there is a possibility, as Oliver Millar

89 *Edward III with the Black Prince after the Battle of Crécy.*

has pointed out, that West made excursions into Froissart's *Chronicles.*

Without doubt these canvases, three of which are on an enormous scale, represent the most significant step forward in an accurate recreation of the Middle Ages made by any painter in late-eighteenth-century England. They are milestones in the emergence of the artist-antiquarian. Henry Angelo, in his *Reminiscences* (1830), records the care that West took over historical accuracy, so much so that at times he 'had found it necessary to depart from the first plans, as he obtained new historical facts, particularly in the armorial bearings'.[3] His biographer tells of West's search, with royal support, for 'historical truth', which led him to the 'inspection of many an ancient volume and much antiquarian research'.[4] Such an approach was revolutionary, and although the paintings may vary in quality they still have the force of an original idea. For the King, West had succeeded in bringing Edward III's legendary victories over the French

'into form and being, with a veracity of historical fact and circumstance which render the masquerades by Vario even a greater disgrace to St George's Hall than they are to the taste of the age in which they were painted'.[5]

Although the armour reflects the study of Grose and visits to the Tower Armouries,[6] the pictures are above all evidence of the supreme importance of the works of Strutt for the development of the artist-antiquarian. Plate xv in *Regal and Ecclesiastical Antiquities* is taken from British Museum Cotton MS. Nero D.6, and depicts Edward III giving his son the Black Prince the conquered provinces of France. The King is attired in armour, and his helmet is encircled by a crown. Over the armour he wears a tabard embroidered with the arms of England and France, and a bejewelled belt is slung across his hips. These figures form the basis for West's representation of Edward and his son throughout the series, although he takes liberties, of course, over the details. In *Edward III entertaining*

90

his Prisoners, the King is in the costume but minus the helmet. In *Edward III with the Black Prince after the Battle of Crécy*, West transforms the tabard into a wide-sleeved short coat and adds a lion to the helmet.

Strutt's book provided West with up-to-date antiquarian information for the first picture he painted for the series, *The Institution of the Order of the Garter*, in which Edward III, the Black Prince and the new Knights gather around an altar at the Order's inauguration. West certainly made use of Elias Ashmole's definitive work (1672) on the Order of the Garter for several figures, notably for the officers. Ashmole narrates that the mantles of the Knights at the inauguration were embroidered all over with garters, but he includes no picture of this costume.[7] Plate XLIII of Strutt's book, however, reproduces an illumination of John Talbot, Earl of Shrewsbury wearing just such a garter-embroidered mantle,

90, 91 *Above,* Edward III and the Black Prince as depicted by Strutt in *Regal and Ecclesiastical Antiquities; below,* Edward III entertaining his Prisoners.

92 *Edward III crossing the Somme.*

kneeling and presenting a book to Henry VI and Margaret of Anjou, and this surely is what West used for the kneeling Garter Knights flanking the altar.

West's greatest debt was to Strutt's work *Honda Angel-cynnan or, A compleat View of the Manners, Customs, Arms, Habits, etc. of the Inhabitants of England, from the Arrival of the Saxons till the Reign of Henry the Eighth*, issued between 1774 and 1776. *The Dress and Habits*, destined to become even more influential, would have been a mine of information, but it did not appear until a decade after, too late for West to use it in the Edward III series. In the second volume of *Honda Angel-cynnan*, a work conceived on the same principles as *Regal and Ecclesiastical Antiquities*, the section dealing with the 'English Aera' covers the period of the Hundred Years War. Eleven chapters are devoted to warfare, including 'Soldiers and Armies of the English', 'The Arrangement of the Army' and 'Warlike Habits'. Costume, sports, pastimes, husbandry,

93, 94 Two battle scenes from Strutt's *Honda Angel-cynnan* . . . (1774–6): *top*, plate XLIII, with the original of the palisading used by West in *Edward III and the Burghers of Calais* (ill. 14); *above*, plate XLVI, showing the archers which appear in reverse in *Edward III crossing the Somme.*

tournaments, regalia, musical instruments and banqueting are all described in detail from original sources, with many illustrations engraved from old manuscripts. Of the sixty plates which illustrate these scenes of English medieval life, over fifty are redrawn from the late-fifteenth-century manuscript *The Pageant of Richard Beauchamp, Earl of Warwick.*

For an example of West's antiquarian approach we can turn to his *Edward III and the Burghers of Calais.* In the bottom right-hand corner there is a strange-looking object with cannon-balls by it. Strutt, in discussing the use of gunpowder, cites Camden: 14

'For', says he (speaking of guns) 'the very time of their first invention is uncertaine, but certaine it is that king Edward the Third used them at the siege of Calice, 1347, for gunnarii had their pay there, as appears by record.'[8]

Turning to Plate VI, figs. 20 and 21 of Strutt's book, we find two cannons of the type West has placed in his picture. Strutt in turn admits lifting them from Plate 42 in Volume III of Montfaucon's *Monumens de la Monarchie Française* (1729–33). The cannons actually date from 1442, but even this does not detract from West's exceptional zeal for historical accuracy. 84

Indeed the whole presentation of West's scenes from the wars, with all their accoutrements, must stem from Strutt:

The kings went royally habited to the wars, with their standards borne before them: thus the Chronicles report of Henry the Fifth, that at Agincourt he rode in the main battle completely armed; his shield quartered with the royal achievements of England and France: upon his helmet he wore a coronet, circled with pearls and precious stones of inestimable price: his horse of fierce courage, prancing as he went; the bridle and furniture was of goldsmith's work, and the caparisons were most richly embroidered, with most victorious ensigns of the English monarchy: before him was borne the royal standard, which was ornamented with gold and glorious colours, with many other banners in warlike order waving in the wind.[9]

Strutt's description reads like a programme for the regal panoply of battle in most of the pictures. *Edward III crossing the Somme* is really Strutt's vision of Henry V at Agincourt. 92

95 *Queen Philippa at the Battle of Nevill's Cross.*

Above all, West's battle scenes reflect his study of the numerous military encounters illustrated by Strutt from *The Pageant of Richard Beauchamp, Earl of Warwick*. In spite of the fact that these illustrations would be more appropriate to the battles fought a century later in the Wars of the Roses, they are the ones West used for his horse accoutrements, weapons, banners, tents and armour. The archers of Strutt's Plate XLVI, for instance, turn up in the distance in *Edward III crossing the Somme,* and the palisading which he uses in a siege scene is fittingly placed behind Edward III and his Queen at the siege of Calais. It could also be argued that West's frieze-like formula for many of the compositions is deliberate archaizing under the influence of medieval art.

This unprecedented marriage of medieval sources with the Grand Manner of late-eighteenth-century English painting was celebrated by Sir Thomas Lawrence in his presidential address to the students of the Royal Academy in 1823:

At an aera when Historical Painting was at the lowest ebb . . . Mr West, sustained by the beneficent patronage of his late Majesty, produced a series of compositions from sacred and profane history, profoundly studied, and executed with the most facile power, which not only were superior to any former productions of English Art, but, far surpassing contemporary merit on the continent, were unequalled at any period below the schools of the Caracci.[10]

94
92
93
4

96

Richard Parkes Bonington

Henry IV and the Spanish Ambassador
1827–8
Oil on canvas, $15\frac{1}{2} \times 20\frac{7}{8}$ in. (39 × 53 cm)
Wallace Collection, London

RICHARD PARKES BONINGTON (1802–28)[1] was born near Nottingham. Owing to the depression in the lace industry the Bonington family left England in 1817 and settled firstly in Calais and later in Paris. In 1819 Bonington entered the studio of Baron Gros at the Ecole des Beaux-Arts, where he remained for a period of two years. He travelled extensively in France and the Low Countries to make drawings which were lithographed for his own *Restes et Fragmens d'Architecture du Moyen Age* and Baron Taylor's

Voyages Pittoresques et Romantiques dans l' Ancienne France (both 1824). In 1825 he came to London, where he met Delacroix, and on their return to France the two shared a studio. In 1826 Bonington travelled to Italy and stayed in Venice. He exhibited at the Royal Academy in 1827, and visited England in that year and again in 1828, the year he died. Although primarily a painter of cities and landscapes, he painted subjects from the literary and historic past charged with a unique charm and nostalgia which had a potent influence on the development of history as a subject for the Victorian genre painter.

Bonington's *Henry IV and the Spanish Ambassador* exists in two versions, both in the Wallace Collection and both reflecting his

97–101 Bonington's sources and inspirations. *Top left*, Johannes Vermeer, *A Lady at the Virginals, with a Gentleman Listening* (c. 1660, Royal Collection). *Top right*, Jean-Auguste-Dominique Ingres, *Henry IV surprised by the Spanish Ambassador while playing with his Children* (1818, Petit Palais, Paris). *Left and below*, details from Peter Paul Rubens, *Marie de' Medici* (c. 1622, Prado), Frans Pourbus, *Henry IV* (1610, Royal Collection), and Van Dyck, *The Children of Charles I* (1637, Royal Collection).

methods of historical recreation. The subject must have been directly inspired by Ingres's canvas painted in 1817 but not exhibited until the Salon of 1824.[2] This is related in theme to a whole series of paintings executed in celebration of the restored monarchy which exalted the virtues of its forebears, the Valois and Bourbon kings of France. Henry IV is commemorated here as the good father not only of his own children but also of his people. Ingres's picture (of which at least two other versions are known) emphasizes this by preserving a degree of formality in its framework: the Queen, Marie de' Medici, sits before a columned state bed. Bonington was surely drawn to this subject not as a morality of monarchy but purely as an informal view of the great. He has therefore jettisoned the overtones of formality and placed

98

102 Léonard Gaultier, *The Regency of Marie de' Medici* (1613).

103, 104 *Left*, Edward Scriven's engraving entitled *Henry Howard, Earl of Surrey*; *right*, the very close copy produced by Bonington in *The Earl of Surrey and the Fair Geraldine* (1825–6, Wallace Collection, London). See also colour plate v.

his characters instead in a room whose debt to his study of seventeenth-century Dutch interiors needs little elaboration. This is tempered by borrowings from and recollections of Van Dyck's *The Children of Charles I* (1637): the draped background, the still life with the jug, the children and their costumes and the little spaniel are all re-echoed. The aristocratic overtones of Van Dyck, however, are reduced in favour of a playful atmosphere reminiscent of Dutch genre scenes of middle-class life. For the figure of Henry IV Bonington could have used any one of Pourbus's famous likenesses of the King, and for Marie de' Medici he has resorted with little alteration to a version of Rubens's famous portrait.

What is the net result? Is it an accurate representation of the past or not? The answer, of course, is that it is not. An engraving of the family of Marie de' Medici dated 1613 gives one a more correct visual point of reference unknown to Bonington. As it is, the painter has combined a likeness of Henry IV of *c.* 1605–10 and one of Marie de' Medici of *c.* 1622 with children in costumes of the 1630s. It is a hotchpotch, and if the atmosphere were not so compelling we would regard the picture as little short of ludicrous.

Henry IV and the Spanish Ambassador provides us with an accurate insight into Bonington's methods as an artist-antiquarian. He made wide use of historical portraits, which he reinterpreted and placed in settings whose inspiration could be either Netherlandish or Venetian. In *François I and Marguerite de Navarre* (1827) he married Titian's portrait of Francis I to a French sixteenth-century chalk drawing of the Queen of Navarre which exists in several versions. *The Earl of Surrey and the Fair Geraldine* (1825–6) incorporates a full-length figure of the poet derived from an engraving of a portrait at Hampton Court then believed to be of him.

Bonington's solitary expedition into the Middle Ages was *Anne Page and Slender* (1826), a Shakespearian scene. No one seems to have noticed that for this picture he made use of Strutt's *Complete View of the Dress and Habits of the People of England*. Anne Page is taken, very little altered, from a plate depicting 'Ladies of High

Rank of the 14th Century', and Slender is based on a figure showing 'Persons of High Rank of the 15th Century'. Bonington has taken off the hat, so that Slender has to clasp its trailing scarf; he has kept the pointed sleeves and fringed edge to the skirt of the upper garment, but made it parti-coloured, and has put Slender into shoes taken from the previous plate, 'Persons of Distinction of the 15th Century'.

Such instances could easily be multiplied among the figures Bonington has lifted and rearranged into compositions designed to evoke reveries of time past.

105–7 Bonington's *Anne Page and Slender* (1826, Wallace Collection, London), together with their originals from Strutt's *Dress and Habits*.

108–10 A detail of the portrait by Titian of François I (c. 1536–9, Louvre), and the chalk drawing of the Queen of Navarre (c. 1540, Musée Condé, Chantilly), on which Bonington based his painting *François I and Marguerite de Navarre* (1827, Wallace Collection, London).

89

111 See also colour plate VI.

William Powell Frith

Coming of Age in the Olden Time 1849
Oil on canvas, $34\frac{1}{2} \times 54\frac{1}{2}$ in. (87.7 × 138.5 cm)
Alexander Gallery, London

WILLIAM POWELL FRITH (1819–1909)[1] was born
at Aldfield, near Ripon in Yorkshire. After an
unsatisfactory early education he entered the
Royal Academy Schools, beginning his career as
a portrait painter. In 1840 he established his
success as a subject painter by exhibiting *Malvolio
before the Countess Olivia* (unlocated) and *Othello
and Desdemona* (unlocated) at the Royal Academy.
Frith stuck closely to literary subjects from
Cervantes, Scott, Molière, Goldsmith, Shakespeare or the *Spectator*. In 1845 he was elected
ARA, and five years later toured Belgium,
Holland and the Rhine. After his return there
occurred that sudden change in subject-matter
which led to his most famous scenes of High
Victorian life: *Life at the Seaside: Ramsgate Sands*

(1854, Royal Collection), *Derby Day* (1858, Tate
Gallery) and *The Railway Station* (1862, Royal
Holloway College). He became an RA in 1854.
During the seventies came two contemporary
moralities in the tradition of Hogarth: the *Road
to Ruin* series (1878) and the *Race for Wealth* series
(1880) (both Baroda, India). Frith lived to a great
age, outliving by decades the popularity of his
own most famous pictures. There is no major
study of this painter, whose attitude of scorn
towards all progressive movements in mid- and
late Victorian art has probably blurred our
recognition of his influence both on them and, in
subject-matter, on the Impressionists.

W. P. Frith, whose smug autobiography is so
much at variance with the warmth of human
observation in his greatest pictures, *Ramsgate
Sands, Derby Day* and *The Railway Station*, was
also a prolific painter of historical scenes within
the genre tradition. In the recent reappraisal of

Frith as an artist these, along with those based on literary sources, have been virtually ignored, left out of consideration as though they were speaking a language far removed from that of the works which we now accept as his masterpieces. But any examination of Frith's historical works will show exactly the opposite: they are, in fact, accurate mirrors of contemporary attitudes reflected back into the past.

It was Frith's historical and literary scenes which established him as a painter of repute in the forties, when he moved in the circle of Charles Dickens and the painter Augustus Egg. At the Royal Academy in 1849 Frith exhibited one of his most acclaimed paintings, *Coming of Age in the Olden Time*. In the courtyard of a grand Elizabethan manor house an excited crowd has gathered to hail the golden youth who stands on the stairs leading up to the entrance to the house. His relatives are near: an old lady, presumably his grandmother, wearing a large ruff, sits on the terrace; behind her stand his parents. At the foot of the steps a man in black reads out the announcement while the rest of the area bustles with incipient revelry: tenants, villagers and country folk gather to listen to the news, others raise their glasses in salute or feast at trestle tables from the ox being roasted in the courtyard (Frith writes that he had been to an ox-roasting). It is a vision of the good Merry England of Olden Times, the society exalted by Disraeli in *Sybil*, when men were tied to the land and cared for by benevolent gentry, before the rottenness of industrialization and its grasping agents came to corrupt the happy and innocent people.

In his autobiography Frith writes that he began this picture in September 1848 and finished it in the April of the following year.[2] Although he says that the house in the composition was made up of elements drawn from Hever Castle, Kent, and Heslington Hall, near York, he has in fact knitted together sections of various buildings from Nash's *Mansions*. The entrance to the right is taken from the porch at Wroxton Abbey, and details of the main entrance arch are lifted from a view of the interior of the courtyard at Hever Castle, while the gabling is adapted from Nash's view of Westwood in Worcestershire.

112–14 Joseph Nash used as a source. Three illustrations from *The Mansions of England in the Olden Time* (1839–49): *top to bottom*, Wroxton Abbey, Oxfordshire, Hever Castle, Kent and Westwood, Worcestershire.

115, 116 The brass of Cicely Page from Fairholt's *Costume in England* (1846), as adapted *(left)* by Frith.

120 Artist unknown, *Elizabeth Talbot, Countess of Shrewsbury* (*c.* 1580, National Trust, Hardwick Hall; detail). Some such portrait must have inspired Frith's depiction of the youth's grandmother.

117, 118 Fairholt's 'Dress of the commonalty in the reign of Edward VI' and his portrait of the Earl of Surrey.

119 Detail of Cornelis Dusart, *Kermesse* (1695, Musées Royaux des Beaux-Arts, Brussels).

Over the costumes Frith claimed to have taken great trouble. Research in the British Museum Print Room, he recounts, could easily be unprofitable, and no readily accessible authorities on dress were at hand to give paid advice on period costume detail, as apparently they were by the time he came to write the autobiography. He must, however, have started with Fairholt's *Costume in England*, which was published two years before. The lady with a large hat is based on Fairholt's picture of a brass of Cicely Page, reproduced as a 'pretty specimen of the dress of a country lady',[3] and variants of his 'dress of the commonalty in the reign of Edward VI' could have furnished Frith with all that he needed to know to costume the people who revel in the courtyard.[4] Certain figures, however, contain more specific references. The aged lady seated at the head of the staircase is surely lifted from some late Elizabethan half-length portrait, the youth wears clothes based on Fairholt's version of a portrait then at Hampton Court, believed to be of the Earl of Surrey and illustrated as typical of aristocratic dress in the reign of Henry VIII,[5] and the little girl running forwards with her apron full of flowers could derive from one of a number of pictures with this motif painted in the early seventeenth century. All these elements are welded together by a compositional scheme derived from Dutch paintings of the *kermesse* and – more surprisingly – from the traditional formula for Christ exhibited to the Populace.

Frith's historical pictures, therefore, give a fascinating glimpse into the methods of the mid-Victorian artist-antiquarian. For his *Knox reproving Mary Queen of Scots*, exhibited in 1844, he had visited what he refers to as 'that delightful hunting-ground for artists', Knole House in Kent.[6] The Queen sits weeping on a sofa based on one of the most famous pieces of Jacobean furniture to survive, the Knole sofa. Returning to the fruitful subject of the travails of Mary Queen of Scots in his *Queen Mary's Last Look at France* (1852), he adapted a French sixteenth-century dress and a bonnet from a costume book published in Paris in 1838.[7]

In 1859, when he was busy on his picture of the highwayman Claude Duval dancing a stately coranto with the beautiful passenger of the coach he has just stopped – a subject derived from Macaulay's *History* – he encountered difficulties over two points in the composition. 'In my

121, 122 Detail of *The Gerbier Family* (*c.* 1630, Royal Collection), from the studio of Rubens, and the same motif echoed *(right)* by Frith.

123, 124 Detail of Mary from Frith's *Knox reproving Mary Queen of Scots* (1844, by permission of Sheffield City Art Galleries), with *(right)* the Knole sofa (National Trust, Knole).

125, 126 *Left*, Frith, *Queen Mary's Last Look at France* (1852, unlocated); *right*, the plate on which her dress is based, from *Costumes Français, depuis Clovis jusqu'à nos jours* (1838).

127 Detail of Frith's *Claude Duval* (1859, City Art Gallery, Manchester).

trouble', he writes, 'I applied myself to an authority on old world costumes – Mr Fairholt – who most kindly supplied me with the descriptions of the dance, accompanied by drawings of the performers.' What more evidence could one have of Fairholt's ubiquitous influence? But even he was unable to solve all the problems. One remained: to find a coach of the

correct date for the picture. Engravings were not enough, and finally an actual coach was discovered in Lord Darnley's collection at Cobham Hall: 'I went and found the quaintest old thing you can conceive, all beguilt and carved, with such great leather straps and buckles . . .'[8]

Frith's autobiography does therefore give us occasional glimpses of how he achieved these elaborate reconstructions. What he does not tell us much about is his motivation in choosing his historical subjects. Like the modern genre paintings, they were obviously powerful and dramatic vehicles for lessons on virtue and vice. *Charles II's Last Sunday* (1857) is as complex a comment as any of the modern subjects, an evocation of a court diametrically opposed to that of Victoria and the Prince Consort, a court of Comus derived from Evelyn's moralizing description written after the death of Charles II:

I am never to forget the unexpressable luxury, & prophanesse, gaming, & all dissolution, and as it were total forgetfullnesse of God (it being Sunday Evening) which this day sennight, I was witnesse of; the King, sitting & toying with his Concubines Portsmouth, Cleaveland, & Mazarine: &c: A french boy singing love songs, in that glorious Gallery, whilst about 20 of the greate Courtiers & other dissolute persons were at Basset round a large table, a bank of at least 2000 in Gold before them, upon which two Gent: that were with me made reflexions with astonishment, it being a sceane of utmost vanity; and surely as they thought would never have an End: six days after was all in the dust.[9]

The reign of Charles II was universally condemned as a triumph of vice, an affront to middle-class morality. Not only did the King indulge in every form of immorality – women, gambling, idleness and frivolity – but, what was worse, he enjoyed it. In 1889 Queen Victoria very reluctantly agreed to purchase a portrait of Charles. As the then Surveyor of the Royal Collection recorded: 'The Queen does not care for Charles II.'[10] The same note of Victorian censure, though often overlooked today, was the moral message of E. M. Ward's delightful *Interview between Charles II and Nell Gwynne, as witnessed by Evelyn* – an encounter which made the diarist 'heartily sorry'.[11]

As in his genre scenes, Frith here deploys the figures with sensitivity, elegance and skill, the central group of the King and his mistresses being flanked by minor ones: the musicians left, the couple dallying right, Evelyn and his companions looking on, and the gamblers beyond. A version of the Knole sofa reappears for the King and the Duchess of Cleveland to sit on, but the overall debt is to the portraiture of Sir Peter Lely. Cleveland is adapted from Lely's languorous and abandoned characterization of her, while Evelyn derives from any of his early portraits of men in sober dress wearing small, plain collars. As in the case of the *Coming of Age*, the costumes and hairstyles, if analysed closely, are seen to range over about four decades; the lady seated on the right, for instance, has a dress cut and laced more in the fashion of 1630 than of 1680. None the less, the immediate overall impression is of startling accuracy which must have made the moral of the subject more powerful to the onlooker at the time.

128–30 For his powerful morality of *Charles II's Last Sunday* (1857, private collection), Frith was indebted to the work of Sir Peter Lely: *above left*, Lely's portrait of the Duchess of Cleveland (*c.* 1664, unlocated); *above right*, the portrait called 'Sir Henry Vane' (*c.* 1650, National Trust, Ham House).

Colour Plates

The quest begins. William Kent's picture of Henry V's meeting with the Queen of France (*c.* 1729–30) includes a likeness of the King taken from an authentic portrait (ill. 5). Royal Collection.

11 **The artist turns antiquarian.** Thomas Stothard, painting Chaucer's Canterbury pilgrims in 1806–7, clothed his figures in costumes derived from Strutt's *Dress and* *Habits of the People of England* (ill. 57) and placed them in a processional frieze based on the paintings on *cassone* chests. Tate Gallery, London. Detail.

III, IV Two details from Ford Madox Brown's
Chaucer at the Court of Edward III
(1856–68). Painted at the height of the
Artist-Antiquarian phase, this massive
visual vehicle incorporates dresses made
up from costume books and portraits
realized from tomb effigies (ills. 59–61).
Tate Gallery, London.

V Bonington's *The Earl of Surrey and the Fair Geraldine* (1825–6) evokes early-sixteenth-century England by marrying a Tudor portrait of the poet (ill. 103) with figures and architecture of the Venetian Renaissance. Wallace Collection, London.

VI Frith's vision of Merry England in *Coming of Age in the Olden Time* (1849) is a compilation of three authentic buildings with figures from portraits and costume books, the composition inspired by Dutch genre painting (ills. 112–22). Alexander Gallery, London. Detail.

VII **Innocence assailed.** Millais's *The Princes in the Tower* (1878) epitomizes the Victorian obsession with violated childhood. Royal Holloway College, University of London. Detail.

VIII **The victimized child-woman.** Delaroche's *The Execution of Lady Jane Grey* (1834) heralded the cult of the nine-day Queen. National Gallery, London. Detail.

IX **Heroine of an age:** Mary Queen of Scots. Sir William Allan's *The Murder of David Rizzio* (1833) is not only a triumph of historical reconstruction, but one of the most powerful evocations of the martyred Queen. Between 1820 and 1897, no less than fifty-six works depicting events in her life adorned the walls of the Royal Academy. National Gallery of Scotland, Edinburgh. Detail.

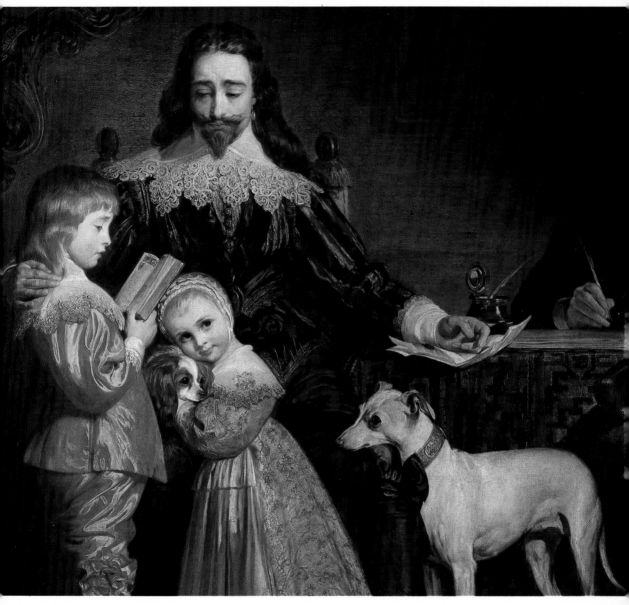

x **Cavaliers and Roundheads.** Yeames's notorious '*And When Did You Last See Your Father?*' (1878) captures this romantic theme in its decline. Walker Art Gallery, Liverpool. Detail.

xi Charles I as the ideal ruler of the *ancien régime* in Maclise's *An Interview between Charles I and Oliver Cromwell* (c. 1836). National Gallery of Ireland, Dublin. Detail.

xii *Overleaf*: Goodall's lyrical *An Episode of the Happier Days of Charles I* (1853) presents the Stuart royal family as prototypes of the bourgeois bliss of Victoria and Albert. Bury Art Gallery.

Part III
Themes and Obsessions

Society in conflict. Oliver Cromwell, hero of nineteenth-century reforming movements, contemplates the body of Charles I in Delaroche's famous picture (1831). Musée des Beaux-Arts, Nîmes. Detail.

The Anglo-Saxons

George Frederick Watts

Alfred inciting the English to resist the Danes 1847
Oil on canvas, 135 × 228 in. (343 × 579 cm)
Houses of Parliament

GEORGE FREDERICK WATTS (1817–1904)[1] came of poor parents and was largely self-taught. As a result of winning a £300 prize for his cartoon of *Caractacus* in the 1843 Houses of Parliament competition, he was enabled to spend four years in Italy, where he made many influential friends. Returning to England in 1847, he became a leading advocate of the revival of fresco painting, his most highly acclaimed work being *The School of Lawgivers* in the New Hall of Lincoln's Inn, begun in 1853. He also offered to decorate Euston Station. After a brief flirtation with Social Realism (*The Irish Famine*, 1849; *Found Drowned*, 1848–50; both Watts Gallery, Compton), he found the ideal vehicle for his ideas in personal allegory. Thereafter followed a steady stream of works almost all on a vast scale – monumental moralities which were to influence the Symbolist movement – besides a continuous flow of portraits and, after 1867, sculpture.

G. F. Watts's picture of *Alfred inciting the English to resist the Danes* was painted for the 1847 competition for the decoration of the new Houses of Parliament. This was the competition devoted to oil paintings. Watts was studying and working in Italy at the time, and began work on the picture in the summer and autumn of 1846, executing at least two hundred drawings for it and completing it in the April of the following year in time for shipment to England. In the competition, the canvas was one of the three which won premiums of £500, the other two being F. R. Pickersgill's *The Burial of Harold* and Edward Armitage's *The Battle of Meeanee*. Subsequently, on the recommendation of Sir Charles Eastlake, the picture was among those purchased for the walls of the committee rooms of the House, where it hangs to this day.

The subject-matter Watts had deliberately chosen as being 'dedicated to patriotism and posterity'. He described it in a letter he wrote to Miss Duff Gordon in December 1846; she had asked for a detailed account, and this Watts gives, as he states, in the manner of a showman:

You ask me to describe my picture of Alfred; the general design you are acquainted with. Alfred stands, as you know, in the centre of the picture, his foot upon the plank, about to spring into the boat. I have endeavoured to give him as much energy, dignity, and expression as possible, without exaggeration. Long-limbed and springy, he is about the size of the Apollo, the other figures are bigger, so you see my composition is colossal. Near to Alfred is a youth who, in his excitement, rends off his cloak in order to follow his King and leader; by the richness of his dress he evidently belongs to the upper class, and I shall endeavour to make that also evident by the elegance of his form, and the grace of his action. Next to him is a youth who is probably a peasant; he grasps a ponderous axe and threatens extermination to the whole Danish race. Contrasted with him you see the muscular back of an older man, who turns towards his wife, who, with a child in her arms, follows distracted at the thought that her child's father is about to rush into danger. He points upward, and encourages her to trust in the righteousness of the cause and the justice of Heaven (religion and patriotism). Behind him two lovers are taking a hurried and tender leave, and beyond them a maiden with dishevelled locks (your sister's hair), whose lover or father has already

131 G. F. Watts, *Alfred inciting the English to resist the Danes.*

departed, with clasped hands is imploring the
protection of Heaven. In the corner a youth is
buckling on his armour; his old mother, with
trembling hands and tearful eyes, hangs about his neck
a cross; the father, feeble, and no longer able to fight
his country's battles, gives his sword with one hand
while with the other he bares his chest, points to his
wounds, and exhorts his son not to disgrace his
father's name and sword; while with glowing cheek
and beating heart the youth responds to his father's
exhortations with all the ardour characteristic of his
age. This I think is my most interesting group . . . You
see I endeavour to preserve a rich base accompaniment
of religious and patriotic feeling. A boy, carried away
by the general enthusiasm, clenches his little fists,
draws his breath, and rushes along with the excited
warriors; which helps to indicate the inspiring effect
of Alfred's harangue . . .[2]

Watts's choice of the Anglo-Saxons as a vehicle
for sentiments rich in 'religious and patriotic
feeling' was shared by the historian Lingard.
Theirs was the period, in his estimation, 'the
most interesting to Englishmen, because it was

the cradle of many customs and institutions,
which exist among us even at the present day'.[3]

The cult of Alfred can already be found in
Hume's *History*, where he appears as a prototype
of the Patriot King:

The merit of this prince, both in private and public
life, may with advantage be set in opposition to that of
any monarch or citizen which the annals of any age or
any nation can present us. He seems indeed to be the
model of that perfect character, which, under the
denomination of a sage man, philosophers have been
fond of delineating, rather as a fiction of their
imagination, than in hopes of ever seeing it really
existing. So happily were they blended; and so
powerfully did each prevent the other from exceeding
its proper boundaries![4]

Alfred is hailed as 'the Great' and as 'the Founder
of the British Monarchy'. In this capacity he
appears among the busts in William Kent's
Temple of British Worthies at Stowe and in
Thomas Arne's stately masque of *Alfred* (1740).
In painting he was taken up by Benjamin West in

132 Benjamin West, *Alfred the Great divides his Loaf
with a Pilgrim* (1779, Worshipful Company of
Stationers and Newspaper Makers).

133 John Francis Rigaud, *The first Interview of King
Edgar and Elfrida* (1796, National Trust, Saltram).

1779 in his *Alfred the Great divides his Loaf with a
Pilgrim*, by Richard Westall in *The Boyhood of King
Alfred* (private collection), and in the renderings
by Francis Wheatley (1792)[5] and David Wilkie
(1806)[6] of *Alfred in the Neatherd's Cottage*.

Interest in the Anglo-Saxons apart from
Alfred hardly rose above searching the histories
for suitable melodramatic sagas, and it was
scenes of this sort which first attracted the
painters of the Gothick Picturesque. Angelica
Kauffmann's *The Interview of King Edgar with
Elfrida, after her Marriage to Athelwold*, exhibited
in 1771, was the first picture on an Anglo-Saxon
theme to be shown at the Royal Academy.
Twenty-five years later, John Francis Rigaud
essayed the same subject. It is presented in the
manner of a scene from a Gothick novel,
depicting the moment when the King realizes
that his friend has tricked him out of marrying
the beautiful Elfrida and married her himself.
Such paintings can hardly be said to be reflective
of any serious interest in the Anglo-Saxons as a
noble race embodying high-minded ideals of
liberty and justice. This exaltation of the race
really began in earnest in 1799 with the appearance of the first volume of Sharon Turner's
History, a book which ran into three editions by
1820.[7] Turner was the first historian to attempt a
reconstruction of Anglo-Saxon society and its
institutions. Through his work the historians of
the Victorian age came to view the Anglo-
Saxons as exponents of a system of government
which was the direct fount of their own
representative institutions. Anglo-Saxon England was seen as the ancestor of the monarchi-
cally ruled but elected government of
nineteenth-century Britain, a burning issue
throughout the period of the Reform Acts and
the extension of the franchise. The Anglo-
Saxons were regarded as a freedom-loving,
democratic and heroic people, a view woven into
literature first by Sir Walter Scott in *Ivanhoe*
(1819)[8] and later by Edward Bulwer Lytton in
Harold, the Last of the Saxon Kings (1848) and
Charles Kingsley in *Hereward the Wake* (1866). It
was a belief shared by establishment and opposition groups alike. Even Tom Paine's influential
Rights of Man (1791) subscribes to this view:
'Conquest and tyranny transplanted themselves

with William the Conqueror from Normandy into England, and the country is yet disfigured with the marks.'[9] During the sixties and seventies the pedantic middle-class cult of the Anglo-Saxons reached its peak in the infants borne to the font as Eadward and Aelfric.[10] Parallel with this popular dissemination of the idea of the Anglo-Saxons went a scholarly reappraisal which reached its climax in J. M. Kemble's *The Saxons in England* (1849), a book actually dedicated to Queen Victoria. The British people, Kemble writes, have inherited their political institutions 'from a period so distant as to excite our admiration, and have preserved them amidst all vicissitudes with an enlightened will that must command our gratitude'. In Kemble's view the Victorians *were* Anglo-Saxons.[11]

The result of all this was a steady flow of works of art celebrating 'our forefathers'. These really began with William Dyce's *St Dunstan separating Edwy and Elgiva* (1839, unlocated),[12] Richard Dadd's *Alfred the Great reflecting on the Misfortunes of his Country* (1840, unlocated) and *Elgiva, the Queen of Edwy, in Banishment* (1840, unlocated),[13] Dyce's *Baptism of St Ethelbert*

134 Alfred Stevens, *King Alfred and his Mother* (*c.* 1848, Tate Gallery, London).

135 Daniel Maclise, *Alfred, the Saxon King disguised as a Minstrel in the Tent of Guthrum the Dane* (1852, Laing Art Gallery, Newcastle-upon-Tyne).

136 Sir John Everett Millais, *Elgiva* (1847, Mr John Lees-Millais).

137 Frederick Richard Pickersgill, *The Burial of Harold* (1847, Houses of Parliament).

(1846), part of the decoration of the south wall of the House of Lords,[14] John Everett Millais's startling *Elgiva* (1847)[15] and Alfred Stevens's *King Alfred and his Mother* (c. 1848).[16] This pre-occupation continued into the fifties, notably in Maclise's *Alfred, the Saxon King disguised as a Minstrel in the Tent of Guthrum the Dane* (1852).[17] The mania for the subject of Edith finding the body of the last Saxon king after the Battle of Hastings in 1066 provoked *Punch*, in connection with F. R. Pickersgill's prizewinning picture (based directly on a Lamentation over the Dead Christ), to congratulate the public that King Harold was buried at last, and to hope that 'British artists would leave off finding his body any more, which they have been doing, in every exhibition, for these fifty years'.[18]

Watts's *Alfred inciting the English to resist the Danes* belongs to the mainstream of this celebration, intensified surely by the nationality of the Prince Consort. The Anglo-Saxons were after all German. No wonder that at the tail end of the cult William Theed should have chosen in 1868 to depict Albert and Victoria as Anglo-Saxons. This astounding tableau could as easily be relabelled 'Alfred the Great and his Queen', so interchangeable had they become.

138 William Theed, sculpture of Victoria and Albert as Anglo-Saxons (1868, Royal Collection).

The Princes in the Tower

Sir John Everett Millais

The Princes in the Tower 1878
Oil on canvas, 58 × 36 in. (147.3 × 91.5 cm)
Royal Holloway College, University of
London

SIR JOHN EVERETT MILLAIS (1829–96)[1] was
trained in the Royal Academy Schools from 1840
to 1848, after which he entered into association
with Rossetti and became one of the founding
members of the Pre-Raphaelite Brotherhood. He
exhibited his first picture in the new manner,
Isabella (Walker Art Gallery, Liverpool) in 1849,
and worked in this style for the next few years,
producing what are generally accepted as his
finest works: *Christ in the House of his Parents*
(1850, Tate Gallery), *The Return of the Dove* (1851,
Ashmolean Museum, Oxford), *Ophelia* (1852,
Tate Gallery) and *The Blind Girl* (1856, City of
Birmingham Museum and Art Gallery). His
election as ARA in 1853 and, more especially, his
marriage in 1855 led to a vigorous pursuit of the
path of fashionable success. He became a leading
society portrait painter, and executed the religious, fancy and historical works which Millais
himself regarded as his masterpieces but which
critics have since condemned. These included
Bubbles (1886, A. & F. Pears Ltd), *The Princes in
the Tower* and *The Boyhood of Raleigh* (1870, Tate
Gallery). In 1885 he was created a baronet, and in
1896 he succeeded Leighton as PRA.

Millais began this picture on a canvas which he
had already painted of the staircase of St Mary's
Tower, Birnham, Perthshire.[2] Subsequently, on
receiving sketches by his son of the Bloody
Tower, he realized that not only was his staircase
too small but it was the wrong way round. Millais

139 See also colour plate VII.

then conducted his own researches and started
again. The Princes were children of professional
models, and the artist records his debt to Planché
for costume detail, in particular the fact that the
King wears the Garter on his left leg.

Millais himself regarded the picture as a
companion to his *Princess Elizabeth in Prison at St
James's* (1879, unlocated), another recurring
subject for those obsessed with 'the persecution
of Royal children, innocent and unoffending,
with jealous cruelty'. The earlier canvas, which
immediately caught the public imagination,
came at the close of a century of interest in the
fate of the Princes in the Tower, Edward V and
his brother Richard, Duke of York. The artist,
drawing on this popular mythology, captures

140 After James Northcote, *The Burial of the Princes in the Tower*.

brilliantly the terror of these two youths as they sense their impending end at the hands of assassins acting on orders from their uncle, Richard of Gloucester. Although the popularity of the theme inevitably owed much to Shakespeare's *Richard III*, and in particular to bowdlerized versions of it, it also drew for nourishment on historians who repeated the story as recounted by Sir Thomas More in his life of Richard.[3] Two deeply emotional scenes preoccupied painters: the parting of the young Duke of York from his mother, who had wisely sought sanctuary in Westminster Abbey, and the actual murder of the innocent children. Narratives of the former vary very little from one historian to another, and Hume is as good a source as any. Here he describes Elizabeth Woodville parting from her younger son:

She was here on a sudden struck with a kind of presage of his future fate: she tenderly took him: she bedewed him with her tears; and bidding him an eternal adieu,

delivered him, with many expressions of regret and reluctance, into their custody.[4]

Such a scene of tearful sentiment was an ideal one for painters of the romantic age, and Samuel Wale (1769, unlocated), John Opie (for Bowyer, engraved 1795), Richard Westall (1800, unlocated) and E. M. Ward (1842, unlocated) all essayed it. James Northcote painted for the Boydell Shakespeare Gallery a number of versions of a similarly touching scene, *The Meeting of the two Princes* (National Trust, Petworth, engraved R. Thew, B. Reading).[5]

This was complemented by 'a scene truly tragical: the murder of the two young princes', and this Hume recounts as follows:

The tyrant then sent for Sir James Tyrrel ... and he ordered Brackenbury (constable of the Tower) to resign to this gentleman the keys and government of the Tower for one night. Tyrrel choosing three associates, Slater, Dighton, and Forest, came in the night-time to the door of the chamber where the princes were lodged; and sending in the assassins, he bade them execute their commission, while he himself staid without. They found the young princes in bed, and fallen into a profound sleep. After suffocating them with the bolster and pillows, they shewed their naked bodies to Tyrrel, who ordered them to be buried at the foot of the stairs, deep in the ground, under a heap of stones.[6]

Although this subject, and others tangential to it, were dealt with by Opie (Royal Shakespeare Theatre),[7] Northcote (the murder, National Trust, Petworth, engraved Legat 1791; the burial, engraved W. Skelton),[8] Thomas Stothard (for Bowyer, engraved 1795) and C. R. Leslie (1830; repetition 1837, Victoria & Albert Museum), the two most famous images are those by Delaroche and Millais.

Of these two, Delaroche's conception (1830)[9] is certainly the more powerful. Millais's canvas has the thrill of an episode from a late Victorian boys' adventure story, but Delaroche's possesses the strength of a reality bred of the French Revolution and the mysterious fate of the Dauphin in the Temple prison. Instead of choosing to depict the actual murder, he moves back in time to an imaginary moment of realization. The Duke of York is reading to his brother the King, who sits on the bed deep in a distant reverie. The younger child has raised his head from his book, and his eyes are filled with fear. A spaniel moves towards the door, beneath which chinks of light and strongly cast shadows suggest incipient action. So compelling is Delaroche's evocation that the viewer never notices that the columns of the bed are inappropriately carved with the Beaufort portcullis and the Tudor rose!

The success of Delaroche's picture was such that the subject was taken up on the Continent by other artists, notably by Hildebrandt in 1835 and P. Miglioretti in 1869. Millais would have seen his subject within this international context, as a direct challenge aiming to supplant in the popular imagination the earlier 'best-selling' canvases on the theme. In order to achieve this he has skilfully married the record of a historical

event with another, perhaps even more potent Victorian obsession, the innocence and vulnerability of childhood. As a motif in romantic painting in Britain it can be followed from Reynolds's *The Age of Innocence* (1788, National Gallery) through the genre painters of the 1850s and 1860s to Yeames's '*And When Did You Last See Your Father?*' (1878) and beyond. Millais resorted to it often, most notoriously in another best-seller, *Bubbles*. Whereas Delaroche's canvas holds us in its power as we contemplate the fate of kings, Millais's casts its spell in emotional and psychological terms, through the terror of two young innocent boys – brothers who tenderly clasp hands – as they sense untold terrors in the darkness which encircles them. Millais achieved his aim. His *Princes in the Tower* has retained its place as one of the most popular and enduring of all Victorian evocations of the British past.

160, x

141 Paul Delaroche, *Edward V and the Duke of York in the Tower* (1831, Wallace Collection, London; small replica of *The Children of Edward IV*, 1830, Louvre).

Lady Jane Grey

Paul Delaroche

The Execution of Lady Jane Grey 1834
Oil on canvas, 97 × 117 in. (246.4 × 297 cm)
National Gallery, London

PAUL DELAROCHE (1797–1856)[1] was born in Paris and trained in the studio of Gros, where Bonington was also a student. He made his début at the Salon of 1822, but only achieved popular success with the long series of great historical pictures painted from 1824 onwards. These included *Flora Macdonald succouring the Young Pretender* (c. 1825, unlocated), *The Death of Queen Elizabeth* (1828, Louvre), *Cardinal de Richelieu* (1829, Wallace Collection), *Cardinal Mazarin mourant* (1830, Wallace Collection), *The Children of Edward IV* (1830, Louvre), *Cromwell gazing at the body of Charles I* (1831, Musée des Beaux-Arts, Nîmes), *The Execution of Lady Jane Grey* and *Le duc de Guise assassiné au château de Blois* (1834, Musée Condé, Chantilly). These made him one of the most acclaimed painters of his generation, and his pictures were eagerly looked forward to each year. Although his career was to go on for another two decades, it was these pictures which set the standard for scenes from history for the artists of mid-Victorian England. Virtually all that Delaroche's art stood for has since gone into total eclipse, but his impact on the Victorian vision of the British past was immense.

The Execution of Lady Jane Grey caused a sensation at the Paris Salon of 1834, when it had already been purchased by Prince Anatole Demidov. On his death, in 1870, it was acquired by an English MP, H. W. Eaton, whose son bequeathed it to the National Gallery.[2] Like Delaroche's other scenes from British history, *The Execution of Lady Jane Grey* had a life and influence totally different on opposite sides of the Channel. For the French, it contained poignant allusions to the horrors of their own immediate revolutionary past; for the mid-Victorians, it joined a stream of paintings and writings which placed Jane Grey among the foremost of their historical heroines.

The picture is, of course, historically inaccurate, for Lady Jane Grey was executed, on 12 February 1554, not in a gloomy Norman hall but outside on a scaffold erected on Tower Green.[3] None the less, this new setting enables Delaroche to surround his fragile heroine with an aureole of saintly light. He is also wrong in showing her helped to the block, to which in fact she resolutely made her own way, although she was attended by two gentlewomen – the ladies who lament to the left in dresses derived from portraits by Holbein of twenty years previously. Although, as Cecil Gould has pointed out, the *livret* of the 1834 Salon refers to a 1588 Protestant Martyrology as the source, this scene could have been created from any reasonable narrative of the event. In spite of all this, Delaroche's recreation of the drama of the nine-day Queen's execution remains overwhelmingly powerful.

In nineteenth-century England, Jane Grey represented an obsessional female type: the victimized child-woman who as a literary character runs direct from the works of Mrs Radcliffe down to Dickens's Florence Dombey. Interest in Jane Grey, however, had its roots as far back as the sixteenth century, when John Foxe eulogized her in his *Acts and Monuments* – still standard Sunday reading throughout the Victorian age: 'let this worthy lady pass for a saint: and let all great ladies which bear her name imitate her virtues'.[4] Bishop Burnet in 1680 categorized her as one 'so humble, so gentle and pious, that all

142 Paul Delaroche, *The Execution of Lady Jane Grey*. See also colour plate VIII.

people both loved and admired her'.[5] In 1715 she was made the subject of a major tragedy by Nicholas Rowe, and by the 1790s could occupy the brush of Northcote (1792), who depicted her for Bowyer's Historic Gallery being subjected to the wiles of Abbot Feckenham, a scene conceived in terms of a tableau from a Gothick horror novel.[6]

Although John Singleton Copley painted *The Offer of the Crown to Lady Jane Grey* in 1806–7 – a picture which owes its compositional formula to an Annunciation[7] – it was not until after 1827 that she became a figure of intense interest to artists, writers and public alike. This phenomenon was to last until the 1870s. The cult was prefaced by C. R. Leslie's influential *Lady Jane Grey prevailed upon to accept the Crown* (1827), painted for the Duke of Bedford five years after the publication of George Howard's *Lady Jane Grey and her Times*.

The scene Leslie depicts is set in Durham House in the Strand on 6 July 1553 when, immediately subsequent to Edward VI's death, the Dukes of Northumberland and Suffolk were sent to Lady Jane Grey to inform her that her cousin had left her the crown. We can take up the

143 James Northcote, *Lady Jane Grey and Abbot Feckenham* (1792, unlocated).

144 John Singleton Copley, *The Offer of the Crown to Lady Jane Grey* (1806–7, unlocated).

story in the words used in the Academy catalogue of 1827:

The Duke of Suffolk, with much solemnity, explained to his daughter the disposition the late King had made of his crown by letters patent . . . and in conclusion, himself and Northumberland fell on their knees, and paid their homage to her as Queen of England. The poor lady, somewhat astonished at their behaviour and discourse, but in no respect moved by their reasons, or in the least elevated by such unexpected honours, answered them, 'that the laws of the kingdom and natural right standing for the king's sisters, she would beware of burthening her weak conscience with a yoke which did belong to them . . . My liberty is better than the chain you proffer me, with what precious stones soever it be adorned, or what gold soever framed . . . And if you love me in good earnest, you will rather wish me a secure and quiet fortune, though mean, than an exalted condition, exposed to the wind, and followed by some dismal fall.'

All the moving eloquence of this speech had no effect; and the Lady Jane was at length prevailed on, or rather compelled by the exhortations of her father, the intercession of her mother, the artful persuasions of Northumberland, and above all, the earnest desires of her husband whom she tenderly loved, to comply with what was proposed to her.[8]

The text has an iconographical tightness which recalls humanist programmes for Renaissance artists. This is the moment Leslie depicts. Jane, the bluestocking, her hand upon a Bible, receives her father-in-law, Northumberland, and the other great lords, all on their knees, while her husband and ambitious mother entreat her to accept the crown they offer.

Wherever possible, Leslie has based his figures on authentic sources: Frances Brandon, Duchess of Suffolk, Jane's mother, is taken from the notorious double portrait by Hans Eworth of her together with her last husband, Adrian Stokes. Jane herself is a free interpretation of the only authentic portrait, an engraving from a series of Protestant heroes and heroines published in 1620 and entitled the *Herwologia*, and John Russell, Earl of Bedford, second from the

145–7 C. R. Leslie's *Lady Jane Grey prevailed upon to accept the Crown* (1827, Woburn Abbey Collection, by kind permission of the Marquess of Tavistock and Trustees of the Bedford Settled Estates), with two of the portrait sources: *below left*, Jane Grey as depicted in the *Herwologia* (1620); *below right*, detail of George Vertue's 1748 engraving after Hans Eworth, *Frances Brandon, Duchess of Suffolk and Adrian Stokes.*

left, is lifted directly from the portrait still at Woburn Abbey, but reversed, with the bonnet removed from his skullcap. The composition, which is based on a formula of suppliants interceding with the Virgin or a saint, is orchestrated in the Venetian manner, with heavy overtones of Titian. Instead of the stiff icons of Tudor England, Leslie was trying to paint the event as though it had been recorded by a master of the Renaissance in northern Italy. And, of course, in the breadth of the brushwork and in the drama of the light there is the influence of his friend Constable.

148 George Cruikshank, 'Jane imploring Mary to spare her Husband's Life'. Illustration from Harrison Ainsworth, *Tower of London* (1840).

Leslie must have worked, at least in part, from made-up costumes, because the observation here is very direct, in contrast to his total uncertainty as to the architectural structure and decoration of the room. A huge column on the left is impossible to relate in any logical way to the bookshelves behind or to the nondescript drapery to the right. Although one senses a theatrical influence (he was passionately interested in the stage), the picture is more than a mere tableau. It is carefully composed, the faces are animated by the psychological tension of the moment, and the light (as in Delaroche's treatment) is deployed to bathe the heroine in an almost supernatural luminosity.

Between 1827 and 1877, twenty-four paintings in all on Jane Grey were exhibited at the Royal Academy. Their themes ranged from her virtues as the exemplary pupil through her spurning of the glories of a crown to her role as a martyr stoutly defending the faith.[9] All these

subjects offered an instant reflection of Victorian conceptions as to feminine sensibility. The nine-day Queen was the perfect *exemplum* for study by the daughters of the middle classes who were educated at home, like their heroine, by a governess.[10] John Callcott Horsley's *Lady Jane Grey and Roger Ascham* (1853), in which he depicts the famous incident when Jane Grey was found reading Plato while the rest of the household hunted (a subject tackled five years before by C. R. Leslie, based on lines in a poem by Samuel Rogers), could be updated to represent any mid-Victorian girl sitting reading with her needlework to hand. The cult owed much to Harrison Ainsworth's colourful dramatization of Jane's last days in his *Tower of London* (1840), which was brilliantly illustrated by Cruikshank, and to *Little Arthur's History of England*, whose author, Maria Callcott, writing in the 1830s, characterized her life thus: 'Some people would have liked Lady Jane [as Queen], first, because they believed their dear young King Edward had wished her to be Queen; and next, because she was beautiful, virtuous and wise, and, above all, a Protestant . . . She was like him in gentleness, goodness and kindness.'[11] But Jane's final position in the Victorian pantheon of perfect womanhood can be summed up best in the opening lines of Agnes Strickland's biography published in 1868: 'Lady Jane Grey is without exception the most noble character of the Tudor lineage. She was adorned with every attribute that is lovely in domestic life, while her piety, learning, courage and virtue qualified her to give lustre to a crown.'[12]

No canvas by a British painter, however, was to rival the potency of Delaroche's dramatic tableau of execution. Its success is due to the artist's oft-used trick of bringing the main action of the picture almost out of the canvas, directly towards the onlooker. Jane is groping her way towards the spectator, gently guided by the Constable of the Tower, the action accentuated by her movement from darkness to light. This picture, in its monumental scale and its combination of historical detail with startling realism allied to a tinge of sentimentality, set the objectives for the British painters of the past in their own set pieces from the 1840s onwards.

149   L. Stocks after John Callcott Horsley, *Lady Jane Grey and Roger Ascham* (1853).

Mary Queen of Scots

Sir William Allan

The Murder of David Rizzio 1833
Oil on canvas, 40½ × 64 in. (103 × 162.5 cm)
National Gallery of Scotland, Edinburgh

SIR WILLIAM ALLAN (1782–1850)[1] is an almost totally forgotten artist. Born in Edinburgh, he later entered the Royal Academy Schools and first exhibited in 1803. Two years later he went to Russia, where he stayed until 1814. On his return to his native Scotland he began to paint scenes from Scottish history and befriended Burns and Scott. He travelled extensively, and his work encompassed subjects as diverse as *Slave Market, Constantinople* (RA 1815, unlocated) and *Lord Byron reposing in the House of a Turkish Fisherman after having swum the Hellespont* (RA 1831, unlocated). Allan became an RA in 1835 and President of the Royal Scottish Academy in 1838. No modern critical assessment or study of his work has ever been undertaken, but the major influence on his painting was Wilkie.

The subject of Mary Queen of Scots occupied the brush of Sir William Allan for a decade, beginning in 1823 when he exhibited his *Knox admonishing Mary Queen of Scots* (unlocated). He followed this in 1824 with *Lord Lindsay compelling Mary to abdicate* (unlocated), in 1827 with *The Landing of Mary Queen of Scots at Leith, 1561* (unlocated) and finally, in 1833, with his masterpiece in mariolatry, *The Murder of David Rizzio*. All these paintings bear witness to an intensive study by Allan of the personal and historical background to each event, representing a tremendous advance on the work of the Gothick Picturesque painters. In many ways *The Murder of*

David Rizzio is a remarkable achievement within the Artist-Antiquarian tradition.

Rizzio was murdered on 9 March 1566 in Mary's cabinet, a small room next to her bedroom, in Holyroodhouse.[3] Within this tiny cabinet she was supping, attended by Rizzio, the Countess of Argyll, Lord Robert Stewart, Arthur Erskine and others. The murderers were let in by Mary's husband, Lord Darnley, who led them up the private stairway from his own apartments below and in through a doorway behind the tapestry hangings. The moment Allan depicts is when Darnley seized his wife and unlocked the grip of the unfortunate Rizzio, who was clinging to her for protection. The luckless secretary was dragged away screaming through her bedroom and savagely butchered to death.

Allan has moved the scene into Mary's bedroom, which he shows as it still survived at the time when the picture was painted. The bed, which is in reality late-seventeenth-century in date, was believed in the nineteenth century to have been the one actually used by the Queen. To the extreme left, the door through which the murderers entered is still open; the table where the party has been dining is to the left; the Countess of Argyll and Mary Seton hide behind Darnley, who prevents the agonized Queen from helping Rizzio. All the murderers are identified: Kerr of Fawdonside with his back to the spectator, Patrick Murray of Tippermuir dragging Rizzio by the cloak, the Earl of Morton pointing towards the door with his sword, and the Earl of Lindsay next to him lifting the green curtain; behind the torchbearer is the Master of Ruthven, his dagger raised to strike, while George Douglas grasps the pathetic Rizzio by the arm. Allan has included Ruthven in complete armour, as he is described in all the contemporary narratives of the murder, ghastly and

150 Sir William Allan, *The Murder of David Rizzio*. See also colour plate IX.

pale after rising from a bed of incurable disease to wreak vengeance.

The picture is remarkably accurate in costume and portrait detail, and stylistically owes much to Opie, who had painted the same scene in 1787 (destroyed, formerly Guildhall Art Gallery). Allan's earliest work, we know, was in the manner of Opie, but there is also a debt to the domestic interiors by his Scottish contemporary Wilkie. In this painting we see the extraordinary fusion of a dramatic scene in sharp chiaroscuro which, through Opie, goes back to gloomy martyrdoms by early-seventeenth-century Bolognese masters, with the small scale and trailing silks of a type of domestic interior going back, via Wilkie, to seventeenth-century Holland.

By 1833, when Allan painted this scene, Mary Queen of Scots had already emerged as *the* heroine above every other from the British past. She was cast in the right mould for the romantic age: she was young, beautiful and accomplished; she was subjected to barbarism, scenes of murder, rape, imprisonment and, finally, execution. In her own age she had been viewed as something far different – precisely what depended on one's religious convictions[4] – and the century which followed evinced virtually no interest in the Queen of Scots at all. Interest began in the second decade of the eighteenth century among historians with the opening of a never-ending wrangle as to the authenticity or otherwise of the Casket Letters, which resulted in Mary becoming widely known as a controversial figure.[5] In 1760 Dr Johnson published a vindication of the Stuarts, and five years later his biographer, James Boswell, commissioned Gavin Hamilton, the leading exponent of the neoclassical style in the 1760s, to paint *Mary Queen of Scots resigning her Crown*. Hamilton's composition, which was painted in Italy and eventually exhibited at the Royal Academy in 1776, represents the beginning of the public cult of the Queen of Scots.

152

151 Normand fils after Sir William Allan, *Knox admonishing Mary Queen of Scots* (1823).

Like Copley and West, Hamilton was an artist-antiquarian, and the portrait of Mary, as mentioned earlier, is carefully composed from a miniature then believed to represent her. The formula for the picture is directly based on the iconography of Christ before Pilate.[6]

Between 1786 and 1798 a dozen paintings appeared on the walls of the Royal Academy, all in the Gothick Picturesque vein, on the subject of Mary. They reflect the changed attitude to the Queen as expounded by her partisans, portraying her as a beautiful, tragic heroine caught in the midst of a web of appalling violence and intrigue. The two most important canvases were those by John Opie, *The Execution of the Queen of Scots* and *The Death of Rizzio* (1787, destroyed 1941, formerly Guildhall Art Gallery; engraved Taylor, 1791). The *Execution*, painted for Bowyer's Historic Gallery, makes no attempt at reportage or historical accuracy, and the Queen could just as well be Marie Antoinette, whose execution must anyway have greatly accelerated public interest in previous queens who died on the scaffold.[7]

152, 153 Gavin Hamilton's *Mary Queen of Scots resigning her Crown* (1765, University of Glasgow), together with the engraving by R. Sheppard of a miniature then thought to represent the Queen.

The prime image of the romantic Mary, however, stems from the novels of Sir Walter Scott. Scott dealt with sixteenth-century Scottish history in two novels, *The Monastery; A Romance* and its sequel *The Abbot*, both of which appeared in 1820. The period covered was from the Battle of Pinkie in 1547 to the Battle of Langside in 1568; *The Abbot* centres on Mary's imprisonment in Lochleven Castle, her escape and her subsequent defeat and flight into England.[8] The theme of the two novels is that of a society in conflict, both sides of which in the end seem to be discredited, and the story ends on the threshold of the Elizabethan peace which Scott moved on to deal with in *Kenilworth*, published the following year. The hero of *The Abbot*, Roland, although he begins as a Catholic and a supporter of Mary, ends by becoming a Protestant and marrying Mary Seton. Mary Queen of Scots is glorified as the romantic heroine of a lost cause, the representative of a passionate world dependent on chivalric loyalty which was to vanish forever with her own person.

Shortly after the publication of these novels, the first of a whole series of biographies of Mary started to appear. These began in 1822 with the first properly documented account, George Chalmers's *The Life of Mary, Queen of Scots*. Chalmers was moved to write about her because he felt that she was 'a calumniated woman, and an injured princess' who lived in corrupt times. The state papers were ransacked to establish the innocency and virtues of this Queen.[9] The correspondence between Allan's subject-matter and the works of Scott and Chalmers cannot be coincidental. Allan, in his painting of scenes from the life of the Queen of Scots, was giving visual expression to this vision of ideal womanhood. 'Who is there', wrote Scott, who knew Allan,[10] 'that, at the very mention of Mary Stewart's name, has not her countenance before him ... a countenance, the like of which we know not to have existed in any other character moving in that high class of life.'[11] Allan's creations of the delicate, romantic Mary contributed to her gradual assumption of the role that she was to occupy by the 1840s – that of forerunner of the perfect Victorian gentlewoman.

154, 155 *Top*, Skelton after John Opie, *The Execution of the Queen of Scots* (1795). *Above*, David Wilkie's drawing of *Mary Queen of Scots and her Infant Son* (1834, National Gallery, Edinburgh).

These paintings heralded an intense interest in the Queen of Scots for the rest of the century. Between 1820 and 1897, fifty-six works on this theme were exhibited at the Royal Academy, and these were just the top of a more sizeable iceberg. In addition, the cult proliferated through thousands of engravings after contemporary portraits and reconstructions of incidents from her life. The subjects of the Academy works, broken down as far as the information allows, were as follows: six of Mary's abdication at Lochleven Castle, six of the murder of Rizzio, seven of encounters with Knox, six of her in captivity, four of scenes connected with her escape from Lochleven, two of her execution, and four each of the Battle of Langside and her farewell to France.[12]

In 1834 Wilkie first began to be intrigued by the subject of the Queen of Scots. His drawing of her being shown the infant James VI[13] utilized the formula of a Virgin and Child, and later he painted the Queen's escape from Lochleven Castle (1837).[14] The two most important canvases from the forties were Frith's *Knox reproving Mary Queen of Scots* (1844),[15] in which the beautiful young Queen sobs at the upbraiding delivered to her, and Ford Madox Brown's *The Execution of the Queen of Scots*,[16] which he began in 1840. During the fifties and sixties she almost became an industry: Joseph Severn's *Mary Queen of Scots at Lochleven Castle* (1850), Frith's *Queen Mary's Last Look at France* (1852) and Herdman's *Execution of Mary Queen of Scots* (1867) are just a few from the vast outpouring on the troubles of this sixteenth-century Scottish Queen.

The Victorian painter, of course, essentially utilized women to stimulate the viewer's sentiments rather than his senses. Sensuality (*pace* Etty and William Frost) was supressed in favour of story-telling scenes extolling woman's virtues as a wife, home-maker and mother,[17] and it was into this mould of the 'perfect lady' that Mary Queen of Scots was surprisingly poured. It was a new idea whose formulation had begun at the close of the previous century. One of the basic evidences

156 Joseph Severn, *Mary Queen of Scots at Lochleven Castle* (1850, Victoria & Albert Museum, London).

157 Ford Madox Brown, *The Execution of the Queen of Scots* (1841, Whitworth Art Gallery, Manchester).

of sensibility in a lady was tears. As the lower classes were regarded as cloddish and incapable of expressing sensitivity, the middle and upper classes found in tears a vehicle to reflect their refined delicacy of emotion. Tears flow abundantly from the eyes of heroines from the middle of the eighteenth century onwards. Mrs Ann Radcliffe, author of *The Mysteries of Udolpho*, portrays the weeping, sentimental heroine at full length in her novels of the 1780s and 1790s. She is frequently 'overcome by a faintness', and retires to her chamber, usually unable to eat. In spite of resolving in dire circumstances not to weep, 'her resolution yields to excess of grief'. Indeed, her chief pleasure is to weep in solitude where no one can see. Appalling afflictions reduce her almost to the point of death, but these woes only 'soften to melancholy'. A lute is to hand, which she 'touches with a fine melancholy expression which comes from the heart'. She is rarely too agitated to find time to compose a sonnet or verse on some aspect of her troubles, though she is so delicate that the least puff of

158 Robert Herdman, *Mary Queen of Scots returning to Scotland* (1867, unlocated).

after her marriage to Bothwell, she wept when she abdicated, torrents flowed during her imprisonment in Lochleven Castle. Tears fell as she crossed from Scotland to England, they continued to flood down the years of imprisonment in England, and from the moment of the reading of the death warrant to her final execution we are afloat in an ocean of tears. No female character in British history bore such a close relationship to those sensitive ideals of upper-middle-class feeling as did the Queen of Scots.

These, of course, are the moments which we have seen every artist choose to celebrate.

When the sails were set, and her galley began to get out to sea, Mary's tears flowed without intermission. Leaning both her arms on the gallery of the vessel, she turned her eyes on the shore she was leaving with longing, lingering looks, crying at every stroke of the oars, 'Adieu, France! Beloved France, adieu!' And thus she remained . . . motionless as a statue, and deaf to all the attempts of her friends to comfort or divert the sad current of her thoughts . . . When darkness approached, she was entreated to descend into the state cabin . . . and partake of supper. But her heart was too full of grief to permit her to taste food.[18]

So runs Agnes Strickland's account. Tears and inability to take food because overcome by emotion are attributes of the sentimental heroine. This is what Frith, Herdman and their contemporaries were placing before the eyes of their audience: an example of genteel, aristocratic sensitivity.

More even than this, pictures of Mary Queen of Scots are evidence of and comments upon the position of women in Victorian society. Mary fitted the bill only ambiguously, for although she was built up as a monument to the female virtues and as an instance of the inability of women to exert power and rule, there was always the lingering possibility that perhaps her defamers were right. Any defence of her virtues suggested an examination of the evidence for her vices – a dabbling into rape, sexual violence and outright murder. And this double image may have considerably increased her potency as a symbol to the suppressed womanhood of mid-Victorian England.

wind would extinguish her. Variants of this type of heroine had an enormous vitality for some decades, culminating in the females of the 1840s and 1850s whose passivity in the midst of their travails was such that they reached a hitherto unbelievable extreme of ignorance, innocence and often downright dimness.

It is hardly surprising that the rise in the cult of Mary Queen of Scots coincided with the advent of this type of heroine in the Gothick novel. Buckets of tears flowed from the eyes of Mary Queen of Scots, instantly winning her the applause of all her many biographers in the nineteenth century. She sobbed as she sailed away from France, she burst into tears when upbraided by John Knox, she wept every day

159 Robert Herdman, *The Execution of Mary Queen of Scots* (1867, Glasgow City Art Gallery and Museum).

Cavaliers and Roundheads

William Frederick Yeames

'And When Did You Last See Your Father?'
1878
Oil on canvas, 48 × 98 in. (122 × 249 cm)
Walker Art Gallery, Liverpool

WILLIAM FREDERICK YEAMES (1835–1918),[1] the son of a British Consul in Russia, was brought to England at the age of thirteen. He studied under Scharf and Westmacott and visited Florence and Rome, returning in 1858. He subsequently became a member of the St John's Wood Clique, whose leader was P. H. Calderon and whose other members included H. S. Marks, D. W. Wynfield, G. A. Storey and G. D. Leslie. Yeames explored both the present and the past in the language of anecdote. His most famous pictures were *Defendant and Counsel* (1895, Bristol City Art Gallery), *Amy Robsart* (1877, Tate Gallery) and the never-to-be-forgotten *'And When Did You Last See Your Father?'* He was elected RA in 1877.

In the Royal Academy of 1878 William Frederick Yeames exhibited what was destined to become one of the most famous of all Victorian evocations of the British past, *'And When Did You Last See Your Father?'*[2] So celebrated did this picture become that it was translated into a wax tableau in Madame Tussaud's, where it stands to this day. Yeames's achievement lay in crystallizing for all time in one potent image the whole saga of romantic, doomed Cavaliers and stern, relentless Puritans, a subject which occupied a central position amongst the themes and obsessions of the Victorian literary and artistic mind. The child, a figure clearly derived from Gainsborough's Blue Boy, stands on a footstool about to answer an inquiry made by the Puritan

160 See also colour plate x.

who leans across the table towards him. The latter is wanting to discover the whereabouts of the boy's father. To the left the ladies of the house, dressed in elegant Van Dyck silks, cling to each other in tearful emotion. They, it is clear, have not answered the dread question. We, the viewers, are held for all time in suspense at this poignant moment when an innocent child might inadvertently betray his father through his own truthfulness. *'And When Did You Last See Your Father?'*, like all Victorian narrative paintings, leaves us to fill in what has gone before and speculate as to what might happen after in a highly tantalizing way.

But why should this scene of confrontation and moral dilemma be set in the England of the Civil War? Yeames's painting is perhaps the sole survivor in the popular imagination of almost fifty years' preoccupation on the part of historians, novelists and artists with the second quarter of the seventeenth century. More works of art were produced depicting scenes connected with Charles I, Oliver Cromwell, Henrietta Maria and the struggle of Cavalier versus Roundhead than for any other period of British history. Yeames's picture came at the tail end of this explosion. On the surface of it, few periods should have been less appealing to High Victorian ideals than that of Caroline and Cromwellian England. Indeed, at first glance the two worlds seem diametrically opposed. As in the case of Mary Queen of Scots, the explanation for this particular obsession is rather complex, and we have to reconnoitre back in time to find out why it should have provided such a rich vehicle for the Victorian imagination. John Singleton Copley's *Charles I demanding in the House of Commons the Five Impeached Members,* a milestone in historical recreation, is also a visual microcosm of eighteenth-century attitudes – ones which the nineteenth century was to inherit and expand.[3]

23

Although Copley's picture was not exhibited until 1795, it was begun fourteen years earlier. Why should this incident, when Charles I went to the House in an attempt to arrest five of its Members, have inspired a major historical composition? David Hume introduces his narrative of the event with these words: 'A few days after, the King was betrayed into another indiscretion, much more fatal; an indiscretion to which all the ensuing disorders and civil wars ought immediately and directly to be ascribed. This was the impeachment of Lord Kimbolton and the five members.'[4] In other words, this incursion into the House was seen to precipitate the final outbreak of Civil War in 1642.

Our view of the War has been formed by the historians of our own day, by R. H. Tawney, Hugh Trevor-Roper and C. V. Wedgwood, and, in a previous generation, by Gardiner and Ranke. To understand Copley's canvas we have to grasp the entirely different significance which the world of the Enlightenment attached to this clash of King and Parliament.[5] These views were inevitably coloured according to whether one was Whig or Tory, but both parties believed that the present system of government in England reflected traditional English 'liberties' fought for and won in the struggle of King and Parliament, a mode of constitutional government set against Continental and especially French 'slavery'. For the Whig historians and propagandists, for patriotic Englishmen and for Continental Anglophiles, England's unique democracy was a source of pride. She alone had maintained and renewed the ancient liberties which freedom-loving invaders had first brought from the forests of Germany to oppose the autocratic might of the Roman Empire. These ancient liberties had always abided until the pretensions of kingship by divine right propagated by the first two Stuart kings had threatened to violate them. So ran the classic Whig scenario. Seen though the eyes of Hume, this canvas celebrates the defence of English liberty:

A sergeant at arms, in the king's name, demanded of the house the five members; and was sent back without any positive answer. Messengers were employed to search for them and arrest them. Their

trunks, chambers, and studies, were sealed and locked. The house voted all these acts of violence to be breaches of privilege, and commanded everyone to defend the liberty of the members. The King, irritated by all this opposition, resolved next day to come in person to the house, with an intention to demand, perhaps seize in their presence, the persons whom he had accused.[6]

We start, therefore, with the confrontation of Roundhead and Cavalier as a constitutional one. The haze of glamorous romance distilled by Yeames a century later did not exist in 1795.

Interest in the Civil War was not renewed until after the close of the Napoleonic Wars, and this time it sprang from a new impulse, the romanticism of Sir Walter Scott. The struggle of Charles I and Cromwell, of Cavaliers and Roundheads, a subject rich in local legend and folklore, was ideal material for the pen of Scott. He treated the Civil War twice, first in 1813 in *Rokeby* and later, in 1826, in *Woodstock; or, The Cavalier. A tale of the year sixteen hundred and fifty-one*. In these, for the first time, the combatants were projected as people of heroic romance.

Rokeby is a narrative poem set in the aftermath of the Battle of Marston Moor. It is dominated by the hostility of Cavaliers and Puritans and deals with the claims of love across such ideological barriers. Loyalty to the King, filial obedience and the demands of rank are inextricably intertwined. But it was not until *Woodstock* that Scott successfully analysed the motivation behind such divisions through the carefully drawn characters of the old Royalist Sir Henry Lee, the moderate Parliamentarian Markham Everard, the dissolute Cavalier Wildrake and the Puritan fanatics Desborough and Harrison.[7] In *Woodstock* Charles I became the perfect aristocrat of the *ancien régime*, a prime exponent of enlightened paternalism and *noblesse oblige*:

. . . if moral virtue and religious faith were to be selected as the qualities which merited a crown, no man could plead the possession of them in a higher or more indisputable degree. Temperate, wise, and frugal, yet munificent in rewarding merit – a friend to letters and the muses, but a severe discourager of the misuse of such gifts – a worthy gentleman – a kind master – the best friend, the best father, the best christian.[8]

So Scott describes Charles through the lips of Alice Lee, the old Royalist's daughter. One can see the Victorian Charles taking shape, the ideal paterfamilias, a tragic symbol of vanishing monarchic and aristocratic society. The Scott vision of noble and loyal Cavaliers is the one which will lead us down to Yeames's '*And When Did You Last See Your Father?*'

The Victorian celebration of Charles I as ideal husband and father found its most compelling visual expression in Daniel Maclise's *An Interview between Charles I and Oliver Cromwell* (*c.* 1836), in which the sad-faced King listens to his son reading while a spaniel, hugged by his daughter, sits on his lap and a hound rests its chin on the royal knee. Oliver Cromwell, in stark contrast, attracts neither children nor animals but sits in gloomy, threatening solitude.[9] A similar vision is Frederick Goodall's lyrical *An Episode of the Happier Days of Charles I* (1853), in which the King, his wife and adorable children sail down the river on a summer's day. In Charles I and his family the viewers were surely meant to be looking at the historical prototype of the middle-class domestic happiness (feeding the swans) of their own Victoria and Albert.

In the aftermath of Scott the Civil War enjoyed a sustained vogue as a background for historical novels and plays.[10] The same year that *Woodstock* was published Horace Smith produced *Brambletye House; or Cavaliers and Roundheads,* a romance also set in the years of the Protectorate. In 1837 G. P. R. James wrote *Henry Masterton; young Cavalier* and Browning in his play *Strafford* described Charles I as 'the man with the mild voice and the mournful eyes'. Shelley had begun a play about Charles I as long ago as 1818, but left it unfinished. Tragedies were, however, written by E. Cobham in 1828, by Mary Russell Mitford in 1840 and the Rev. A. T. Gurney in 1846. This obsession within the theatre was to find its most enduring form in Vincenzo Bellini's light-hearted opera *I Puritani di Scozia,* based on the play *Têtes Rondes et Cavaliers* by François Ancelot and Xavier Boniface Saintine.

161 Daniel Maclise, *An Interview between Charles I and Oliver Cromwell* (*c.* 1836, National Gallery of Ireland, Dublin). See also colour plate XI.

The latter had its début at the Théâtre Italien in Paris in 1835, reflecting a similar French preoccupation with the personalities and events of Stuart England. This had begun in 1818 with Balzac's play on Charles I and Cromwell, which was followed by Villemain's *Histoire de Cromwell* (1819). In 1826 Victor Hugo began his famous *Cromwell* and in 1826–7 Guizot published his influential *Histoire de la Révolution d'Angleterre,* translated into English in 1845 by William Hazlitt. The French interpretation of the Civil War strengthened and influenced the Victorian. Guizot believed that it was a precursor of the French Revolution of 1789: 'They struggled for liberty against absolute power, for equality against privilege, for progressive and general interests ... the first would never have been thoroughly understood had not the second taken place.'[11] The French interest in the Great Rebellion was from the start essentially a political one, a historical autopsy on the Revolution. Along with this they did, of course, derive from the translation of Walter Scott's works the haze of romantic melodrama which attended any saga of Cavaliers and Puritans.

As in the case of Lady Jane Grey, Paul Delaroche occupied a key position in the new mythology. He painted no less than three major canvases on the subject of the English Civil War:

172, XIII *Cromwell gazing at the body of Charles I* (1831), *The Mocking of Charles I* (1837) and *Strafford on his Way to Execution* (1837). The first of these was subsequently exhibited at the Royal Academy in London, while the second was purchased by the Earl of Ellesmere; all three were subjects for best-selling prints. Delaroche always denied that his pictures had any explicit contemporary reference, maintaining that they were merely scenes of noble suffering and heroism from the past, but surely they could never have been painted without the French interest in the Great Rebellion. Charles I explained Louis XVI, just as Cromwell accounted for the phenomenon of Napoleon. Cromwell looks down on the corpse of Charles I like a figure mourning over the dead Christ. In *The Mocking of Charles I* the Cromwellian soldiers jeer at the King in a direct parody of the mocking of Christ. In such images, which drew upon the most potent emotions within the make-up of the nineteenth-century mind, powerful statements were implicit on the nature and abuse of power, on social change and revolution and their dire consequences. In England these canvases were widely admired, but the images were read, like those of Lady Jane Grey, within a very different historiographical context.

Within the prototypes of Cromwell and Charles and of Cavaliers and Puritans the Victorians had their vehicle *par excellence* for

162 Paul Delaroche, *The Mocking of Charles I* (1837, Duke of Sutherland).

163 Charles West Cope, *Speaker Lenthall asserting the Privileges of the Commons against Charles I* (1866, Houses of Parliament).

living out their own dilemmas, the dilemmas they faced as the middle classes gradually won ascendancy and power passed to them from the old landed gentry, as radical and revolutionary movements such as Chartism rose to threaten the established social hierarchy, as the new self-made upper classes born of the purple of commerce and manufacture fought for acceptance in the closed world of the old nobility and county families. Between about 1820 and 1900, something like a hundred and seventy-five paintings appeared on the walls of the Royal Academy connected with Charles I and his family, Oliver Cromwell and the Civil War. No other period could match this for intensity of public interest.

We see this preoccupation at its finest in the great series of paintings by C. W. Cope commissioned for the Peers' Corridor in the new Houses of Parliament and executed during the 1850s and 1860s.[12] These monumental paintings, much maligned and victims of wretched experiments in medium, are supreme achievements of the Victorian vision of the British past, brilliant recreations of lost moments in time within the Artist-Antiquarian tradition. They unfold the whole saga: Charles I demanding the arrest of 163 the five Members (1866), the King raising his 164 standard at Nottingham (1861), the setting off of the train-bands from London to Gloucester (1865), the siege of Basing House (1862), the expulsion of the Fellows of an Oxford College (1865) and the burial of Charles I at Windsor 165 (1857). To these we can add the endless canvases on every conceivable battle and event in the

164 Charles West Cope, *Charles I erecting his Standard at Nottingham, 1642* (1861, Houses of Parliament).

period by A. C. Gow, J. S. Lucas, T. F. Marshall, Ernest Crofts, Augustus Egg or John Gilbert exhibited year by year at the Academy. So obsessive was the interest that a painter like Crofts rarely produced anything else except Civil War battle scenes. He almost lived in the 1640s.

What was the basis for this obsession, and how did it differ from that of the previous century? Until the publication of S. R. Gardiner's magisterial history in the sixties, the Victorian view of the significance of these events can best be approached through the work of Henry Hallam, and in particular his *Constitutional History of England* (1827), which became a standard work. Hallam followed the eighteenth century in his cult of the British Constitution and of ancient liberties defended. To him as a Whig historian, history was the handmaid of politics

and a subject which invited its readers not, as we do today, to stand aside but, on the contrary, to take sides and pass judgment. When he describes the outbreak of the Civil War, he asks 'whether a thoroughly upright and enlightened man would rather have listed under the royal or parliamentary standard'.[13] For Hallam, the upright and virtuous man of the seventeenth century was no different from the same being in his own age, and history was there for morals to be drawn. For him the period's fascination and importance lay in this birth of Constitution. Writing of this special British glory in an earlier book, his *Europe during the Middle Ages*, he states:

No unbiased observer, who derives pleasure from the welfare of his species, can fail to consider the long and uninterruptedly increasing prosperity of England as

165 Charles West Cope, *The Burial of Charles I* (1857, Houses of Parliament).

the most beautiful phenomenon in the history of mankind. Climates more propitious may impart more largely the mere enjoyments of existence; but in no other region have the benefits that political institutions can confer been diffused over so extended a population; nor have any people so well reconciled the discordant elements of wealth, order, and liberty . . .[14]

All over Europe in Hallam's day the British Constitution was studied as a model to be followed, as Britain alone had escaped the woes of revolution and revolt which still continued to convulse the mainland. Henry Hallam served on the commission for the decoration of the Houses of Parliament from 1841 until his death in 1859. It is his view of history which enables us to understand the choice of historical subject-matter and its placing within the House. Walk-

ing down the Peers' Corridor past scenes of violent conflict gave the Victorian no feeling of unease, for these scenes reflected battles for basic liberties won long ago and inspired a calm confidence in the destiny of this island and its ideal parliamentary democracy.

This, then, was the central idea which animated the Victorian preoccupation with the seventeenth century. But it could also be reversed; the seventeenth century could be seen as a mirror in time of present conflicts, manifested in the meeting of Charles I and Cromwell or Cavalier face to face with Puritan. Many of these tableaux invite the onlooker to read the scene in a variety of ways. They deliberately present the dilemma and leave us the agonizing choice between two worlds. One of the most famous of these is William Shakespeare Burton's *A Woun-* 166 *ded Cavalier*, which caused a sensation at the Royal Academy in 1856. Painted under heavy Pre-Raphaelite influence, it is now the only painting by which Burton is remembered. In it a Puritan girl comes to the aid of a Royalist, while her husband or brother (it is not clear which), Bible in hand, stands unmoved. John Everett Millais's *The Proscribed Royalist, 1651* (1853),[15] in which a young Puritan girl gives succour to a Cavalier in hiding, reiterates exactly the same theme, though less successfully. So too does the picture with which we started our pursuit of Cavaliers and Roundheads, '*And When Did You Last See Your Father?*' Yeames, when he wrote of how he had come to paint the picture, gave no clues as to the tradition on which he was drawing and which, if taken away, would irretrievably

diminish the impact. All he wrote was as follows:

I had, at the time I painted the picture, living in my house a nephew of an innocent and truthful disposition, and it occurred to me to represent him in a situation where the child's outspokenness and unconsciousness would lead to disastrous consequences, and a scene in a country house occupied by the Puritans during the Rebellion in England suited my purpose.[16]

By 1878 the theme of Cavaliers and Roundheads had been reduced to what seems to us little more than an episode from a children's adventure story. In this painting we catch the dying echoes of one of the most potent of all themes in Victorian painting, a vehicle by which artists had been able to express some of the central ideals and contradictions of their own age.

166 William Shakespeare Burton, *A Wounded Cavalier* (1856, Guildhall Art Gallery, London).

167 William Henry Simmons after Sir John Everett Millais, *The Proscribed Royalist, 1651* (1853).

Oliver Cromwell

Ford Madox Brown

St Ives, AD 1630. Cromwell on his Farm
1874
Oil on canvas (arched top), $55\frac{1}{2} \times 41\frac{1}{2}$ in.
(141×105.5 cm)
Lady Lever Art Gallery, Port Sunlight, by
courtesy of Merseyside County Council

FORD MADOX BROWN (1821–93)[1] was born in
Calais and studied at the Academies at Bruges,
Ghent and Antwerp under two pupils of David
and the academic master Baron Wappers. Later
he studied in Paris and was influenced both by
the works in the Louvre and by contemporary
French romanticism. He travelled to Rome via
Basle, where he came under the spell of Holbein
and the Nazarenes. On settling in England he
befriended Rossetti, Millais and Holman Hunt,
but he never officially became a member of the
Pre-Raphaelite Brotherhood. His two most
famous and most Pre-Raphaelite works were *The
Last of England* (Birmingham City Art Gallery)
and *Work* (Manchester City Art Gallery), both
started in 1852. Later he was associated with the
Morris firm and decorated the Great Hall of
Manchester Town Hall.

St Ives, AD 1630. Cromwell on his Farm was
commissioned by Mr Brockbank of Manchester
in 1872, and Ford Madox Brown completed it by
March 1874.[2] The description by Forbes Robertson, Senior is worth quoting because it was
inspired by the artist himself:

On a white horse, which grazes leisurely by the
roadside before us, sits a stalwart man of saturnine
visage, in the prime of lusty manhood.

He is attired in the sober costume worn by
thoughtful men in the early part of Charles I's reign, is
booted in buff, and his beaver is slouched . . . Before
him burns a heap of weeds and stubble, which those
two labourers have grubbed from the hedges they
have been trimming, and it is the flames thereof that
have arrested the attention of their master, and on
which he now gazes so earnestly yet so absently.

In vain may the buxom wench, sent by her mistress,
who stands with her two children by the garden
terrace in front of the goodly manor-house yonder to
the right, raise her voice . . . to tell the master that
dinner waits.

He hears, and heeds her no more than the little lamb
does that nibbles contentedly the herbage by the
horse's nose, or than the pig that fancies something
good is going on in her neighbourhood, and comes
scampering up, with her squeaking litter, among the
very horse's feet.

By the consenting fall of the lines of the mouth and
the weird speculation in those eyes, he of the white
horse sits evidently spell-bound; and that which fixes
him is no fairy dance, no pleasing phantasy, but the
soul-sobering vision of the prophet or seer.

We have seen where we are in time; but where are
we in place, and who is he? . . .

As it is, we are standing on the lands of the Manor of
Sleep Hall; all these, to the river side, are its meadows,
used, as we see, for grazing purposes, and yonder lady,
with her two children, is its mistress . . . Her husband
is the melancholy man before us on the white horse,
and his name is Oliver Cromwell.

He has not been long back from Parliament, and it
will be ten or eleven years before he sits there again. In
the meanwhile his notions about kingcraft have been
sadly shaken, and he has made up his mind to devote
himself to the interests of his family and of his grazing
farm, and, above all, of his soul . . .

'Living neither in any considerable height nor yet in
obscurity, I did endeavour', said he afterwards in a
famous speech in Parliament, 'to discharge the duty of
an honest man.'

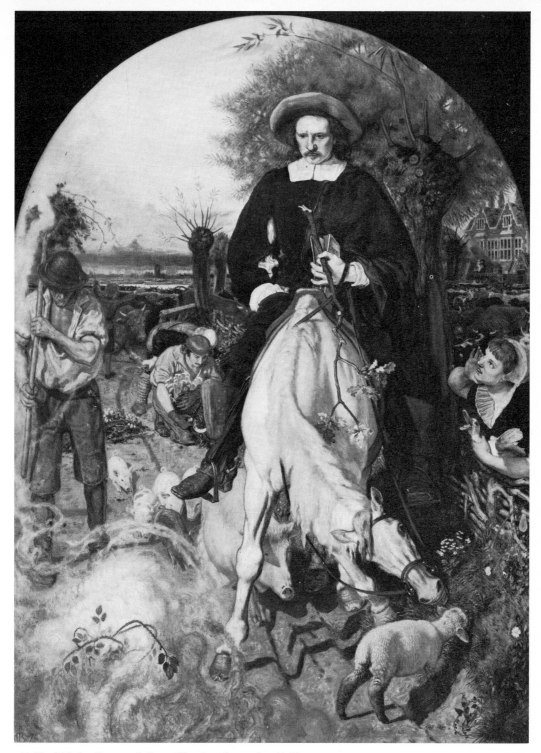

168 Ford Madox Brown, *St Ives, AD 1630. Cromwell on his Farm.*

169 Ford Madox Brown, *Cromwell discussing the Protection of the Vaudois with Milton and Andrew Marvell* (1878, Nottingham Castle Museum).

Oliver Cromwell, as we see him here, is supposed by the artist to be returning from a neighbourly visit, and, on his homeward road, to have opened his Bible at these passages:

'Lord, how long? Wilt thou hide Thyself for ever?'
'And shall Thy wrath burn like fire?'

Pondering on the texts, he comes all at once on the burning stubble, and the concrete fact, so palpable to his outward eyes, answers readily to the vision within, and the man lapses, in the saddle where he sits, into a religious trance . . .[3]

The description provides a tremendous insight into the layers contained within the picture's subject-matter. Although its colouring is of the seventies, the design and execution are of the fifties and relate to Brown's Pre-Raphaelite days. He even returned to the habit of painting in the open air, working in the countryside around Morris's Kelmscott. The fact is that *Cromwell on his Farm* was first started in 1853, twenty years before, at exactly the same time that he began work on his better-known picture *The Last of England*. The theme of the former arose intially out of a deep personal depression which, in later life, Brown compared to the religious melancholy he attempted to depict in his picture of Cromwell. He once wrote to a friend about this:

I have suffered so much myself from imaginary nervousness, and every friend I have has suffered so exactly in the same way, that I cannot help thinking that I should be in some way helpful to you as a comparison.

No man ever does any good in the world without passing through the phase some time between the ages of thirty and forty. This is what I endeavoured to depict in the *Cromwell on his Farm*, which seems so little understood by ordinary mortals.[4]

The picture is therefore both a personal and a public allegory of doubt, a crisis of faith. This surely is also reflected in its iconographical formula, with its direct echoes of a Conversion of St Paul. But why should Cromwell be Brown's chosen vehicle to present this dilemma of the present? The artist without doubt had an obsession with Cromwell. In 1878 he returned to him in *Cromwell discussing the Protection of the Vaudois with Milton and Andrew Marvell*, and he planned to execute several other pictures illustrative of Cromwell's career.[5] He even chose the name Oliver for his son, who died in the year in which *Cromwell on his Farm* was completed.

Our initial clue to this mania is the key figure in his canvas *Work*, also belonging to the early fifties – Thomas Carlyle, the historian, whose best-selling *Letters and Speeches of Oliver Cromwell* was published in 1845. These formulated the Victorian idea of the Lord Protector, which was a total reversal of that held by the previous century.[6] To the Enlightenment Cromwell had been, in the words of David Hume, 'a mixture of so much absurdity with so much penetration . . . tempering such violent ambition and such enraged fanaticism with so much regard to justice and humanity'.[7] This is the Cromwell whom West painted in 1783 in his *Oliver Cromwell ordering the Mace to be taken away*.

Scott's Cromwell in *Woodstock* (1826) takes us some way towards the Victorian cult figure:

He was of middle stature, strong and coarsely made, with harsh and severe features . . . His manner of speaking . . . was energetic and forcible, though neither graceful nor eloquent . . . It was also remarked of Cromwell, that though born of a good family . . . the fanatic democratic ruler could never acquire, or else disdained to practise, the courtesies usually exercised among the higher classes in their intercourse with each other. His demeanour was so blunt as sometimes might be termed clownish . . .[8]

Scott goes on to say, in line with his eighteenth-century predecessors, that no one would ever know where his religion ended and his hypocrisy began. Evangelical in religion, a self-made man, anti-aristocratic and anti-establishment by inclination, a reformer of passionate moral conviction, Cromwell had all the ingredients to make him the hero of the reformers, liberals and new men of nineteenth-century Britain.

The most important early collection of unbiased material on Cromwell to be published was Mark Noble's *Memoirs of the Protectoral House of Cromwell* (1784), but it was not until the 1830s and 1840s that the reappraisal of Cromwell became a major preoccupation of historians. During the forties Thomas Carlyle began to regard Cromwell as 'a great and true man' and 'one of the greatest souls ever born of English kin'. His famous edition of the *Letters and Speeches* billed Puritanism, to the reversal of Hume and the Enlightenment, as 'the last of our Heroisms',[9] and the Lord Protector was finally apotheosized, by the glory of Carlyle's passionate rhetoric, as a great national hero leading the country from darkness into light. No subsequent appraisal of Cromwell went untouched by Carlyle's impassioned partisanship.

In 1836 Daniel Maclise exhibited *An Interview between Charles I and Oliver Cromwell*, but it was not until after 1840, coinciding exactly with the new spate of literature, that Cromwell appeared with any degree of regularity as a permanent ingredient of Academy historical mythology. As such he was to continue until the 1870s.

The figure which emerges in these pictures is a very different one from the bigoted maniac of the eighteenth century. Augustus Egg painted Cromwell on the eve of the battle of Naseby (1859) like Christ undergoing the Agony in the Garden. Bathed in prophetic moonlight, the future Lord Protector is shown in a state of religious ecstasy. In 1863 Charles Lucy recreated the Cromwellian court, another aspect of the cult, portraying the Protector as the head of an ideal household, a pattern for middle-class

170 Benjamin West, *Oliver Cromwell ordering the Mace to be taken away* (1783, Collection of the Montclair Art Museum).

171 Augustus Leopold Egg, *Cromwell before Naseby* (1859, Royal Academy of Arts). Detail.

behaviour of the present. Later, in 1867, David Wilkie Wynfield evoked the piety of Cromwell's death in a scene based on one of Carlyle's great set pieces, drawing this time on the iconography of the Death of the Virgin. The Cromwell cult took on overtones of almost religious veneration as sacred iconography was automatically transferred to him.

172 Paul Delaroche, *Cromwell gazing at the Body of Charles I* (1831, Musée des Beaux-Arts, Nîmes).

The Victorian Cromwell was therefore a man of heroic stature.[10] Of Ford Madox Brown it was written that 'intellect made him a Socialist of an extreme type',[11] and with this as a lead it is hardly surprising to discover that the statue erected to Cromwell in Manchester (Mr Brockbank who commissioned *Cromwell on his Farm* was a Manchester man) was paid for by the wife of Abel Heywood, the city's leading radical publisher and an active Chartist.[12] Cromwell not only epitomized the self-made man, he expressed the idea of popular sovereignty and represented the exercise of power by someone of exemplary moral standards. Within a wider context, his achievements abroad in terms of foreign policy and maritime power foreshadowed the great age of the British Empire. (This is what Brown celebrates in *Cromwell discussing the Protection of the Vaudois*.) The relationship between his popularity among artists and his glorification by the exponents of radicalism cannot surely be a coincidence.

Cromwell emerged within the context of popular leadership with the rise of the Chartists, a working-class movement which sprang from the earlier failure of attempts at trade unionism and the frustrations evoked by the limitations of the 1832 Reform Bill. In 1838 the Chartists codified their demands for universal male suffrage, equal electoral districts, paid Members of Parliament, a secret ballot and annual Parliaments. After that year the campaign rose to a crescendo with mass demonstrations and torchlight processions. The movement was at its most dynamic through the forties until its ultimate failure in the year of revolutions, after which support fell away as control passed into the hands of extremists and Victorian England entered its economic heyday.

Throughout the 1840s Cromwell was held up as *the* great hero to the followers of Chartism, who overtly associated themselves in a direct line of descent from the reforming groups of his time. Thomas Cooper lectured regularly on Cromwell in the Chartist interest up and down the country; so also did one of their greatest leaders and orators, Henry Vincent. Bearing all this in mind, one can see the significance of these images of Cromwell, and understand what could be read in England into Delaroche's *Cromwell gazing at the Body of Charles I* (1831), perhaps the most potent and gruesome of all the tableaux. Every history of the period accepts the unlikely account that Cromwell sat up with Charles I's coffin. Even S. R. Gardiner incorporates the story into his otherwise exemplary and precisely documented narrative of the Stuart period. The vivid account Merle d'Aubigné gives in his history captures the mingling of horror and destiny this composition was intended to evoke:

But there was a solemn lesson in his sovereign's lifeless corpse. He opened the coffin himself, and sadly gazed upon the cold inanimate body, without cruelty, or anger, or exultation, but reverential fear, as he thought of the judgements of God . . . And who was it that lay before him? . . . A descendant of kings, – a mighty prince –, a ruler of three kingdoms . . . Cromwell before the dead body of Charles I. is a scene worthy to be described by a Milton, or a Shakespeare, or by some genius still more sublime than even they.[13]

There is a footnote to the Cromwell cult in the Victorian age. As the Lord Protector was rewritten into the part of a national saviour of radical reform, the Puritans assumed a new role as the forerunners of middle-class morality. David Hume had spoken of the Civil War as motivated by 'gloomy enthusiasm' which had 'poisoned' the body politic and led to 'puritanical

173 David Wilkie Wynfield, *The Death of Oliver Cromwell* (1867, Victoria & Albert Museum, London).

absurdities'. The Enlightenment naturally had no time for what it regarded as the bigotry and downright hypocrisy of seventeenth-century evangelical movements. As, however, evangelical morality reasserted its sway over the upper and middle classes during the opening decades of the nineteenth century, the way was opened for a radical reassessment of Puritanism. Carlyle's conception of Cromwell greatly influenced the first favourable account, T. B. Marsden's *The History of the Early Puritans*, published in 1850. In 1856 the embarkation of the Pilgrim Fathers was depicted by C. W. Cope on the walls of the Houses of Parliament. The flag bears the motto 'Freedom of worship', and the placing of the Pilgrim Fathers as part of Victorian national mythology in the House reflects this total revolution in attitudes as vividly as does Brown's vision of Cromwell the prophet and seer.

174 Charles West Cope, *The Embarkation of the Pilgrim Fathers* (1856, Houses of Parliament).

Epilogue:
The Victorian Image

The loyal to their crown
Are loyal to their own far sons, who love
Our ocean-empire with her boundless homes
For ever-broadening England, and her throne
In our vast Orient, and one isle, one isle,
That knows not her own greatness . . .
TENNYSON, 'To the Queen', *Idylls of the King*

I CAME to this book from my research on the Elizabethan age, and all the time I was writing it I was becoming more and more aware of the parallels between the two eras. And this in no false sense, but as providing a clue to a different way of looking at the art and culture of Victorian Britain. Perhaps an approach through the Elizabethan era could prove to be just as fruitful as the more conventional ones which regard the Victorian age either as our own century projected back to many of its seminal roots, or as the eighteenth century brought forward to a fulfilment.

The Elizabethan age and the Victorian were both intensely nationalistic, bent on creating mythologies powerful enough to hold together a divided people. The Elizabethans focused on their cult of the Virgin Queen, an ambiguous Virgin-Mother figure whose mystique and celebration in literature, festival and the visual arts bound together a kingdom rent asunder by religion. The nineteenth century found in Victoria a Mother Empress who could above all be the pattern of the domestic virtues which sustained the ethics of behaviour for the whole of society, irrespective of class or religion. Kemble, the Anglo-Saxon historian, described her as 'fearless in the holy circle of her domestic happiness, secure in the affections of a people whose institutions have given to them all the blessings of an equal law'.[1] Both ages developed new national historical mythologies. The Eliz-

abethan found its most vivid expression in the chronicles of Hall and Holinshed as transmuted by the playwrights – the exaltation of the Tudor myth as a symbol of the nascent nationalism. The Victorian equivalent would range from Macaulay's *History of England* to Dickens's *A Child's History of England* (1851–3), and from whatever political stance it was viewed the saga was that of the evolution of Britain from feudal slavery to elected representative government.

In the Victorian age, as in the sixteenth century, there was an isolation from Europe and an expansion of empire. The stability of England, in comparison with the religious civil wars or endless revolutions prevalent elsewhere in these two periods, made this country the envy of the Continental mainland. Those who watched and hoped for a solution to the terrible division of Catholic and Protestant found in Elizabeth Tudor a symbol of hope to set against outright intolerance, against the extremes of Counter-Reformation thought with its stifling of intellectual speculation, against the hideous obscurantism and bloody persecution of Philip II's Spain. From the Low Countries, from Germany, from *politique* France, from tolerant Poland, from Italy and above all from Venice, all that was liberal in the stream of European humanist thought looked towards England. So, three hundred years later under Victoria, England was similarly looked to, this time for her liberal system of representative government, the model for those who aspired to overthrow the absolutist régimes re-established from the previous century. Whether in Byron's Greece, Garibaldi's Italy or the France of 1830, 1848 or 1870, it was to Britain that the nationalistic liberation movements looked, not only for refuge but for intellectual support and as a focal point for their ideals. It is these themes of ancient

152

British liberties that are proclaimed again and again in the stories and pictures of King Alfred, the death of Harold at the Battle of Hastings, the signing of Magna Carta, the events of the Civil War or the Glorious Revolution of 1688.

The imperial saga was equally rich for both Queens. The Elizabethan period was the first heroic age of colonial endeavour in the New World, but it was clothed with the sanctions of the historic Tudor imperial myth, with the Queen as the descendant of the ancient House of Troy now laying claim to an empire which, if we are to believe some of the more extreme messianic prognostications or the visual symbolism of her portraits, was to be global. She was Spenser's 'most royall queen or empresse':

Great lady of the greatest isle, whose light,
Like Phoebus lamp throughout the world doth shine . . .[2]

Was Gloriana so very different from Tennyson's vision of Victoria at her Jubilee?

> *Fifty times the rose has flower'd and faded,*
> *Fifty times the golden harvest fallen,*
> *Since our queen assumed the globe, the sceptre.*
>
> > *She beloved for a kindliness*
> > *Rare in fable or History,*
> > *Queen and Empress of India,*
> > *Crown'd so long with a diadem*
> > *Never worn by a worthier . . .*[3]

Although the Victorian age rejected Elizabeth I because she epitomized its female vices – spinsterhood, vanity and behaviour ill befitting a lady – I cannot but believe that the celebration and cult of the Virgin Queen had a powerful influence on the cult of Victoria.

The theme of sea empire, to take one thread, can be traced down from Spenser's 'Cynthia, queen of seas and lands' to Tennyson's eulogy of Queen Alexandra as 'Bride of the heir of the Kings of the Sea'.[4] And it is to this tradition, of course, that G. F. Watts's *Alfred inciting the English to resist the Danes* belongs, as vividly as do the endless canvases of Nelson's victories. When it came to the imperial saga, even Oliver Cromwell could somehow be fitted in as a forerunner of imperial greatness.

So, too, both ages were obsessed by romance. In each case this was directly related to the papering over of vast social changes, in the sixteenth century the rise of the gentry and the establishment of a new post-Reformation aristocracy, in the nineteenth the advent of the new middle classes, particularly the urban industrialists. Both periods found in medieval romance and neo-Gothicism a façade with which to cover up this re-ordering of the social structure. For the Elizabethans it was manifested in their passion for tilts and tournaments, their love for romances of chivalry and the neo-Gothic style of their architecture. For the Victorians it was equally reflected in the transitory art of festival, whether in the form of the Eglinton Tournament or the masquerade balls given by Victoria, as well as in the literature pouring down from the Scott tradition and in the visual arts from Pugin to the Pre-Raphaelites. And, of course, all the pictures dealt with in this book are a direct reflection of this overwhelming ethos of romance. But it was romance tempered by new antiquarian standards. It is fascinating that not for a long time did the aim of accuracy in historical reconstruction become irreconcilable with a romantic view of the past. Indeed, it might be said to have strengthened it. As Jerome Hamilton Buckley has written: 'to . . . whatever use the past might be put, each historical reference was expected to rest upon a studious regard for fact and an ability to enter, at least for one moment, imaginatively, even empathically into the life of another society'.[5]

As a consequence of their romantic ideals, both eras fostered a worship of the lady, bolstered and propagated in each case by the fact of the Queen regnant. The romantic cult of womanhood in the Elizabethan age combined the heroine of medieval romance with the Neoplatonized lady of Castiglione's *Courtier*. The women of the Victorian age were idolized as ideal wives and mothers, untouchable as were the consorts of medieval knights enshrined in their bowers. Their dream idealizations were the ladies of Tennyson or Burne-Jones, pale-faced, bewimpled and dressed in trailing robes. Winterhalter's Queen Victoria, wan in white, silhouetted in the twilight with a rose clasped to her bosom, is closer than a first glance would suggest to the Ermine Portrait of Elizabeth I. Encased in her ruff and studded with jewels, holding the olive branch of *pax*, Elizabeth is yet the heroine of her knights, and the little ermine of chastity alluding to this fact nestles on the sleeve of her dress. In each of the two Queens, therefore, the artificial chivalry of her age found its nodal point.

Elizabethan women of the upper classes, however, enjoyed a freedom and status unknown to the women of Victorian Britain. This representation may account for the overwhelming preoccupation in Victorian history paintings with womanhood and woman's proper role. Mary Queen of Scots and Lady Jane Grey, both tough, humanist-educated women holding their own in a man's world, are deliberately distorted to approximate to a view of women as inferior beings in a male-dominated society. *Pace* Victoria herself, their kingdom was the fireside and the nursery. Children also are distorted to fit into a romantic notion of the innocence of childhood. Whether we are looking at a medieval king and his brother or a little Cavalier boy in blue, they are not depicted as they would have been in their own ages – miniature adults – but as fragile beings uncorrupted as yet by the sin of adult life.

These pictures, which aimed at portraying the national past so vividly, are therefore key documents in unravelling what one might call 'the Victorian image'. Passionately patriotic, overtly romantic, they drew to themselves one further, even more potent thread from the make-up of the Victorian mind – that of religion. Just as the cult of the Virgin Elizabeth replaced in the minds of her subjects the cult of the Virgin Mary, so the celebration of the heroes and heroines of Great Britain's past had strongly religious overtones. Now, in a post-nationalistic age, we can see how the myths of nationalism were crucial for holding together the thought-assumptions of the teeming masses which made up the modern state. That they developed religious overtones is hardly surprising. Lady Jane Grey, Mary Queen of Scots, King Alfred, Harold, the Princes in the Tower, Charles I, Oliver Cromwell, even Bonnie Prince Charlie were all, in their varying ways, 'saints', and these pictures are celebrations of their virtues, their agonies and ecstasies and, often, their 'martyrdom'. This is reinforced by the artists' deliberate use in tackling these subjects of formulae derived from sacred iconography. Surely here we are touching the root of a vital part of the Victorian imagination.

These scenes from our national history have long lost their potency for us. It has been eroded by two world wars, by the collapse and dissolution of empire, by demands for devolution, by a revolution in the teaching of history both in universities and, even more, in schools. These pictures now remain as monuments to the lost era which strove so boldly to relive its own past. They speak to us of optimism and heroism, of pride in the past and tranquillity within the present in that second greatest of all our ages, the reign of Queen Victoria.

Appendix: Subjects from British history from the Ancient Britons to the outbreak of the Napoleonic Wars exhibited at the Royal Academy, 1769–1904

The following listing under subject-matter is an analysis of all the main topics from British history represented in the Royal Academy exhibitions between 1769 and 1904. Inevitably, there will be overlaps and omissions. Overlaps occur in the case of subjects which also have a literary connotation, such as Richard III or Cardinal Wolsey; omissions can result from the inadequacy of the picture's title. Subjects or periods of minimal interest have been left out, as have also works whose subject is a reverie of time past as against a specific event. I have included sculpture where it seems relevant.

The list has been compiled verbatim from Algernon Graves, *The Royal Academy of Arts*, London, 1905–6, a complete dictionary of exhibitors at the Academy since its foundation. The letters 'qu.' in brackets indicate that the dictionary entry includes a quotation from a literary source.

The Ancient Britons

1783 (423) Conrad Martin Metz, *Queen Boadicea preparing to engage the Romans*

1787 (579) Conrad Martin Metz, *Boadicea* (Cowper's Poems)

1793 (311) Samuel Woodford, *Caractacus before Claudius*

1815 (178) Samuel Drummond, *Boadicea rallying the Britons; a sketch*

1831 (55) Henry Perronet Briggs, *The Progress of Civilisation. The Ancient Britons instructed by the Romans in the mechanical arts* (painted for the Mechanics' Institute, Hull)

1841 (1248) William Calder Marshall, *Caractacus before Claudius*

1844 (1359) William Calder Marshall, *Caractacus before Claudius*

1847 (1391) George Gammon Adams, *An Ancient Briton as a Spy*

1850 (553) William Holman Hunt, *A converted British family sheltering a Christian missionary from the persecution of the Druids*

1856 (1233) John Thomas, *Queen Boadicea inciting the Britons to avenge the loss of their liberty, and the wrongs inflicted on her children and herself* (qu.)

1862 (996) William Calder Marshall, *The Young Briton . . .*

1864 (991) Thomas Thornycroft, *Colossal head of Boadicea, a part of a chariot group now in progress*

1865 (294) Sir John Everett Millais, *The Romans leaving Britain* (qu.)

1868 (620) Wilfrid Vincent Herbert, *Captives from Britain in the Arena of the Flavian amphitheatre, Rome, reign of Domitian* (qu.)

1878 (1390) James Elder Christie, *Introduction of Christianity into Britain; Christian missionaries interrupting a human sacrifice*

1884 (245) Lawrence Alma-Tadema, *Hadrian in England, visiting a Romano-British pottery*

1891 (1011) Thomas Davidson, *Captive Britons in Rome*

The Anglo-Saxons

1769 (117) Samuel Wale, *St. Austin preaching Christianity to King Ethelbert and Queen Bertha in the Isle of Thanet; a sketch*

1770 (116) Angelica Kauffmann, *Vortigern, King of Britain enamoured with Rowena, at the banquet of Hengist, the Saxon general*

1771 (113) Angelica Kauffmann, *The interview of King Edgar with Elfrida, after her marriage with Athelwold*

1772 (227) William Wynne Ryland, *Vortigern falling in love with Rowena . . .* (after Angelica Kauffmann)

1774 (114) William Hamilton, *King Edgar's first interview with Elfrida*

(309) Samuel Wale, *St. Augustine preaching to K. Ethelbert and Q. Bertha in the Isle of Thanet*

1778 (331) Benjamin West, *William de Albanac presents his three daughters (naked) to Alfred the third King of Mercia . . .* (qu.)

1779 (204) John Hamilton Mortimer, *The meeting of Vortigern and Rowena*

1786 (411) Thomas Burgess, *The Death of Duke Athelwold after his marriage with Elfrida*

1788 (135) John Francis Rigaud, *Vortigern and Rowena, or the first settlement of the Saxons in England*

1793 (260) William Bromley, *The insolence of Dunstan to King Edwy*

1795 (19) Henry Tresham, *St. Augustine preaching to King Ethelbert*

1796 (80) John Francis Rigaud, *The first interview of King Edgar and Elfrida*

1799 (311) Henry Singleton, *St. Austin preaching the Gospel to King Ethelbert and Queen Bertha, in the Isle of Thanet*

1806 (99) Henry Tresham, *St. Augustine's mission to King Ethelbert*

1830 (1252) A. Roach, *Godiva, the wife of Leofric, Earl of Leicester, riding through Coventry to remove an oppressive tax from his people*

1834 (475) Herbert Luther Smith, '*Non Angli, sed Angeli*' (qu.)

1836 (575) George Jones, *Godiva's Return*

1838 (1048) John Jewell Penstone, *Saxon Bride*

1839 (471) William Dyce, *St. Dunstan separating Edwy and Elgiva* (qu.)

1842 (372) Thomas Bicken, *Peeping Tom*, '*Fair Godiva, wife of Leofric, a potent Earl . . .*'

(1249) Ferdinand Pickering, *Peeping Tom* (qu.)

1843 (582) John Martin, *Canute the Great rebuking his courtiers* (qu. Hume)

1845 (445) James Sant, *Gregory passing through the slave market at Rome* (qu.)

(628) Gustavus Ellinthorpe Sintzenich, *The last moments of the Venerable Bede, while translating the Gospels into Saxon, A.D. 735* (qu.)

1846 (400) Gustavus Ellinthorpe Sintzenich, *St. Augustin preaching Christianity to King Ethelbert and Queen Bertha in the Isle of Thanet A.D. 597*

(547) Thomas Roods, *The mother of Elgiva, Edwy's Queen, interceding with Odo, Archbishop of Canterbury, on behalf of her daughter*

1847 (174) Thomas George Duvall, *The Charity of King Canute the Great* (qu.)

(613) Sir John Everett Millais, *Elgiva* (qu.)

1848 (328) J. Hadwen Wheelright, *The assassination of Edward the Martyr*

1849 (329) George Patten, *The destruction of idolatry in England* (qu.)

(511) William James Grant, *The last act of one of the early missionaries* (qu.)

1854 (1386) William Calder Marshall, *Godiva* (Tennyson)

1857 (608) William Cave Thomas, *Canute listening to the monks singing at Ely* (qu.)

1866 (109) Sir Edwin Henry Landseer, '*Lady Godiva's prayer*' (qu.)

1867 (158) John Rogers Herbert, *St. Edmund, King of East Anglia, on the morning of his last battle with the Danes, by whom he was captured and martyred near Bury, November 20th, A.D. 890*

(226) George Jones, *Godiva with her gentlewoman to wait upon her, gallops through the town*

1868 (188) Paul Falconer Poole, *Custance sent adrift by the constable of Alla, King of Northumberland* (qu. Chaucer)

(926) William Theed, *Group of Her Majesty the Queen and H.R.H. the Prince Consort in early Saxon costume . . .*

(1047) Count Prosper d'Epihay, *The Saxon's Challenge; a sketch in bronze*

1869 (880) Charles Goldie, *The interview of St. Augustine and King Ethelbert* (qu.)

(1211) William Calder Marshall, *The Venerable Bede translating the Gospel of St. John* (qu.)

1871 (230) Edward Henry Courbould, *Ladie Godiva*

1872 (358) Heywood Hardy, *The Saxons' tribute to King Edgar* (qu.)

1877 (112) Andrew Benjamin Donaldson, *Edric, the fisherman, presents a fish as a token from St. Peter of the consecration of Westminster Abbey* (qu.)

1879 (1042) Charles Goldie, *The last hours of the Venerable Bede* (qu.)

1882 (558) Valentine Cameron Prinsep, *Death of Siward the Strong, Earl of Northumberland* (qu.)

1889 (326) George Adolphus Storey, *Godiva* (qu.)

1892 (411) Edward Blair Leighton, *Lady Godiva* (Tennyson)

(1325) Stephen B. Carlill, *St. Augustine preaching to the Saxons*

1893 (901) George McCulloch, *Lady Godiva's Sacrifice*

1902 (388) James Doyle Penrose, *The last chapter (Bede)* (qu.)

(674) Robert Spence, *Legend of the founding of Durham by St. Cuthbert* (qu.)

1904 (1033) Miss Mary Winefride Freeman, *The dedication of St. Edward the Confessor*

Alfred the Great

1771 (208) Samuel Wale, *King Alfred making a code of laws, dividing the Kingdom into counties, and encouraging the Arts and Sciences; a stained drawing*

1779 (341) Benjamin West, *Alfred the Great divides his Loaf with a Pilgrim*

1800 (423) Richard Westall, *Queen Judith reciting to Alfred the Great, when a child the songs of the bards, describing the heroic deeds of his ancestors*

1814 (352) Henry Pierce Bone, *The wife and sons of Hastings, the Danish chief, brought prisoners before Alfred the Great, etc.*

1840 (450) Richard Dadd, *Alfred the Great in disguise of a peasant*

1842 (491) William Simson, *Alfred dividing his last loaf with the pilgrim* (qu.)

1850 (451) William Cave Thomas, *Alfred giving a portion of his last loaf to the pilgrim*

(1299) Thomas Thornycroft, *Alfred the Great encouraged to the pursuit of learning by his mother*

1852 (122) Daniel Maclise, *Alfred, the Saxon King (disguised as a minstrel) in the tent of Guthrum the Dane* (qu.)

1863 (1060) Edward Bowring Stephens, *Alfred the Great in the neatherd's cottage (statue)* (qu.)

Harold

1831 (484) George Jones, *Harold's body discovered after the battle of Hastings, by Edith Sweneshals and two monks* (qu.)

1834 (194) William Hilton, *Editha and the monks searching for the body of Harold* (qu.)

1836 (103) Abraham Cooper, *The death of Harold at the Battle of Hastings* (qu.)

1846 (1068) H. G. Smith, *Editha and the monks discovering the body of Harold, after the battle of Hastings*

1849 (862) William Maw Egley, *Harold, the Earl, and the good Alfred . . .* (qu.)

1851 (580) John Cross, *Edward the Confessor leaving his crown to Harold* (qu.)

(619) John Cross, *Harold's Oath to William* (qu.)

1865 (929) Miss Alyn M. Thornycroft, *Edith seeking the body of Harold*

1882 (800) John Alfred Vinter, *The burial of Harold*

William the Conqueror

1775 (328) Samuel Wale, *Several of the bishops, nobility, and principal citizens of London swearing allegiance to King William at Berkhamsted Abbey*

1778 (29) Thomas Burgess, *William the Conqueror dismounted by his eldest son*

1808 (592) Benjamin West, *The citizens of London presenting the crown to William; a sketch*

1849 (470) Henry Hall Pickersgill, '*Robert proposed to a young girl . . . She was the mother of William the Conqueror*'

1858 (457) John Cross, *Coronation of William the Conqueror* (qu.)

1883 (1672) Mark Roche, *William the Conqueror at the Battle of Hastings, charging the standard defended by Gyrth, the brother of Harold*

1886 (1050) St. George Hare, *William the Conqueror* (qu.)

1897 (529) St. George Hall, *Courtship of William the Conqueror* (qu.)

1898 (449) John Seymour Lucas, *William the Conqueror granting a charter to the citizens of London*

1899 (670) George Elgar Hicks, *The Bayeux Tapestry: Queen Matilda with her Norman and Saxon Maidens, working the Bayeux Tapestry*

Henry II, Eleanor and the Fair Rosamund

1772 (192) Edward Penny, *Rosamund and Queen Eleanor*

1779 (75) John Downman, *Fair Rosamund*

1839 (940) Thomas Price Downes, *Queen Eleanor obliging Fair Rosamund to take poison*

1859 (901) James Archer, *Fair Rosamund and Queen Eleanor*

1867 (620) James Archer, *Henry II and Fair Rosamund*

Richard I

1791 (92) Thomas Stothard, *Richard Ist returning from Palestine*

(108) Thomas Stothard, *Richard First's treatment of Isaac, prince of Cyprus*

1806 (63) Henry Singleton, *Richard I. receiving his brother, Prince John, after his rebellion* (qu. Rapin)

1808 (593) Benjamin West, *The intercession of the Queen Mother with Richard the First to pardon his brother John; a sketch*

(682) T. M. Simpson, *Richard I, at the point of death, orders the release of the regicide*

1828 (128) Abraham Cooper, *Richard I, called Coeur-de-Lion, at the Battle of Ascalon in the act of unhorsing Saladin* (qu.)

1835 (395) Solomon Alexander Hart, *King Richard the First of England, surnamed Coeur de Lion, and the Soldan Saladin* (qu. Scott)

1840 (124) Abraham Cooper, *Richard Coeur de Lion reviewing the Crusaders in Palestine* (qu.)

1854 (414) James N. Glass, *Richard, Coeur de Lion, on his way to Jerusalem*

1856 (1021) Henry Chawner Shenton, *Richard Coeur de Lion forgiving Bertrand de Gourdon* (from J. Cross's picture in the House of Lords)

1862 (57) Henry William Pickersgill, *Blondel in search of his master, Richard Coeur de Lion*

King John

1832 (379) William N. Hardwick, *King John and the bishops, etc.*

1860 (74) Solomon Alexander Hart, *Archbishop Langton, after a Mass in the Cathedral of St. Paul's in London on 25th August, 1214 . . .* (qu.)

1876 (1318) Wilfrid Vincent Herbert, *Runnymede, near Windsor, A.D. 1215; eve of the signing of Magna Charta*

1883 (1237) Philip Harry Newman, *Magna Charta; design for wall painting*

Edward III and the Black Prince

1775 (243) John Francis Rigaud, *The entry of Edward, Prince of Wales (commonly called the Black Prince), into London with his royal prisoner*

1787 (19) Benjamin West, *The original institution of the most noble order of the garter by Edward III; a finished sketch*

1788 (130) John Francis Rigaud, *Edward III receiving the King of France in Westminster Hall*

1792 (8) Benjamin West, *The first ceremony, when Edward the Third instituted the most noble order of the Garter*

(66) Benjamin West, *Edward IIId passing the river Soame*

1793 (16) Benjamin West, *King Edward III embracing his son, Edward the Black Prince, after the battle of Cressy*

(74) Benjamin West, *Philippa, Queen Consort to Edward III, at the battle of Nevill's Cross, near Durham where David, King of Scotland, was made prisoner*

1794 (8) Benjamin West, *Edward, the Black Prince receiving John, King of France, prisoner, after the battle of Poictiers*

1808 (493) Augustus Earle, *Battle of Poitiers*

1817 (209) Francis Philip Stephanoff, *Edward the Black Prince conducting his prisoner John, King of France, in triumph to Westminster after the Battle of Poictiers*

1818 (497) Benjamin Burnell, *Portrait of Edward, The Black Prince . . .*

1824 (14) Henry Perronet Briggs, *Edward III, Queen Isabella, and the Earl of March* (qu.)

1839 (254) James Ramsay, *The entry of the Black Prince into London, with French King and his son prisoners . . .*

1842 (404) Benjamin Robert Haydon, *Edward the Black Prince thanking Lord James Audley for his gallantry in the battle of Poictiers* (qu.)

1846 (1042) Charles West Cope, *Small cartoon of Edward III conferring the Order of the Garter on Edward the Black Prince* (House of Lords)

1848 (509) William James Grant, *Scene in the tent of Edward the Black Prince, after the battle of Poitiers* (qu.)

1851 (380) Ford Madox Brown, *Geoffrey Chaucer reading the 'Leading of Custance' to Edward III and his court, at the Palace of Sheen, on the anniversary of the Black Prince's forty-fifth birthday, etc.*

1852 (47) Charles Landseer, *The death of Edward III* (qu.)

1881 (428) Robert Alexander Hillingford, *'Ich Dien'* (qu.)

1903 (492) Eyre Crowe, *The windmill of Crecy* (qu.)

Edward III and the Burghers of Calais

1788 (89) Benjamin West, *Queen Philippa soliciting her husband, Edward the Third, to save the lives of the brave burghers of Calais*

1790 (497) Richard Westall, *Queen Philippa interceding for the brave citizens of Calais*

1791 (509) Richard Westall, *The brave Burghers of Calais taking leave of their friends at the gate*

1814 (122) Edward Bird, *Queen Philippa supplicating King Edward to spare the lives of the six burghers of Calais, etc.*

1834 (565) George Jones, *Philippa relieving the burghers of Calais*

1859 (480) Henry Holiday, *The burgesses of Calais, A.D. 1347* (qu.)

Richard II

1787 (154) James Northcote, *Sir William Walworth, Lord Mayor of London, A.D. 1381, in the presence of Richard II, then 15 years old, kills Wat Tyler at the head of the insurgents, who are appeased by the heroic speech of the King*

1788 (466) J. Carter, *The Death of Richard II* (ref. to Rapin)

1793 (172) Henry Singleton, *The reception of Richard IId's Queen on her landing at Dover* (Rapin)

1811 (18) William Hilton, *John of Gaunt reproving Richard II, etc.*

(251) Charles Alfred Stothard, *The assassination of Richard II* (qu.)

1835 (570) John Zephaniah Bell, *Richard II giving the Charter to the Goldsmiths' Company*

1843 (659) Charles Blair Leighton, *The assassination of Richard II*

1852 (499) F. W. Oliphant, *Dying interview of John of Gaunt with Richard II* (qu. Shakespeare)

1876 (165) Sir John Gilbert, *Richard II resigning his crown to Bolingbroke, etc.*

Henry V

1779 (203) John Hamilton Mortimer, *The Battle of Agincourt*

1791 (18) Thomas Stothard, *Henry 5th's marriage to Catherine of France*

1826 (242) Frank Howard, *Country wedding in the time of Henry V : the procession returning from church* (qu.)

1828 (629) Thomas Stothard, *Frame containing four designs from Monstrelet : The Duke of Burgundy soliciting and vowing amity to the family of the young Duke of Orleans – The marriage of Henry 5th with Catherine, daughter to the King of France – Battle of Agincourt – Coronation of Henry 6th*

1835 (462) George Jones, *Henry V visiting the camp, and encouraging his soldiers the night before the battle of Agincourt* (qu.)

1880 (482) Robert Alexander Hillingford, *England's welcome to Henry V after Agincourt* (qu.)

1884 (258) Sir John Gilbert, *The morning of the battle of Agincourt* (qu.)

1888 (1115) Samuel Edmund Waller, *The morning of Agincourt* (qu.)

The Wars of the Roses

1779 (37) Thomas Burgess, *The Earl of Warwick swearing allegiance to Edward IV after the battle of Ferry Bridge*

1785 (402) Thomas Burgess, *After the defeat of Ferrybridge, the Earl of Warwick killing his horse in the presence of King Edward*

1791 (43) Thomas Burgess, *The Earl of Warwick swearing allegiance to Edward IV*

1798 (220) Henry Fuseli, *Richard III in his tent the night preceeding the battle of Bosworth . . .* (Shakespeare)

1811 (204) Henry Fuseli, *Richard III starting from the apparation of those whom he had assassinated, etc.* (Shakespeare)

1824 (220) Abraham Cooper, *Battle of Shrewsbury* (description)

1825 (70) Abraham Cooper, *Bosworth Field* (description)

1830 (417) Henry Singleton, *Richard's dream the night previous to the battle of Bosworth field* (Shakespeare)

1832 (987) J. A. Mitchell, *Death of Richard Nevill, Earl of Warwick, called the Kingmaker, with his two faithful friends, the Duke of Somerset and the Earl of Oxford . . .*

1834 (526) William N. Hardwick, *The Murder of Clarence* (Shakespeare)

1842 (413) John Wood, *King Henry VI taking refuge in a cottage after the battle of St. Alban's* (qu.)

1863 (140) Frederick Richard Pickersgill, *Isabella, Duchess of Clarence, urging her husband to abandon the cause of the House of York, and support that of Lancaster, A.D. 1470*

1871 (501) John Pettie, *Scene in the Temple Garden* (Shakespeare)

(541) Andrew Benjamin Donaldson, *After a battle – period: War of the Roses*

1874 (1280) F. A. Heath, *Choosing the roses in the Temple Garden* (after Pettie)

1896 (217) Charles J. Adams, *Bringing the body of Richard III to Leicester, etc.*

Margaret of Anjou, Queen of Henry VI

1787 (473) John Henry Ramberg, *Queen Margaret of Anjou landing at Weymouth after the battle of Tewkesbury*

1798 (3) F. Vieira, *Queen Margaret and the Robber*

1802 (429) Richard Westall, *Margaret of Anjou and her son, Edward Prince of Wales . . . after the battle of Hexbury*

1809 (440) Samuel Drummond, *Queen Margaret attacked by robbers*

1812 (140) Henry Pierce Bone, *Margaret of Anjou after the Battle of Hexham* (qu.)

1829 (181) Henry Perronet Briggs, *Queen Margaret of Anjou, being defeated at the battle of Hexham, flies with the young prince into a forest, where she meets with robbers*

1843 (439) Samuel Drummond, *Margaret, Queen of Henry VI with the Prince of Wales, her son, attacked by robbers*

1846 (600) John Archibald Casey, *Deliverance of Margaret of Anjou in the Gulf of Solway* (qu. Strickland)

1848 (62) Charles Landseer, *Queen Margaret and the robber of Hexham* (qu.)

1875 (227) Sir John Gilbert, *Tewkesbury Abbey: Queen Margaret carried prisoner to Edward after the battle of Tewkesbury*

1882 (533) William Christian Symons, *Margaret of Anjou and the robber of Hexham* (qu.)

1901 (217) James Doyle Penrose, *Margaret of Anjou and the robber* (qu.)

Edward IV and Lady Elizabeth Grey

1776 (156) Angelica Kauffmann, *Lady Elizabeth Grey imploring of Edward IV the restitution of her deceased husband's lands, forfeited in a dispute between the houses of York and Lancaster* (Rapin)

1793 (255) Richard Westall, *Lady Elizabeth Gray imploring of Edward IV the restitution of her husband's lands*

1796 (115) John Francis Rigaud, *Lady Elizabeth Grey petitioning King Edward the fourth for her husband's lands*

1797 (312) John Downman, *Edward IV on a visit to the Duchess of Bedford, is enamoured of Lady Elizabeth Grey* (Hume)

1798 (26) John Opie, *Elizabeth Grey petitioning Edward IV for the restoration of her estates*

1846 (520) Miss Ambrosini Jerôme, *Lady Elizabeth Grey pleading to Edward IV for the restoration of the inheritance of her children* (qu.)

1853 (469) Alexander Johnston, *Edward IV's first interview with Elizabeth Woodville* (Hume)

The Princes in the Tower, Edward V and the Duke of York

1769 (118) Samuel Wale, *The Queen Dowager of King Edward in the Sanctuary delivering up the Duke of York to the Cardinal Archbishop of Canterbury*

1776 (312) Samuel Wale, *The Duke of York, taken from his mother, the Dowager of Edward the Fourth, out of the Sanctuary of Westminster, to be conveyed to the Tower to his brother, by order of Richard, Duke of Gloucester*

1786 (116) John Francis Rigaud, *The Queen Dowager of England, widow of Edward the IVth, delivering her son, the Duke of York, to the Cardinal* (qu. Rapin)

(188) James Northcote, *King Edward the Vth and his brother Richard, Duke of York, murdered in the Tower by order of Richard III*

1797 (629) Henry Singleton, *Edward V and his brother the Duke of York entering the Tower*

1800 (429) Richard Westall, *Cardinal Bourchier, Archbishop of Canterbury, and Rotherham, Archbishop of York, endeavouring to persuade the Queen, Elizabeth Grey, to suffer her son, the Duke of York, to leave the sanctuary of Westminster . . .*

1821 (22) James Northcote, *The burial of Edward Fifth and his brother Richard of York, who were murdered in the Tower of London, June the 9th, 1483, by the order of King Richard III, etc.*

(217) James Northcote, *The marriage of Richard of Shrewsbury, Duke of York, brother of King Edward the Fifth to the Lady Anne Mowbray, only daughter of John Lord Mowbray, Duke of Norfolk, on the 15th of January, 1477*

1842 (237) Edward Matthew Ward, *Queen Elizabeth, widow of Edward IV, delivering the young Duke of York into the hands of Bourchier, Archbishop of Canterbury, and Rotherham, Archbishop of York, at the Sanctuary, Westminster* (qu.)

(534) Miss Sarah Elizabeth Thorn, *Elizabeth, Queen of Edward IV, parting with her youngest son . . .* (Hume)

1850 (491) John Cross, *The burial of the two sons of Edward IV in the Tower, 1483*

1853 (169) Henry Courtney Selous, *The rustle of the tapestry – scene in the Tower of London, Anno Domini 1483* (qu.)

1864 (565) Mrs. Edward Matthew Ward, *'The Tower, ay, the Tower'* (qu. Strickland)

1868 (150) Edward Matthew Ward, *Royal Marriage, 1477* (qu.)

1878 (21) John Everett Millais, *The Princes in the Tower*

1883 (1546) L. Fabbrucci, *The Princes in the Tower*

1893 (210) Philip Hermogenes Calderon, *Elizabeth Woodville, widow of Edward IV, parting with her younger son, the Duke of York* (qu.)

Henry VIII and his Queens

1781 (118) Henry Fuseli, *Queen Catherine's vision* (Shakespeare)

1790 (542) Richard Westall, *Catherine of Arragon, at her trial, accusing Cardinal Wolsey*

1791 (369) John Graham, *Anne Bollen on her way to execution, taking leave of Princess Elizabeth*

1794 (148) Thomas Stothard, *The interview between Henry VIII and the Emperor Charles V*

1795 (172) Samuel Drummond, *Henry VIII visits his first wife*

(415) Samuel Drummond, *Henry VIII affected at the death of his first wife*

1810 (370) Arthur Perigal, *Queen Catherine delivering to Capucius her farewell letter to Henry the Eighth* (Shakespeare)

1817 (17) George Henry Harlow, *The Court for the trial of Queen Catherine* (Shakespeare)

1822 (74) Francis Philip Stephanoff, *Henry VIII and Francis the First crowned victors at the Tournament of the Cloth of Gold*

1825 (208) Francis Philip Stephanoff, *Henry VIII crowned victor at the Tournament of the Cloth of Gold* (sketch for window)

1826 (378) William Derby, *Queen Catherine Parr after her reconciliation with Henry VIII, supplicating the pardon of her enemies, who were about to carry her, under the King's warrant, to the Tower* (qu.)

1827 (429) George Cattermole, *Trial of Queen Catherine*

1833 (253) Samuel Drummond, *Henry VIII, Anne Boleyne, Lady Jane Seymour and Princess Elizabeth – Harry receiving the news of his first wife's death*

1838 (645) Charles Fournier, *Anne Boleyn, the morning of her execution* (qu.)

1841 (34) Samuel Drummond, *Anne Boleyne as maid of honour to Katherine of Arragon*

(1101) Sir John Gilbert, *Holbein painting the portrait of Anne Boleyn*

1842 (1246) Henry Cook, *Queen Catherine's reception of the Cardinals* (Shakespeare)

1848 (479) Edward Armitage, *Henry VIII and Catherine Parr, etc.*

(542) Henry Nelson O'Neil, *Catherine of Arragon on appealing to Henry VIII* (Shakespeare)

1853 (559) Henry Nelson O'Neil, *Katherine's Dream* (Shakespeare)

(560) William James Grant, *The incident which led to the Reformation: Queen Catherine first discovers Henry's love for Anne Boleyn*

1854 (1402) William Theed, *Katharine of Arragon pleading before Henry VIII* (bas-relief for the Palace of Westminster)

1856 (585) E. Deveria, *The birth of Edward VI, and the death of his mother, Jane Seymour*

1857 (425) Henry Le Jeune, *The Vision of Queen Katherine* (Shakespeare)

1858 (953) Frederick Cowie, *Henry VIII and Holbein* (qu.)

1863 (431) David Wilkie Wynfield, *Rival Queens* (qu.)

1864 (489) William James Grant, *Katherine Parr* (qu.)

1865 (350) George Adolphus Storey, *A Royal challenge* (qu.)

(555) Daniel Pasmore, *The happy days of Anne Boleyn; The interior painted Hever Castle*

1866 (547) David Wilkie Wynfield, *Anne Boleyn and Percy* (qu.)

1870 (891) Marcus C. Stone, *Henry VIII and Anne Boleyn observed by Queen Katharine* (qu.)

1871 (104) Marcus C. Stone, *The Royal Nursery, 1538* (qu.)

(182) Edward Matthew Ward, '*Anne Boleyn at the Queen's stairs, Tower*' (qu.)

1872 (470) William Powell Frith, *Henry the Eighth and Anne Boleyn deer shooting in Windsor Forest, etc.*

(497) David Wilkie Wynfield, *The arrest of Anne Boleyn* (qu.)

1874 (1020) Sir John Gilbert, *The field of the Cloth of Gold* (qu.)

(1243) John Ballin, *Henry VIII and Anne Boleyn* (after V. Paloky)

1878 (559) Henry Nelson O'Neil, *Catherine's Dream* (Shakespeare)

1880 (985) John Laslett Pott, *The trial of Queen Catherine*

1889 (293) Sir John Gilbert, *Ego et rex meus* (qu.)

1894 (1286) Miss Kathleen E. Coud, *Queen Catherine*

1900 (96) Edward Austin Abbey, *The Trial of Queen Katherine*

Cardinal Wolsey

1805 (266) J. Smart, *Cardinal Wolsey on his death bed at Leicester Abbey* (qu.)

1812 (259) John Augustus Atkinson, *Cardinal Wolsey received into the Abbey of Leicester*

1826 (355) Robert Trewick Bone, *Cardinal Wolsey at the court of Francis I, negotiating the meeting of that king with Henry VIII of England at the field of the Cloth of Gold, etc.*

1828 (487) Robert Trewick Bone, *The Dukes of Norfolk and Suffolk demanding the great seal of Cardinal Wolsey, etc.*

1834 (285) Solomon Alexander Hart, *The quarrel scene between Cardinal Wolsey and the Duke of Buckingham* (Shakespeare)

1836 (391) Francis Philip Stephanoff, *Death of Cardinal Wolsey*

1840 (21) Thomas Musgrove Joy, *The Cardinals Wolsey and Campeius endeavouring to reconcile the mind of Queen Catherine to her divorce* (Shakespeare)

1841 (1175) Samuel West, *Cardinal Wolsey leaving London after his disgrace* (qu.)

1848 (11) Charles West Cope, *Cardinal Wolsey* (painted for Prince Albert)

1869 (130) John Pettie, *The disgrace of Cardinal Wolsey* (Shakespeare)

1874 (1380) John Laslett Pott, *Dismissal of Cardinal Wolsey*

1877 (201) Sir John Gilbert, *Cardinal Wolsey at Leicester Abbey, etc.*

1889 (293) Sir John Gilbert, *Ego et rex meus* (qu.)

Sir Thomas More

1836 (353) Solomon Alexander Hart, *Lord Chancellor Sir Thomas More receiving the benediction of his father, Judge More, in the Court of King's Bench*

1840 (1073) Baron Henry de Triqueti, *Sir Thomas More expounding the scriptures to his family before his execution* (qu.)

1844 (364) John Rogers Herbert, *Sir Thomas More and his daughter* (qu.)

1845 (16) Solomon Alexander Hart, *The parting of Sir Thomas More from his daughter Margaret Roper* (qu.)

1854 (478) Thomas A. Woolnoth, *The separation of Sir Thomas More and his family* (qu.)

1859 (290) W. A. Atkinson, *Sir Thomas More leaving home for the last time, etc.*

1861 (608) John Evan Hodgson, *A visit to Holbein's studio – Sir Thomas More and his daughters looking at his portrait*

1863 (522) William Frederick Yeames, *The meeting of Sir Thomas with his daughter after his sentence of death* (qu.)

1881 (242) Walter Field, *Sir Thomas More in his garden at Chelsea visited by Henry VIII*

1890 (1677) Paul Hardy, *His Majesty King Henry VIII visits Sir Thomas More at Chelsea*

1895 (1656) Ludwig Cauer, *Sir Thomas More; statuette, bronze*

Lady Jane Grey

1794 (63) Samuel Medley, *Dr. Fechenham's last visit to Lady Jane Grey* (qu. Camden)

1808 (1) John Singleton Copley, *The offer of the crown to Lady Jane Grey by the Dukes of Northumberland and Suffolk and other Lords, deputies of the Privy Council* (qu.)

1827 (85) Charles Robert Leslie, *Lady Jane Grey prevailed on to accept the crown* (qu.)

1834 (460) Henry Pierce Bone, *Lady Jane Grey in prison* (after Northcote)

1839 (1) Marshall Claxton, *Lady Jane Grey in the Tower refusing to accede to the Roman Catholic faith* (qu.)

(389) Solomon Alexander Hart, *Lady Jane Grey at the place of execution* (qu.)

1841 (284) Joseph Bouvier, *Lady Jane Grey in the Brick Tower. 'Most gentle, most unfortunate, crowned but to die.'*

1844 (425) Edward Daniel Leahy, *Lady Jane Grey summoned to her execution* (qu.)

1846 (1314) James Clarke Hook, *The controversy between Lady Jane Grey and Feckenham, who was sent to her from the Queen, two days before her death, to convert her to Romanism, etc. etc.*

1847 (564) Miss Mary Clark, *Lady Jane Grey in the Brick Tower*

1848 (157) Charles Robert Leslie, *Lady Jane Grey 'who in her chamber sat, musing with Plato, etc.'* (qu. Rogers)

1853 (171) John Callcott Horsley, *Lady Jane Grey and Roger Ascham* (qu.)

1854 (1305) George P. Manley, *An incident in the early life of Lady Jane Grey* (qu.)

1860 (204) Solomon Alexander Hart, *Lady Jane Grey, a prisoner in the Tower of London refusing to accede to the solicitations of Fakenham, Queen Mary's Confessor, to abandon the Protestant faith*

(543) J. D. Marshall, *Lady Jane Grey and her tutor, in the park at Woodstock*

1861 (631) William James Grant, *The Tower, February 1553: the last reliques of Lady Jane Grey*

1863 (618) Joseph Bouvier, *Edward VI and Lady Jane Grey. 'Lady Jane being of equal age, etc.'*

1864 (908) Charles Augustus William Wilke, *Lady Jane Gray on her way to execution . . .* (qu.)

1866 (562) Francis John Wybird, *Lady Jane Grey* (qu.)

1867 (143) John Callcott Horsley, *Lady Jane Grey and Roger Ascham* (qu.)

1868 (363) William Frederick Yeames, *Lady Jane Grey in the Tower* (qu.)

(467) Mrs. Edward Matthew Ward, *Sion House, 1553* (qu.)

1871 (395) Robert Thorburn, *Lady Jane Grey* (qu.)

(445) G. F. Folingsby, *Lady Jane's victory over Bishop Gardiner* (qu.)

1877 (225) Miss Maria Burnham Brook, *Lady Jane Grey*

(1343) Miss Eleanor Bell, *Lady Jane Grey and Roger Ascham*

Elizabeth I

1794 (20) Benjamin West, *Queen Elizabeth going in procession to St. Paul's Cathedral after the destruction of the Spanish Armada*

1796 (300) Henry Singleton, *Essex's indignation* (qu. Rapin)

1803 (485) Joseph Collyer, *The Baptism of Queen Elizabeth* (qu. Shakespeare)

1807 (304) George Henry Harlow, *Queen Elizabeth striking The Earl of Essex*

1821 (8) Charles Robert Leslie, *May Day in the reign of Queen Elizabeth* (qu.)

1824 (35) Mrs. Ansley, *Queen Elizabeth giving Ring to the Earl of Essex, etc.*

1828 (250) Samuel Drummond, *The gallantry of Sir Walter Raleigh*

1835 (342) John Wood, *Shakespeare reading one of his*

plays to Queen Elizabeth

1836 (542) John Wood, *Elizabeth in the Tower, after the death of her sister, Queen Mary* (qu. Hume)

1840 (510) David Scott, *Queen Elizabeth viewing the performance of the 'Merry Wives of Windsor' in the Globe Theatre* (qu.)

1846 (437) John Hollins, *The circumnavigator Drake receiving the honour of knighthood from Queen Elizabeth on board his ship, the Golden Hind, at Deptford 1581* (qu.)

(1224) Dean Wolstenholme Jnr., *'In April, 1556, Princess Elizabeth was escorted from Hatfield House . . .'* (qu.)

1847 (1078) Musgrave Lewthwaite Watson, *Proclamation of the Royal Exchange, by command and in the presence of Queen Elizabeth*

1848 (529) Augustus Leopold Egg, *Queen Elizabeth discovers she is no longer young* (qu.)

1849 (75) Frederick Cowie, *Queen Elizabeth at Kenilworth* (Scott)

1853 (1340) William Theed, *Sir Walter Raleigh spreading his cloak as a carpet for Queen Elizabeth* (bas-relief for the Palace of Westminster)

1857 (53) William James Grant, *From the early life of Queen Elizabeth* (qu.)

1858 (1045) William James Montaigne, *How Queen Elizabeth passed her last days* (qu.)

(1236) William Theed, *Elizabeth knighting Drake on board his own vessel at Greenwich* (bas-relief for the Palace of Westminster)

1864 (450) James Hayllar, *The Queen's Highway in the 16th Century* (qu.)

(507) Thomas Falcon Marshall, *Queen Elizabeth in the Tower* (qu.)

(512) John Evan Hodgson, *Queen Elizabeth at Purfleet. The squadron under Lord Howard, is sailing down the Thames to attack the Armada: and she bids God-speed to her sailors*

1865 (189) David Wilkie Wynfield, *The last days of Queen Elizabeth* (qu.)

(527) James Hayllar, *Queen Elizabeth's toothache* (qu.)

1866 (314) William Frederick Yeames, *Queen Elizabeth receiving the French ambassadors after the news of the Massacre of St. Bartholomew*

1869 (60) Marcus C. Stone, *The Princess (afterwards Queen) Elizabeth obliged to attend mass by her sister Mary* (qu.)

1872 (560) John Laslett Pott, *Shakespeare reading before Queen Elizabeth*

1875 (389) David Wilkie Wynfield, *Queen Elizabeth and Essex* (qu.)

1877 (75) Henry Nelson O'Neil, *Shakespeare reading 'A Midsummer Night's Dream' to Queen Elizabeth*

1879 (13) Tito Conti, *The Duke D'Anjou contemplating the portrait of Queen Elizabeth*

1880 (573) David Wilkie Wynfield, *At Traitor's Gate* (qu.)

(1437) Henry Daniel Chadwick, *In the reign of Queen Elizabeth*

Mary Queen of Scots

1776 (124) Gavin Hamilton, *Mary, Queen of Scots resigning her crown*

1786 (51) John Howes, *The Earls of Shrewsbury and Kent reading to Mary, Queen of Scotland the warrant for her Execution*

1787 (26) John Opie, *Assassination of David Riccio*

(205) Richard Westall, *Mary, Queen of Scots, taking leave of Sir Andrew Melville on her way to execution*

(224) John Graham, *The Murder of David Riccio* (Hume)

1788 (15) Mather Brown, *The Warrant read to Mary, Queen of Scots*

(419) John Graham, *Mary, Queen of Scots making her escape with George Douglas from Loch Leven Castle, etc.*

1789 (481) Richard Westall, *The flight of Mary Queen of Scots*

(485) Richard Westall, *Mary, Queen of Scots, when a child, embarking for France*

1791 (546) Richard Westall, *Mary, Queen of Scots, at the Battle of Langside*

(568) John Francis Rigaud, *Mary Queen of Scots going to the place of execution*

(569) John Francis Rigaud, *Mary, Queen of Scots at prayers on the scaffold*

(570) John Francis Rigaud, *Mary Queen of Scots at the block*

(571) John Francis Rigaud, *Mary, Queen of Scots beheaded*

1792 (22) John Graham, *Mary Queen of Scots the morning before her execution*

(466) John Francis Rigaud, *The sheriff entering the chapel of Mary Queen of Scots the morning of her execution*

(467) John Francis Rigaud, *The funeral Procession of Mary Queen of Scots*

(468) John Francis Rigaud, *The entombing of Mary, Queen of Scots*

1793 (181) Samuel Medley, *The death warrant read to Mary, Queen of Scots*

1797 (552) Samuel Drummond, *Death of David Rizzio*

1808 (714) Miss J. Hay, *Mary Queen of Scots*

1820 (28) Henry Singleton, *The departure of Mary Queen of Scots from France* (qu.)

1821 (389) W. Sharp, *The Murder of David Rizzio* (qu.)

1823 (34) Sir William Allan, *Knox admonishing Mary Queen of Scots*

1824 (285) Sir William Allan, *Lord Lindsay compelling Mary to abdicate*

1827 (315) Sir William Allan, *Landing of Mary Queen of Scots at Leith, 1561*

1829 (1106) W. Beattie, *Knox admonishing Mary, Queen of Scots (embossed silver plate)* (after Sir William Allan)

1831 (56) Abraham Cooper, *Mary Queen of Scots meeting the Earl of Bothwell between Stirling and Edinburgh* (qu.)

1833 (16) Sir William Allan, *Murder of David Rizzio*

1834 (303) H. Andrews, *Mary Queen of Scots at Battle of Langside*

1837 (119) Sir David Wilkie, *Mary Queen of Scots escaping from Loch Leven Castle* (qu. Scott)

(437) Edward Daniel Leahy, *Mary Queen of Scots' escape from Lochleven Castle* (qu.)

(455) Charles Landseer, *The Battle Langside* (qu. Scott)

(514) John Hayes, *Mary Queen of Scots, when a prisoner at Lochleven Castle, was forced to sign her abdication in favour of Murray as Regent* (Scott)

1839 (800) Douglas Morison, *The Palace of Linlithgow: Rizzio playing before Mary Queen of Scots*

1841 (429) William Simson, *Mary, Queen of Scots, and her retinue returning from the chase to the castle of Stirling in 1562* (qu.)

1842 (256) B. R. Haydon, *Mary Queen of Scots, when an infant, stripped by order of Mary of Guise, her mother, to convince Sadler, the English Ambassador, that she was not a decrepid child, which had been insinuated at court*

(391) John Archibald Casey, *Nostrodamus predicting the future fate of Mary Queen of Scots* (qu.)

1843 (1045) C. Stonhouse, *Mary, Queen of Scots forced into signing the resignation of the crown* (Scott)

1844 (73) Alfred E. Chalon, *John Knox reproving the ladies of Queen Mary's court* (qu.)

(312) Richard Ansdell, *Mary Queen of Scots returning from the Chase to Stirling Castle*

(328) William Powell Frith, *One of the interviews that took place between John Knox and Mary Queen of Scots, respecting her marriage to Darnley* (qu.)

1848 (940) Joseph Middleton Jopling, *Mary Queen of Scots in prison* (qu. Burns)

1850 (569) Joseph Severn, *The Abdication* (qu. Scott)

1852 (396) Ebenezer Butler Morris, *John Knox and Mary, Queen of Scotland* (qu.)

1853 (1338) William Theed, *Mary, Queen of Scots, looking back at the coast of France* (bas-relief for the Palace of Westminster)

1854 (1311) Henry Courtney Selous, *A Scene at Holyrood, 9th March, anno domini, 1566* (qu.)

(1401) William Theed, *The Escape of Mary Queen of Scots from Lochleven Castle* (bas-relief for the Palace of Westminster)

1855 (361) Alexander Johnston, *The abdication of Mary Queen of Scots* (qu.)

1856 (1376) William Theed, *The Murder of Rizzio* (bas-relief for the Palace of Westminster)

1861 (565) Alfred Clay Barron, *Imprisonment at Loch Leven Castle* (qu. Scott)

1862 (337) Henry Nelson O'Neil, *Mary Stuart's farewell to France* (qu.)

1863 (386) Mrs. Edward Matthew Ward, *'Queen Mary quitted Stirling Castle . . .'* (qu. Strickland)

1865 (258) Edward Matthew Ward, *The night of Rizzio's murder* (qu. Froude)

1866 (473) Alexander Johnston, *Mary of Scotland at the Priory of Inschemachame in 1547* (qu.)

1868 (50) Alfred Barron Clay, *Imprisonment of Mary, Queen of Scots* (qu.)

(348) Charles Lucy, *The forced abdication of Mary, Queen of Scots at Lochleven Castle, July 25, 1567* (qu.)

(673) Eyre Crowe, *Mary Stuart, February 8th 1587* (qu. Strickland)

1870 (5) Thomas E. Roberts, *The Captivity of Queen Mary*

1871 (58) Laslett John Pott, *Mary Queen of Scots being led to execution* (qu.)

(136) Frederick Richard Pickersgill, *Queen Elizabeth's commissioners accusing Mary Stuart of having participated in the murder of her husband* (qu.)

(193) John Callcott Horsley, *Mary Queen of Scots in captivity* (qu.)

1872 (479) George Kilburne, *Holyrood, 26th May, 1563* (qu. Strickland)

(1090) Thomas Frank Heaphy, *Queen Mary Stuart at Tutbury Castle* (qu.)

1875 (211) Alfred W. Elmore, *Mary Queen of Scots and Christopher Norton at Bolton Castle* (qu.)

(901) Robert Herdman, *The first conference between Mary Stuart and John Knox, Holyrood, 1561* (qu.)

1877 (282) Alfred W. Elmore, *Mary Queen of Scots and Darnley at Jedburgh* (qu.)

1878 (281) Henry Nelson O'Neil, *Loch Leven A.D. 1568*

1885 (195) William Powell Frith, *John Knox at Holyrood* (qu.)

1891 (250) Andrew Carrick Gow, *After Langside: Queen Mary's farewell to Scotland*

1893 (178) William Powell Frith, *L'Adieu de Marie Stuart. 'Adieu, charmant pays de France, etc.'*

1896 (1719) Philip Harry Newman, *Design for stained glass. Mary Queen of Scots flight to England*

1897 (1613) Charles Oliver Murray, *Mary Queen of Scots leaving England* (after A. C. Gow)

The Civil War

1811 (498) John Frearson, *The Monument of William of Wykeham, saved from destruction by an officer in Cromwell's army . . .*

1817 (26) George Arnald, *Battle of Edgehill* (one of a series: nos. 51, 55, 253, 260, 292, 344, 362)

1818 (398) George Arnald, *The Army under Cromwell marching to Winchester, etc.*

1819 (20) Abraham Cooper, *The Battle of Marston Moor, near York, fought in the year 1644, representing the leaders of both parties, taken from authentic family portraits, and the best recorded accounts of that disastrous conflict, etc.*

1821 (246) George Arnald, *The Battle of Naseby*

1822 (143) Abraham Cooper, *Rupert's standard at Marston Moor*

1823 (118) Abraham Cooper, *The Death of a cavalier at Marston Moor*

(151) Abraham Cooper, *Arthur, Lord Capel defending Colchester for the King* . . .

(547) John Augustus Atkinson, *Montrose taking leave of his Followers, etc.*

(660) John Augustus Atkinson, *Montrose cutting his way through the convenanters at the battle of Selkirk*

1825 (527) John Augustus Atkinson, *Cromwell's decisive charge at the battle of Marston Moor*

1826 (23) James Ward, *Battle near Boston, Lincolnshire* (qu.)

1827 (113) John Renton, *King Charles the First setting up his standard at Nottingham in 1642; a sketch*

1831 (364) W. Bailey and W. Barraud, *Skirmish of Cavaliers and Roundheads*

1832 (37) George Arnald, *Battle of Naseby, sketch*

(392) H. Milling, *The retreat of the baggage-wagon from the battle of Naseby, fought 1645*

1833 (132) Abraham Cooper, *The retreat at Naseby*

1836 (374) Charles Landseer, *The Plundering of Basing House, Hants; taken and destroyed by Cromwell, October 14, 1645* (qu.)

1837 (505) Thomas Woodward, *The Battle of Worcester*

1839 (347) Thomas Woodward, *King Charles' standard at the battle of Worcester*

1841 (182) Abraham Cooper, *The Fight at Cropedy Bridge, June 29, 1644* . . .

(243) Thomas Woodward, *A detachment of Cromwell's cavalry surprised in a mountain pass*

1842 (436) Richard Ansdell, *Death of Sir William Lambton at Marston Moor*

(1225) William Brough, *The Countess of Derby refusing to surrender Lathom House to Fairfax's summons to capitulation*

1843 (597) Francis Philip Stephanoff, *The Countess of Derby defending Lathom House when besieged by Fairfax*

1844 (58) Abraham Cooper, *Prince Rupert routing the besiegers at Newark on the morning of the 22nd March, 1644*

1845 (275) Charles Landseer, *The Eve of the Battle of Edgehill* (qu.)

1847 (10) James Ward, *The discomforture of Charles II at the Battle of Worcester* (qu.)

1851 (176) Frederick Richard Pickersgill, *The raising of the standard of Charles I. at Nottingham; a sketch for a picture*

1852 (44) Abraham Cooper, *The rout at Marston Moor*

1853 (396) Edward Matthew Ward, *The Executioner tying Wishart's book around the neck of Montrose* . . . (qu.) (for the Houses of Parliament)

1853 (487) D. W. Deane, *An incident in the Civil Wars – concealment of the fugitive, destruction of compromising documents*

1855 (1556) J. Holt, *Rupert's standard at Marston Moor* (after A. Cooper)

1859 (40) Augustus Leopold Egg, *The night before Naseby*

(930) Henry Wallis, *Back from Marston Moor*

1862 (86) Abraham Cooper, *The Battle of Naseby, fought June 14, 1645, etc.*

(657) Thomas Falcon Marshall, *The eve of the Battle of Edgehill 1642* (qu.)

1863 (565) Charles Goldie, *True to Death* (qu.)

1864 (204) Philip Hermogenes Calderon, *John Hampden, June 27, 1643* (qu.)

1865 (136) Abraham Cooper, *The Battle of Edgehill* (qu.)

(616) George Dunlop Leslie, *The defence of Lathom House, 1644* (qu.)

1867 (425) Charles Lucy, *The intercepted embarkation of John Hampden and his friends A.D. 1637* (qu.)

1870 (224) Charles Landseer, *Surrender of Arundel Castle to Sir William Waller, January 6th, 1643* (qu.)

1873 (643) Sir John Gilbert, *Naseby* (qu.)

1874 (445) Mrs. Edward Matthew Ward, *The defence of Lathom House* (qu.)

1875 (93) John Seymour Lucas, *Oxford, 1650*

1877 (528) Ernest Crofts, *Ironsides returning from sacking a cavalier's house*

1878 (931) John Seymour Lucas, *An Ambuscade – Edgehill*

1881 (354) John Seymour Lucas, *Charles I before Gloucester* (qu.)

(551) John Laslett Pott, *Before Naseby* (qu.)

1882 (840) Eyre Crowe, *The Defence of London in 1643* (qu.)

1887 (147) W. Frank Calderon, *John Hampden (mortally wounded at Chalgrove Field, June 18th, 1643)* (qu.)

1888 (746) Ernest Crofts, *Marston Moor* (qu.)

1889 (82) Ernest Crofts, *The Knight's farewell* (qu.)

(523) Ernest Crofts, *Hampden riding away from Chalgrove Field*

(651) Stanley Berkeley, *For God and the King; an incident in the Civil War*

1898 (2) Ernest Crofts, *To the rescue; an episode of the Civil War*

1901 (558) H. Randolph Rose, *Hampden* (qu.)

1904 (223) Ernest Crofts, *Prince Rupert and his staff at Marston Moor* (Carlyle)

Charles I

1790 (478) Richard Westall, *Charles I refusing his assent to the militia bill*

1801 (97) Samuel Woodford, *Charles the First . . . was allowed an interview with his children . . . at which Cromwell was present, July, 1647*

1825 (293) Francis Philip Stephanoff, *The children of Charles restored to him after he had been seized by the Army* (qu.)

1827 (113) John Renton, *King Charles the First setting up his standard at Nottingham in 1642; a sketch*

1836 (262) Daniel Maclise, *An interview between Charles I and Oliver Cromwell* (qu.)

1838 (530) John Bridges, *King Charles I, after the last*

interview with his children, the Princess Elizabeth and the Duke of Gloucester

1841 (507) Frank Stone, *The stolen interview of Charles Ist, when Prince of Wales, with the Infanta of Spain* (qu.)

(999) Edward Matthew Ward, *Cornet Joyce seizes the King at Holmby, June 3, 1647* (qu.)

(1211) Ferdinand Pickering, *A Visit to Vandyck* (qu.)

1842 (267) Samuel West, *Charles I receiving instructions from Rubens, whilst sketching the portraits of his Queen and Child* (qu.)

(458) William Fisk, *The trial of Charles I in Westminster Hall, January 27, 1648–9* (qu.)

(1206) Samuel Blackburn, *The Earl of Strafford in the Tower, receiving intelligence from Carleton, secretary to Charles I, that the King had assented to his death* (qu.)

1843 (1293) William Fisk, *Charles I passing through the banqueting house, Whitehall, to the scaffold, January 30, 1648–9* (qu.)

1844 (188) Claudius Jacquand, *Charles I à Holmby* (qu.)

1846 (113) Thomas Jones Barker, *Charles I and Henrietta, his Queen, reposing after the Chase in Windsor Forest*

1847 (421) Alexander Johnston, *The Burial of Charles I* (qu.)

1848 (607) Robert Hannah, *Harvey demonstrating to Charles I the circulation of the blood from the heart of a deer* (qu.)

1853 (248) Frederick Goodall, *An episode of the happier days of Charles I*

1857 (16) Charles Lucy, *Burial of King Charles the First*

1867 (468) James Archer, *In the Time of Charles I; portraits*

1870 (226) Alexander Hohenloe Burr, *King Charles the first at Exeter* (qu.)

1872 (42) Sir John Gilbert, *King Charles I leaving Westminster Hall after sentence of death had been passed* (qu.)

(107) John Laslett Pott, *Charles I leaving Westminster Hall after his trial*

1873 (845) Harding C. Smith, *King Charles at Cothele on the Tamar*

1877 (19) Andrew Carrick Gow, *The tumult in the House of Commons, March 2nd, 1629* (qu.)

1881 (354) John Seymour Lucas, *Charles I before Gloucester* (qu.)

1883 (1502) Ernest Crofts, *Charles I on his way to execution* (qu.)

1884 (353) William Powell Frith, *'Cruel Necessity'* (qu.)

1886 (2) Henry Gillard Glindoni, *Dismissal of Archy, the King's Jester* (qu.)

1889 (260) Andrew Carrick Gow, *The Visit of King Charles I to Kingston-upon-Hull, 1642* (qu.)

1890 (216) Ernest Crofts, *Whitehall, January 30th, 1649*

1892 (331) Ernest Crofts, *Charles I at Edgehill* (qu.)

1896 (106) Henry Gillard Glindoni, *The Black Tribunal, Jan. 29, 1648*

Henrietta Maria

1848 (191) Charles Landseer, *Henrietta Maria, Queen of England, and the Prince of Wales assisting at the toilet of Mademoiselle de Montpensier* (qu.)

1849 (8) Augustus Leopold Egg, *Henrietta Maria in distress, relieved by Cardinal de Retz* (qu. Strickland)

1850 (593) Thomas Woolnoth, *The meeting of Henrietta Maria, wife of Charles I, with her mother, Marie de Medicis* (qu. Strickland)

1860 (249) William James Grant, *A page from the Civil War* (qu.)

1862 (583) Mrs. Edward Matthew Ward, *Scene at the Louvre in 1649. The despair of Henrietta Maria at the death of her husband, Charles I* (qu. Strickland)

1864 (477) William Frederick Yeames, *La Reine Malheureuse* (qu.)

1869 (854) Alexander Hohenloe Burr, *The Escape of Queen Henrietta* (qu.)

The Children of Charles I

1825 (293) Francis Philip Stephanoff, *The children of Charles the First restored to him after he had been seized by the Army* (qu.)

1850 (571) Charles Lucy, *The parting of Charles I with two youngest children, the day previous to his execution* (qu.)

1851 (720) Charles Lucy, *The Royal Captives of Carisbrooke, A.D. 1650* (qu. Strickland)

1855 (161) Charles West Cope, *Royal Pensioners at Carisbrooke Castle, 1650* (qu.)

1863 (531) J. P. Downes, *Last Moments of the Princess Elizabeth, daughter of Charles I* (qu.)

1868 (613) George Elgar Hicks, *Escape of the Countess of Morton to Paris with Henrietta, infant daughter of Charles I* (qu.)

(672) James Hayllar, *The orphans of Charles I at Carisbrooke* (qu.)

1876 (153) Solomon Alexander Hart, *Dinner-time at Penshurst in the year 1655* (qu.)

1895 (378) Miss Margaret Dicksee, *The Children of Charles I. After the execution of the King, his younger children, Elizabeth and Henry, were confined in Carisbrooke Castle. There the little Elizabeth languished for a short time, dying within a year of her father's tragic fate*

1901 (860) Miss Irlam Briggs, *Elizabeth, second daughter of King Charles I, died 8th September, 1656* (qu.)

Oliver Cromwell

1783 (62) Benjamin West, *Oliver Cromwell ordering the mace to be taken away when he expelled the long parliament*

1801 (97) Samuel Woodford, *Charles the First . . . was allowed an interview with his children . . . at which Cromwell was present, July, 1647*

1806 (585) Joseph Collyer, *Oliver Cromwell dissolving the Long Parliament*

1826 (23) James Ward, *Battle near Boston, Lincolnshire* (qu.)

1836 (262) Daniel Maclise, *An interview between Charles I and Oliver Cromwell* (qu.)

(369) E. F. Lambert, *Cromwell – a scene from Woodstock* (qu. Scott)

1840 (134) William Fisk, *Cromwell's family interceding for the life of Charles I*

1842 (548) Augustus Leopold Egg, *Cromwell discovering his chaplain, Jeremiah White, making love to his daughter Frances* (qu.)

1844 (389) Henry James Townsend, *The fatal letter of Charles I intercepted by Cromwell and Ireton* (qu.)

1846 (658) William Carpenter, *Oliver Cromwell at Thurloe's Chambers, Lincoln's Inn* (qu.)

1849 (166) Charles Lucy, *Mrs. Claypole, Cromwell's favourite daughter, on her deathbed at Hampton Court, admonishing him to repent of his sins and guiltiness, A.D. 1659*

1850 (369) Paul Delaroche, *Cromwell looking at the dead body of Charles I*

(409) Thomas Musgrove Joy, *'Suspended between these fears . . .' (Cromwell refusing the crown)*

1851 (127) Charles Landseer, *Cromwell, attended by Fairfax, reading a letter found in the King's cabinet, taken at the battle of Naseby . . .* (qu. Hume)

1853 (1183) Richard Hamilton Essex, *Interior of Trinity Chapel, Canterbury Cathedral: Oliver Cromwell taking away the sword from the monument of Edward the Black Prince*

1854 (375) Richard Norbury, *Cromwell on the night after the Battle of Naseby, perusing the private letters and papers of the King, which were taken at the battle*

(1295) Samuel Blackburn, *Cromwell, Milton and Mary Powell, his wife* (qu.)

1858 (1122) Robert Graves, *Cromwell resolving to refuse the Crown* (after C. Lucy)

1861 (449) James Gow, *A Volunteer for Cromwell*

1863 (628) James Hayllar, *Life or death?* (qu.)

1867 (55) Charles Landseer, *Oliver Cromwell, with some of his officers, visits the house of Sir Walter Stewart, called Allerton, on 1st May, 1651* (qu. Carlyle)

(494) David Wilkie Wynfield, *Oliver Cromwell the night before his death* (qu. Carlyle)

(957) Samuel Bellin, *Cromwell at Hampton Court* (after C. Lucy)

1868 (410) David Wilkie Wynfield, *Oliver Cromwell's first appearance in the Parliament* (qu.)

1872 (368) Charles West Cope, *Oliver Cromwell receiving a deputation of Ministers and Elders, accompanied by the Dutch Ambassador* (qu.)

1873 (322) Solomon Alexander Hart, *The conference between Manasseh Ben Israel and Oliver Cromwell* (qu.)

1877 (497) Ernest Crofts, *Oliver Cromwell at Marston Moor*

1880 (1267) Charles William Sherborn, *Oliver Cromwell; ideal portrait*

1882 (1681) Henry Rich Pinker, *Oliver Cromwell at Marston Moor; equestrian statue, bronze*

1883 (201) Ernest Crofts, *At the sign of the Blue Boar, Holborn* (qu.)

(729) Professor Cretius, *Cromwell prevented from leaving England for America by an order from the King*

1885 (1645) Charles Oliver Murray, *Cromwell's first visit to John Milton* (after D. Neal)

1892 (708) Rudolf Lehmann, *Cromwell at Ripley Castle* (qu.)

1895 (674) Eyre Crowe, *Thomas Carlyle looking at the Duke of Buccleuch's miniatures of Cromwell, his wife and daughter*

1900 (82) Ernest Crofts, *Oliver Cromwell at the storming of Basing House* (qu.)

Cavaliers

1846 (495) Henry and William Barraud, *A Royalist Family taken prisoners by the Puritans*

1850 (20) J. D. Croome, *A young cavalier*

(234) James Digman Wingfield, *The Cavalier's song on the Terrace . . .* (qu.) *. . . Haddon Hall*

1853 (520) John Everett Millais, *The proscribed royalist, 1651*

1856 (413) William Shakespeare Burton, *A Wounded Cavalier*

1859 (641) Matthew James Lawless, *A cavalier in his cups* (qu.)

(1185) William Henry Simmons, *The proscribed Royalist* (after Millais)

1862 (432) Miss Rebecca Solomon, *Fugitive Royalists* (qu.)

(610) George Dunlop Leslie, *The cavaliers escape* (qu.)

1865 (76) Frederick Richard Pickersgill, *A royalist family, 1651, 'Unfriended'*

1869 (77) James Archer, *Against Cromwell; a Royalist Family playing at Soldiers*

1874 (597) James Gow, *Memoirs of a Cavalier*

1876 (467) William E. Miller, *A little Royalist; pastel study*

1877 (1227) William Frederick Yeames, *The fair royalist*

1878 (329) William Frederick Yeames, *'And when did you last see your father?'*

(1347) John Ballantyne, *A young cavalier*

1893 (599) Claude Calthrop, *Cavaliers in hiding*

Roundheads and Puritans

1848 (308) Charles Lucy, *The landing of the primitive Puritans, or pilgrim fathers on the coast of America, A.D. 1620* (qu.)

(661) James W. Glass, *Roundheads and Royalists*

1852 (224) Vernon Hughes, *A soldier of the Commonwealth*

1857 (503) Charles West Cope, *The Pilgrim Fathers.
Departure of a Puritan family for New England* (qu.)
1859 (73) Charles Lucy, *Puritan Emigrants – an
English pastor's family*
(921) Eyre Crowe, *The Roundhead* (qu.)
1861 (277) Charles Rossiter, *Puritan Purfiers*
1865 (575) James Archer, *The Puritan Suitor*
1867 (657) George Henry Boughton, *Early Puritans
of New England, going to worship armed, to protect
themselves from Indians and wild beasts*
1872 (513) Robert Dudley, *'The Puritans were peculiar
in aspect and conduct but showed great affection on
occasions'*
1873 (556) Arthur Hill, *The little Puritan*
1877 (189) Henry Gillard Glindoni, *The Puritan*
1883 (748) Alfred Walter Bayes, *The Puritan Father's
first Sunday in New England, etc.*
1886 (87) Frederick Goodall, *Puritan and cavalier*
1889 (2132) Andrew C. Lucchesi, *A Puritan bust*
1894 (153) Ernest Crofts, *Roundheads Victorious*
1890 (396) George Henry Boughton, *The Puritans'
first winter in New England; watching for the 'Fortune'
relief ship*
1892 (12) Francis David Millet, *Between two fires*

Charles II

1828 (259) Henry Liverseege, *Wildrake presenting
Colonel Everard's challenge to Charles II* (qu. Scott)
1835 (269) John Joseph Barker, *Beauties of the Court
of Charles II*
1837 (66) Charles Robert Leslie, *Charles II and Lady
Bellenden* (qu. Scott)
1842 (278) Charles Landseer, *The departure of Charles
II from Bentley in Staffordshire, the house of Colonel
Lane* (qu. Clarendon)
1844 (180) Claudius Jacquand, *Charles à New
Shoreham, après la bataille de Worcester* (qu.)
(494) Alexander Chisholm, *Charles II offering to
purchase some miniatures from Mrs. Oliver, wife of
Isaac Oliver, miniature painter – Walpole's Anecdotes*
1847 (10) James Ward, *The discomfiture of Charles II
at the battle of Worcester* (qu.)
(634) Thomas Jones Barker, *The Beauties of the Court
of Charles II, portraits*
1848 (550) William Carpenter, *Charles II in Holland
before the Restoration* (qu.)
1854 (587) Edward Matthew Ward, *Interview between
Charles II and Nell Gwynne, as witnessed by Evelyn*
(qu.)
1858 (919) Thomas Musgrove Joy, *An incident in the
life of Charles II at the Hague* (qu. Pepys)
1861 (169) Edward Matthew Ward, *Antechamber at
Whitehall, during the dying moments of Charles II* (qu.
Macaulay)
(240) James Digman Wingfield, *The Court of Charles
II; the King has been seen walking with the Queen again*
1864 (152) James Goodsell Middleton, *Nell Gwynn
directing the attention of Charles II to a disabled soldier*

1867 (132) William Powell Frith, *King Charles the
Second's last Sunday* (qu. Evelyn)
(435) Eyre Crowe, *Charles II knighting the loin of beef*
(555) Alfred Barron Clay, *The Return to Whitehall,
May 29th, 1660*
1868 (456) Thomas Falcon Marshall, *In the woods of
Boscobel, after the defeat of Worcester in 1651* (qu.)
1873 (400) Edward Matthew Ward, *The landing of
Charles II at Dover* (Houses of Parliament)
1874 (252) Edward Matthew Ward, *Charles II and
Lady Rachel Russell* (qu.)
1877 (709) Edward Matthew Ward, *Forgotten; Court
of Charles II*
1885 (813) David Wilkie Wynfield, *The Royal
Fugitive* (qu.)
1889 (164) Ernest Crofts, *The Boscobel oak*
1890 (793) Charles William Bartlett, *The Twenty-ninth
of May – Incident in the Restoration, etc.*
1898 (270) Ernest Crofts, *Charles II at Whiteladies
after the battle of Worcester*
1899 (204) William Powell Frith, *Charles II and Lady
Castlemaine* (qu. Pepys)
(1466) Miss Minna Bolinbroke, *Charles II at Salisbury*
1900 (32) Roland Holyoake, *Charles II and Nell
Gwynn* (qu.)

Lord William Russell

1790 (249) John Downman, *Lord William Russell
(who suffered innocently) in Newgate, with his wife,
Lady Rachel, and children; the day prior to his being
beheaded*
1825 (127) Sir George Hayter, *The Trial of William,
Lord Russell at the Old Bailey, 1683* (qu.)
1842 (215) Henry M. Cooper, *Lady Rachel Russell
entreating her husband to petition the King for pardon*
1845 (546) Alexander Johnston, *'Dr. Tillotson
(afterwards Archbishop of Canterbury) administering
the sacrament to Lord William Russell (and his Lady
Rachel Russell) at the Tower . . .'* (qu.)
1847 (585) John Bridges, *Lord William Russell's last
interview with his family, the day before his execution,
1683, etc.*
1852 (14) Charles Lucy, *The parting of Lord and Lady
Russell, A.D. 1683* (qu.)
1861 (103) Charles West Cope, *The parting of Lord
and Lady Russell* (qu.)
1873 (712) Charles Lucy, *The parting of Lord William
and Lady Russell, A.D. 1683* (qu.)

James II

1780 (58) Benjamin West, *Battle of the Boyne*
(73) Benjamin West, *Destruction of the French Fleet at
La Hogue, 1692*
1831 (85) Samuel Drummond, *King James the Second,
the Countess of Dorchester, and Kitty Chervil*
(Colyton)
1833 (204) Richard Westall, *The death of King James
the Second . . .*

1850 (350) Edward Matthew Ward, *James II in his Palace of Whitehall, receiving the news of the landing of the Prince of Orange in 1688* (qu.)

1865 (890) F. A. Heath, *King James II receiving intelligence of the landing of the Prince of Orange* (after Ward)

1869 (190) Alexander Johnston, *The flight of the Queen of James II* (qu. Macaulay)

1882 (30) John Pettie, *The Duke of Monmouth's interview with James II* (qu. Macaulay)

1888 (273) Andrew Carrick Gow, *A lost cause: flight of King James II after the battle of the Boyne*

1898 (407) Eyre Crowe, *James II at La Hogue, May 1692* (qu.)

Jacobites and Bonnie Prince Charlie

1834 (326) William Simson, *Prince Charles Edward Stuart at the battle of Preston, 1745* (qu.)

(562) Frederick Clarke, *St. Germain en Laye A.D. 1698: King James II, Prince Charles Edward, etc. etc. on the terrace*

1840 (136) Sir William Allan, *Prince Charles Edward in Adversity*

(482) Thomas Duncan, *Prince Charles Edward and the Highlanders entering Edinburgh after the battle of Preston* (qu.)

1843 (263) Thomas Duncan, *Prince Charles Edward asleep in one of his hiding places, after the battle of Culloden, protected by Flora MacDonald and Highland outlaws, who are alarmed on their watch*

1844 (577) Ronald Robert McIan, *'In the month of July, 1746, Prince Charles Edward Stuart was concealed and protected by the seven men of Glenmoriston'* (qu.)

1846 (374) Alexander Johnston, *The introduction of Flora McDonald to Prince Charles Edward Stuart after his retreat from the battle of Culloden . . .*

(1480) George Mossman, *Prince Charles Edward Stuart after Culloden*

1847 (942) Gustavus Ellinthorpe Sintzenich, *After the battle of Culloden*

1855 (134) John Lamont Brodie, *The escape of Prince Charles Edward and Flora Macdonald to Skye* (qu.)

1858 (942) Philip Hermogenes Calderon, *Flora Macdonald's farewell to Charles Edward* (qu.)

1859 (1141) William Fisk, *Fugitives escaped from the Massacre of Glencoe, Feb. 15, 1692*

1862 (669) Frank William Warwick Topham, *An affray during the Rebellion, 1745*

1864 (118) Sir John Everett Millais, *'Charlie is my darling'*

1868 (521) Charles Sillem Lidderdale, *The exiled Jacobite* (qu.)

1869 (96) Eyre Crowe, *The Jacobite*

(211) Mrs. Edward Matthew Ward, *Scene from the childhood of the Old Pretender* (qu. Strickland)

(701) Charles Sillem Lidderdale, *In hiding after Culloden*

(723) Alexander Johnston, *Flora Macdonald* (qu.)

1872 (413) John B. Macdonald, *Prince Charles in hiding* (qu.)

(589) Alfred Walter Bayes, *Making a Jacobite*

(1081) H. Townley Green, *A Jacobite's Farewell* (qu.)

(1139) Frederick Havill, *Charles Edward, Comte D'Albanie*

1874 (952) Robert Alexander Hillingford, *During the Wandering of Charles Edward Stuart* (qu.)

1875 (71) John Adam Houston, *Fugitives from Culloden*

(1217) John Pettie, *Jacobites, 1745*

1878 (10) Claude Calthrop, *Meeting of Scottish Jacobites* (qu.)

(584) Richard Beavis, *Halt of Prince Charles after Culloden*

1880 (442) Robert Herdman, *Charles Edward seeking shelter in the house of an adherent; an incident in the rising of 1745*

1881 (949) Arthur Beckingham, *The Right of Search 1745*

1882 (440) John Watson Nicol, *Before Culloden*

(786) Andrew Carrick Gow, *A Jacobite Proclamation*

1884 (347) John Everett Millais, *An Idyll, 1745*

(881) John Seymour Lucas, *After Culloden: rebel hunting*

1886 (646) Charles Edward Johnson, *Raising the Standard, 'You're welcome, Charlie Stuart'*

1888 (273) Andrew Carrick Gow, *A lost cause: flight of King James II after the Battle of the Boyne*

1891 (281) George William Joy, *Flora Macdonald's farewell to Prince Charles, 'Will ye no come back again?'*

1892 (89) John Pettie, *'Bonnie Prince Charlie'*

(281) W. Lockhart Bogle, *Prince Charles Edward Stuart in the cave of the robbers of Glen Moriston, etc.*

1894 (361) Allan Stewart, *Prince Charles' last look of Scotland*

1896 (794) G. O. Reid, *Dalquharn receiving the sword from Prince Charlie*

1897 (97) Andrew Carrick Gow, *Waiting for Prince Charlie*

Notes

JWCI = Journal of the Warburg and Courtaulds Institutes

Part I: The Century of History

Introduction: The Victorian Vision

1 This unhelpful attitude to the study and appreciation of history painting in Britain is enshrined above all in E. K. Waterhouse, *Painting in Britain 1530 to 1790*, London, 1969 ed., pp. 187ff.: 'the idea took an intolerable time to die'.

History Writing and History Painting

1 On eighteenth-century historians and their attitude to the past see A. J. Grant, *English Historians*, London, 1906, pp. xxxi–xxxvi, 13–32; *The Evolution of British Historiography*, ed. J. R. Hale, Cleveland, N.Y., 1964, pp. 22–34, 142–66.

2 Henry St John, Viscount Bolingbroke, *Letters on the Study and Use of History*, London, 1752, p. 15.

3 M. Jourdain, *The Work of William Kent*, London, 1948; John Summerson, *Architecture in Britain 1530–1830*, London, 1963 ed., pp. 200–204, 237–9.

4 Oliver Millar, *The Tudor, Stuart and Early Georgian Pictures in the Collection of Her Majesty the Queen*, London, 1963, I, pp. 27–8.

5 *Ibid.*, I, pp. 171–2, nos. 505–7.

6 *Ibid.*, I, p. 50, nos. 6 and 7.

7 Quoted Grose Evans, *Benjamin West and the Taste of his Times,* Illinois U.P., 1959, p. 31.

8 *Walpole Society*, XXVII, 1938–9, p. 74, no. 159.

9 John Sunderland, 'Mortimer, Pine and Some Political Aspects of English History Painting', *Burlington Magazine*, CXVI, 1974, pp. 317–26.

10 Paul de Rapin-Thoyras, *Histoire d'Angleterre*, The Hague, 1724–36, IV, pp. 10–11.

11 The best account of Pine is in the *Dictionary of National Biography*.

12 For Mortimer see Benedict Nicolson, *John Hamilton Mortimer ARA, 1740–79*, Towner Art Gallery, Eastbourne and Iveagh Bequest, Kenwood, 1968.

13 *Walpole Society, op. cit.*, p. 73, no. 142.

14 Hume, *op. cit.*, I, pp. 160–61. He writes that 'the English themselves, by the accession of Edward, were delivered for ever from the dominion of foreigners' (p. 161). Sunderland (*op. cit.*, pp. 321–2) makes this a definitely antimonarchical subject. As a subject it could be read more than one way.

15 Hume, *op. cit.*, II, p. 142.

16 A drawing for this is in the Vorarlberger Landesmuseum, Bregenz, rep. *Angelika Kauffmann und ihre Zeitgenossen,* Vorarlberger Landesmuseum, Bregenz and Österreichisches Museum für angewandte Kunst, Vienna, 1969, p. 76 (80a), pl. 232.

17 Rapin-Thoyras, *op. cit.*, I, pp. 96–111.

18 T. S. R. Boase, 'Macklin and Bowyer', *JWCI*, XXVI, pp. 170–74.

19 On Boydell see T. S. R. Boase, 'Illustrations of Shakespeare's Plays in the Seventeenth and Eighteenth Centuries', *JWCI*, X, 1947, pp. 94ff.; W. Moelwyn Merchant, *Shakespeare and the Artist*, London, 1959 (with an appendix giving locations of Boydell paintings as then known); Winifred H. Friedman, 'Some Commercial Aspects of the Boydell Shakespeare Gallery', *JWCI*, XXXVI, 1973, pp. 396–401; Hans Hammelman, *Book Illustrators in Eighteenth-Century England*, ed. T. S. R. Boase, Yale U.P., 1975, pp. 8–9; Winifred H. Friedman, *Boydell's Shakespeare Gallery*, Garland reprint, Harvard U.P., 1976, thesis.

20 For Bowyer see Boase, 'Macklin and Bowyer', *op. cit.*, pp. 174ff.

21 Mary Webster, *Francis Wheatley*, London, 1970, p. 147 (98), fig. 129; p. 178 (E 110).

22 David Irwin, *English Neoclassical Art*, London, 1966; and, more particularly, *Romantic Art in Britain, Paintings and Drawings 1760–1860*, Detroit Institute of Arts and Philadelphia Museum of Art, 1968.

23 Hume, *op. cit.*, III, p. 227.

24 Boase, 'Macklin and Bowyer', *op. cit.*, p. 177. Ada Earland, *John Opie and his Circle*, London, 1911, p. 335. Engraved W. Bromley, 1800.

25 David Irwin, 'Gavin Hamilton: Archaeologist, Painter and Dealer', *Art Bulletin*, XLIV, 1962, pp. 87–102.

26 Dora Wiebenson, 'Subjects from Homer's Iliad in Neoclassical Art', *Art Bulletin*, XLVI, 1964, pp. 29–30; *Romantic Art in Britain, op. cit.*, pp. 46–7, no. 11.

27 Frances A. Yates, *The Valois Tapestries*, London, 1959, p. 21, pl. II(b).

28 Charles Mitchell, 'Benjamin West's "Death of General Wolfe" and the Popular History Piece', *JWCI*, VII, 1944, pp. 20–33.

29 John Galt, *The Life, Studies and Works of Benjamin West*, London, 1820, p. 48.

30 Allen Staley, 'The Landing of Agripinna at Brundisium with the Ashes of Germanicus', *Bulletin, Philadelphia Museum of Art*, LXI, no. 287–8, 1965–6, pp. 10–19; *Romantic Art in Britain, op. cit.*, pp. 98–9 (49).

31 The list of works in Galt, *op. cit.*, pp. 216–34 contains not only the many versions and sketches of several of the pictures but also other subjects from British history: King John and the barons with Magna Carta; the death of Sir Philip Sidney; the destruction of the Spanish Armada; the pardoning of John by his brother King Henry.

32 Henry Angelo, *Reminiscences*, London, 1904 ed., I, pp. 152–3.

33 Jules Prown, *John Singleton Copley, 1774–1815*, Washington D.C./Cambridge, Mass., 1966.

34 *Ibid.*, I, pp. 342ff.

35 *Ibid.*, II, p. 349 note 25, from the Assembly Minutes of the Royal Academy, II, pp. 77–8, 10 December 1779. Here Copley intercedes to save, from the old House of Lords building which was about to be demolished, some tapestries 'supposed to represent with uncommon truth and accuracy the costume, civil, religious and military, of the Country about the period of the fourteenth century; a Work of incalculable use to Artists . . .'.

36 On the historical novel see Avram Fleishman, *The English Historical Novel. Walter Scott to Virginia Woolf*, Johns Hopkins U.P., 1971, pp. 37ff.; George Lukács, *The Historical Novel*, London, 1969 ed., pp. 15ff.

37 Martin Kemp, 'Scott and Delacroix, with Some Assistance from Hugo and Bonington' in *Scott Bicentenary Essays*, ed. Alan Bell, Edinburgh, 1973, pp. 213–27.

38 Quoted by Hale, *op. cit.*, p. 36.

39 On which see Fleishman, *op. cit.*; J. C. Simmons, 'Of Kettledrums and Trumpets: The Early Victorian Followers of Scott', *Studies in Scottish Literature*, VI, 1965, pp. 47–59.

40 S. M. Ellis, *The Solitary Horseman or the Life and Adventures of G. P. R. James*, London, 1927.

41 Curtis Dahl, 'History on the Hustings: Bulwer-Lytton's Historical Novels of Politics' in *From Jane Austen to Joseph Conrad, Essays collected in Memory of James T. Hillhouse*, ed. Robert C. Rathburn and Martin Steinmann, Jr, University of Minnesota Press, 1958, pp. 60–71.

42 G. P. Gooch, *History and Historians in the Nineteenth Century*, London, 1913; Grant, *op. cit.*, pp. xxxixff., 192ff.; Hale, *op. cit.*, pp. 39ff., 197ff.; Emery Neff, *The Poetry of History*, Cambridge U.P., 1967; Jerome Hamilton Buckley, *The Triumph of Time. A Study of the Victorian Concepts of Time, History, Progress, and Decadence*, Harvard U.P., 1967, especially chapter II; *The Varieties of History, from Voltaire to the Present*, ed. Fritz Stern, 1972 ed., pp. 16–20; Olive Anderson, 'The Political Uses of History in mid-nineteenth-century England', *Past and Present*, 36, 1967, pp. 87–105.

43 Valerie E. Chancellor, *History for their Masters*, Bath, 1970.

44 John Lingard, *The History of England*, London, 5th ed., 1849, I, pp. xxvii–xxviii.

45 Peter Conrad, *The Victorian Treasure-House*, London, 1973, especially chapter II.

46 This phenomenon needs greater research, particularly the interrelationship of literature, theatre and the visual arts. A study similar to the present one devoted to theatrical productions could be equally revealing.

47 George Craik and Charles MacFarlane, *The Pictorial History of England* (1837–44). The introduction states that it is 'enriched with appropriate woodcuts . . . copied from illuminated manuscripts of the period to which they belong . . . views of scenes . . . taken from prints or drawings as near the period as could be obtained . . . portraits and facsimiles . . . and, here and there, cuts from historical pictures' (the latter include Fuseli's *Caractacus*, Stothard's *Boadicea*, Tresham's *St Augustine preaching*, Smirke's *Canute rebuking the Courtiers*, etc.).

48 T. S. R. Boase, 'The Decoration of the New Palace of Westminster', *JWCI*, XVII, 1954, pp. 319–58.

49 Based on an analysis of the lists in Algernon Graves, *The Royal Academy of Arts*, London, 1905–6.

50 Andrew Shirley, *Bonington*, London, 1940; *R. P. Bonington, 1802–1828*, Castle Museum and Art Gallery, Nottingham, 1965 (ed. Marion Spencer).

51 Quoted by W. T. Whitley, *Art in England*, 1820–37, Cambridge, 1930, p. 147.

52 Robert Rosenblum, 'Painting under Napoleon, 1789–1799' in *French Painting 1774–1830: The Age of Revolution*, Grand Palais, Paris, Detroit Institute of Arts, Metropolitan Museum of Art, New York, 1975, pp. 168ff.

53 Robert Rosenblum, *Ingres*, London, 1967, pp. 12ff., and commentaries on pls. 22, 26, 27 and 29.

54 Henri Delaborde and J. Goddé, *Oeuvre de Paul Delaroche*, Paris, 1858.

55 Whitley, *op. cit.*, p. 246. Scott, of course, knew Wilkie: Carola Oman, *The Wizard of the North, The Life of Sir Walter Scott*, London, 1973, p. 282.

56 C. R. Leslie, *Autobiographical Recollections*, ed. Tom Taylor, London, 1860, I, p. xxv; II, pp. 106, 111.

57 Martin Butlin and Evelyn Joll, *The Paintings of J. M. W. Turner*, Yale U.P., 1977, I, p. 173 (338).

58 Graham Reynolds, *Victorian Painting*, London, 1966, p. 111.

59 Robert Rosenblum, *Transformations in Late Eighteenth-Century Art*, Princeton U.P., 1967, and the same author's 'Painting under Napoleon, 1789–1799' and 'Painting During the Bourbon Restoration' in *French Painting 1774–1830: The Age of Revolution*, *op. cit.*, pp. 161–73, 231–44.

60 As quoted in *The Varieties of History*, ed. Fritz Stern, New York, 1973 ed., p. 15.

The Recreation of the Past

1 The following account is based on Joan Evans, *A History of the Society of Antiquaries*, Oxford, 1956.

2 Horace Walpole to Cole, September 1778, quoted *ibid.*, p. 155.

3 *Ibid.*, p. 42.

4 Robert Raines and Kenneth Sharpe, 'The Story of King Charles I: Part I', *Connoisseur*, CLXXXIV, 1973, p. 46.

5 Reynolds to Lord Hardwick, concerning a proposal for a picture on the subject of the interview between James II and the Duke of Monmouth, 5 March 1783, quoted in Frederick W. Hilles, *The Literary Career of Sir Joshua Reynolds*, Cambridge, 1936, pp. 101–2.

6 In Henry Hallam's *The Principles which may regulate the selection of subjects for painting in the Palace of Westminster* it was stipulated that the subjects should reveal the human form 'to a considerable extent uncovered', with the result that the 1843 competition subject-matter never passed the Plantagenet period. 'If', Hallam wrote, '[an artist] is compelled to exhibit modern dress, the naked form is entirely hid, and the drapery is already disposed by the tailor' (*Parliamentary Papers*, 1844, XXI, p. 189).

7 On Strutt see *Dictionary of National Biography* and the introduction to the 1903 edition of his *Sports and Pastimes of the People of England*.

8 Joseph Strutt, *The Regal and Ecclesiastical Antiquities of England . . .*, London, 1773, title page.

9 *Ibid.*, p. 26 and note.

10 *Ibid.*, p. iii.

11 Joseph Strutt, *A Complete View of the Dress and Habits of the People of England*, ed. J. R. Planché, London, 1842, I, p. vii.

12 J. R. Planché, *History of British Costume*, The Library of Entertaining Knowledge, London, 1834, p. xii.

13 *Ibid.*, p. xi.

14 *Ibid.*, p. 198, compiled from Strutt, *Dress and Habits, op. cit.*, II, pls. CXVIII, CXIX. Other figures lifted and adapted from the same source are p. 116 from pl. XCVIII (redrawn and with a head reversed); p. 132 from pl. XCVI; p. 188 from pl. XCIII; p. 201 from pl. CXXVII; p. 206 from pls. CXXII, CXXIII; p. 218 from pl. CXXIV (reversed); p. 220 from pl. CXXXVIII; p. 230 from pl. CXXXV; and from *Regal and Ecclesiastical Antiquities* p. 190 from pl. XLIII; p. 199 from pl. XLVII.

15 F. W. Fairholt, *Costume in England. A History of Dress from the Earliest Period until the Close of the Eighteenth Century*, London, 1860 ed., preface.

16 The following are from *Dress and Habits*: p. 161 from II, pl. CXXXII; p. 142 from pl. LXXVI and pl. XCIII with one figure reversed; p. 183 from pls. CXXXII, CXXVIII; p. 136 from pl. XCIV; p. 89 from pl. LXII; and from *Regal and Ecclesiastical Antiquities*, p. 168 from pl. XXXIII; p. 110 from pl. XIX.

17 Fairholt, *op. cit.*, p. 142.

18 Alfred John Kempe, *Introduction and Descriptions for Stothard's Monumental Effigies of Great Britain*, 1832.

19 Francis Grose, *A Treatise on Ancient Armour and Weapons . . .*, London, 1786, sig. A2.

20 Samuel Rush Meyrick and Charles Hamilton Smith, *The Costume of the Original Inhabitants of the British Islands, from the earliest periods to the sixth century*, London, 1815.

21 Samuel Rush Meyrick, *A Critical Inquiry into Antient Armour, as it existed in Europe, but particularly in England, from the Norman Conquest to the Reign of King Charles II*, London, 1842 ed., preface, pp. x, xii–xiii. Meyrick, of course, denounces Grose's work.

22 *Ibid., loc. cit.*, where he expresses gratitude to Scott for information on Scottish armour and refers to him as 'his good friend'.

23 Roger Smith, 'Bonnard's *Costume Historique* – a Pre-Raphaelite Source Book', *Costume*, VII, 1973, pp. 28–37.

24 Leonée Ormond, 'Dress in the Painting of Dante Gabriel Rossetti', *Costume*, VIII, 1974, pp. 26–9.

25 W. M. Thackeray, *Critical Papers in Art, Stubbs' Calendar, Barber Cox*, London, 1904, p. 121.

26 *Ibid., loc. cit.*

27 *Ibid.*, p. 221.

28 J. R. Planché, *Recollections and Reflections*, London, 1872, I, pp. 225–6.

29 *Ibid.*, I, pp. 228–9.

30 *Ibid.*, I, p. 229.

31 *Ibid.*, I, p. 231.

32 *Ibid.*, I, pp. 332–3.

33 Many artists were dabbling with amateur theatricals, e.g. Frith, Millais and E. M. Ward designing costumes for them, as recorded in Mrs E. M. Ward, *Memories of Ninety Years*, ed. Isabel McAllister, n.d., p. 49. See p. 42 for Wilkie arranging historical tableaux from Scott's novels.

34 Evans, *op. cit.*, pp. 62–3.

35 *Ibid.*, p. 64.

36 *Art Journal*, XII, 1850, p. 68.

37 As quoted in Edmund Lodge, *Portraits of Illustrious Personages of Great Britain*, Bohn Edition, London, 1849–50, I, p. vii.

38 Richard and Samuel Redgrave, *A Century of British Painters*, London, 1947 ed., p. 339: 'he was able to dispose loose drapery on his model . . . as to enable him to represent his costume without the aid of the milliner'.

39 Information kindly communicated by Mr Richard Ormond.

40 *Specimens of Ancient Furniture drawn from existing authorities by Henry Shaw F.S.A., with descriptions by Sir Samuel Rush Meyrick K.H.*, London, 1836, prospectus.

41 *Daniel Maclise, 1806–1870*, Arts Council Exhibition, National Portrait Gallery, London and National Gallery of Ireland, Dublin, 1972 (catalogue and introduction by Richard Ormond), p. 95 (100).

42 C. K. Adams and W. S. Lewis, 'The Portraits of Horace Walpole', *Walpole Society*, XLII, 1970, p. 25 (B7).

43 Joseph Nash, *The Mansions of England in the Olden Time*, ed. J. Corbet Anderson, 1869–72, II, quoting Nash: 'I have carefully abstained from introducing any subject that is not a genuine specimen of the style peculiar to its age . . . The figures introduced, both as regards their costumes and occupations, are all from authority; and the object of their introduction has been not merely an eye to pictorial effect, but a desire to identify the characters and habits of a people that have now passed away, and to represent, in its various peculiarities, the very age and body of the time.'

44 See *Dictionary of National Biography*, s.v. Cattermole.

45 Dated 1 March 1851; quoted by Ford M. Hueffer, *Ford Madox Brown: A Record of His Life and Work*, London, 1896, I, p. 72. Kindly communicated by Mr Richard Ormond.

46 Quoted in *Romantic Art in Britain, Paintings and Drawings 1760–1860*, Detroit Institute of Arts and Philadelphia Museum of Art, 1968, p. 297.

47 Letter to J. Comyns Carr, 1873, quoted by Richard and Leonée Ormond, *Lord Leighton*, Yale U.P., 1973, p. 85.

Conclusion: Decline and Eclipse

1 G. A. Storey, *Sketches from Memory*, London, 1899, p. 250.

2 *Ibid., loc. cit.*

3 As quoted in *The Varieties of History*, ed. Fritz Stern, New York, 1973 ed., p. 15.

Part II: Recreators and Recreations

Benjamin West

1 John Galt, *The Life, Studies and Works of Benjamin West*, London, 1820; Alfred Neumeyer, 'The Early Historical Paintings of Benjamin West', *Burlington Magazine*, LXXIII, 1938, pp. 162–5; Charles Mitchell, 'Benjamin West's "Death of General Wolfe" and the Popular History Piece', *JWCI*, VII, 1944, pp. 20–33; Edgar Wind, 'Penny, West and "The Death of General Wolfe"', *JWCI*, X, 1947, pp. 159–62; James T. Flexner, 'Benjamin West's American Neo-Classicism', *The New York Historical Society Quarterly*, XXXVI, 1952, pp. 4–41; Grose Evans, *Benjamin West and the Taste of his Times*, Illinois U.P., 1959; Allen Staley, 'The Landing of Agripinna at Brundisium with the Ashes of Germanicus', *Bulletin, Philadelphia Museum of Art*, LXI, no. 287–8, 1965–6, pp. 10–19.

2 Oliver Millar, *Later Georgian Pictures in the Collection of Her Majesty the Queen*, London, 1969, I, nos. 1158–66; David Irwin, *English Neoclassical Art*, London, 1966, pp. 95–6.

3 Henry Angelo, *Reminiscences*, London, 1904 ed., I, pp. 152–3.

4 Galt, *op. cit.*, II, p. 72.

5 *Ibid.*, II, p. 52.

6 Information kindly supplied by Mr Claude Blair.

7 Elias Ashmole, *The Institution, Laws & Ceremonies of the Most Noble Order of the Garter*, London, 1672, p. 186: 'In this *Roll* are divers things mentioned to be adorned with *Garters*, which were provided against the first grand Feast of St. George, and among the rest are *Robes* for the *Sovereign* of the *Order*; namely his *Mantle, Surcoat*, and *Hood* . . . adorned with embroidered *Garters*, containing the Motto, *Honi soit qui mal y pense*'.

8 Joseph Strutt, *Honda Angel-cynnan or, A compleat View of the Manners, Customs, Arms, Habits, etc. of the Inhabitants of England, from the Arrival of the Saxons till the Reign of Henry the Eighth*, London, 1774–6, II, p. 32.

9 *Ibid.*, II, pp. 42–3.

10 J. T. Smith, *Nollekens and His Times*, London, 1828, II, p. 384.

Richard Parkes Bonington

1 Albert Dubuisson and C. E. Hughes, *Richard Parkes Bonington*, London, 1924; Roger Fry, 'Bonington and French Art', *Burlington Magazine*, LI, 1927, pp. 268–74; Andrew Shirley, *Bonington*, London, 1940; A. P. Oppé, *Burlington Magazine*, LXXIX, 1941, pp. 99–101; *R. P. Bonington, 1802–1828*, Castle Museum and Art Gallery, Nottingham, 1965 (ed. Marion Spencer); Martin Hardie, *Water-colour Painting in Britain*, II, *The Romantic Period*, ed. Dudley Snelgrove with Jonathan Mayne and Basil Taylor, London, 1967, pp. 173ff.

2 Robert Rosenblum, *Ingres*, London, 1967, pp. 12–13, figs. 5 and 6; for the various versions of Ingres's painting see Emilio Radius and Ettore Camesasca, *L'Opera Completa di Ingres*, Milan, 1968, no. 93.

William Powell Frith

1 W. P. Frith, *My Autobiography and Reminiscences*, London, 1887; *An Exhibition of Paintings by William Powell Frith, R.A., 1819–1909*, Corporation Art Gallery, Harrogate and Whitechapel Art Gallery, London, 1951 (catalogue with introduction by Jonathan Mayne).

2 Frith, *op. cit.*, I, pp. 185ff.

3 F. W. Fairholt, *Costume in England*, London, 1860 ed., p. 208.

4 *Ibid.*, p. 198.

5 *Ibid.*, p. 192.

6 Frith, *op. cit.* I, p. 96.

7 *Costumes Français, depuis Clovis jusqu'à nos jours*, Paris, 1838, II, opp. p. 72.

8 Frith, *op. cit.*, I, pp. 305–6.

9 John Evelyn, *Diary*, 6 February 1685.

10 Oliver Millar, *The Queen's Pictures*, London, 1977, p. 190.

11 Evelyn, *Diary*, 2 March 1671, which Ward quotes.

Part III: Themes and Obsessions

The Anglo-Saxons

1 M. H. Spielman, *The Work of G. F. Watts*, Pall Mall Gazette Extra, 1886; H. Macmillan, *The Life and Work of George Frederick Watts, R.A.*, London, 1903; M. S. Watts, *George Frederick Watts*, London, 1912; see *G. F. Watts. A Nineteenth-Century Phenomenon*, Whitechapel Art Gallery, London, 1974 (chosen by John Gage, introduction by Chris Muller), appendix I for bibliography.

2 Watts, *op. cit.*, I, pp. 76ff.

3 John Lingard, *The History of England*, London, 5th ed., 1849, I, p. xiv.

4 David Hume, *The History of England*, Edinburgh, 1818 ed., I, pp. 76ff.

5 For Bowyer's Historic Gallery: Mary Webster, *Francis Wheatley*, London, 1970, p. 147 (98).

6 *Paintings and Drawings by Sir David Wilkie, R.A., 1785–1841*, National Gallery of Scotland, Edinburgh and Royal Academy, London, 1958 (catalogue and introduction by John Woodward), p. 23 (29).

7 Avram Fleishman, *The English Historical Novel. Walter Scott to Virginia Woolf*, Johns Hopkins U.P., 1971, pp. 56–7.

8 In *Ivanhoe*, Scott type-cast them thus: 'It seemed to the author that the existence of the two races in the same country, the vanquished distinguished by their plain, homely, blunt manners, and the free spirit infused by their ancient institutions and laws; the victors, by the high spirit of military fame, personal adventure, and whatever could distinguish them as the Flower of Chivalry, might, intermixed with other characters belonging to the same time and country, interest the reader by the contrast, if the author should not fail on his part' (*The Waverley Novels*, Edinburgh, 1879 ed., XVI, *Ivanhoe*, I, p. 5). See also Christopher Hill, 'The Norman Yoke' in *Democracy and Labour: Essays in Honour of Donna Torr*, ed. John Saville, 1954, pp. 11–66.

9 Quoted by Derek Beales, *From Castlereagh to Gladstone*, New York, 1969, p. 58.

10 Olive Anderson, 'The Political Uses of History in mid-nineteenth-century England', *Past and Present*, 36, 1967, pp. 87–105.

11 J. M. Kemble, *The Saxons in England*, London, 1849, I, pp. v–vi.

12 *Centenary Exhibition of the Work of William Dyce, R.A. (1806–1864)*, Aberdeen Art Gallery and Thomas Agnew & Sons, London, 1964 (catalogue and introduction by Charles Carter).

13 *The Late Richard Dadd 1817–1886*, Arts Council Exhibition, Tate Gallery, etc., 1974–5 (catalogue and introduction by Patricia Allderidge), p. 54 (40).

14 R. J. B. Walker, *A Catalogue of paintings, drawings, sculpture and engravings in the Palace of Westminster*, 1962 (typescript), part IV, pp. 28–9.

15 *Millais*, Walker Art Gallery, Liverpool and Royal Academy, London, 1967 (catalogue and introduction by Mary Bennett), p. 22 (6).

16 Kenneth Romney Towndrow, *The Works of Alfred Stevens in the Tate Gallery*, London, 1950, p. 67 (72) and related studies (nos. 73–9).

17 *Daniel Maclise, 1806–1870*, Arts Council Exhibition, National Portrait Gallery, London and National Gallery of Ireland, Dublin, 1972 (catalogue and introduction by Richard Ormond), pp. 97–8 (102).

18 Walker, *op. cit.*, part IV, p. 75. See also the entry by Allen Staley on Ford Madox Brown's *The Body of Harold brought before William the Conqueror (Wilhelmus Conquistador)* (1844–61, Manchester City Art Gallery) in *Romantic Art in Britain, Paintings and Drawings 1760–1860*, Detroit Institute of Arts and Philadelphia Museum of Art, 1968, pp. 296–8 (210).

The Princes in the Tower

1 M. H. Spielman, *Millais and His Works*, Edinburgh and London, 1898; John Guille Millais, *The Life and Letters of Sir John Everett Millais*, London, 1899; Mary Lutyens, *Millais and the Ruskins*, London, 1967; *Millais*, Walker Art Gallery, Liverpool and Royal Academy, London, 1967 (catalogue and introduction by Mary Bennett).

2 Spielman, *op. cit.*, p. 134 (150); Millais, *op. cit.*, II, pp. 88, 91, 102; Bennett, *op. cit.*, p. 55 (93).

3 On the historiography of the murder of the Princes in the Tower see Paul Murray Kendall, *Richard III*, London, 1955, p. 393ff.; *Richard III*, National Portrait Gallery, London, 1973 (catalogue by Pamela Tudor-Craig), pp. 51–4.

4 David Hume, *The History of England*, Edinburgh, 1818 ed., III, pp. 271–2.

5 Winifred H. Friedman, *Boydell's Shakespeare Gallery*, Garland reprint, Harvard U.P., 1976, pp. 164–5, 230–31.

6 Hume, *op. cit.*, III, p. 280.

7 T. S. R. Boase, 'Macklin and Bowyer', *JWCI*, XXVI, 1963, p. 177.

8 Friedman, *op. cit.*, *loc. cit.*

9 On which see *French Painting 1774–1830: The Age of Revolution*, Grand Palais, Paris, Detroit Institute of Arts, Metropolitan Museum of Art, New York, 1975, pp. 389–90 (44) and bibliography. Replica in the Wallace Collection, London.

Lady Jane Grey

1 See p. 170, note 54.

2 See Cecil Gould, *Delaroche and Gautier. Gautier's Views on the Execution of Lady Jane Grey and on other compositions by Paul Delaroche*, National Gallery, London, 1975.

3 See the most recent biography, Hester W. Chapman, *Lady Jane Grey*, London, 1962, pp. 204ff.

4 For a short account of later attitudes see *ibid.*, pp. 173–4.

5 Gilbert Burnet, *The History of the Reformation of the Church of England*, Oxford, 1829, II, pp. 469–70.

6 T. S. R. Boase, 'Macklin and Bowyer', *JWCI*, XXVI, 1963, p. 177.

7 Jules Prown, *John Singleton Copley, 1774–1815*, Washington D.C./Cambridge, Mass., 1966, II, p. 376.

8 George Scharf, *A Descriptive and Historical Catalogue of the Collection of Pictures at Woburn Abbey*, 1890, pp. 247–8; C. R. Leslie, *Autobiographical Recollections*, ed. Tom Taylor, London, 1860, II, pp. 181–2.

9 See list, p. 161.

10 See p. 173, note 17 for bibliography on Victorian concepts of womanhood.

11 Maria, Lady Callcott, *Little Arthur's History of England*, London, 1955 ed., pp. 163–4. Original edition 1835.

12 Agnes Strickland, *Lives of the Tudor Princesses*, London, 1868, p. 94.

Mary Queen of Scots

1 The best account of Allan is that in the *Dictionary of National Biography*.
2 *Catalogue of Paintings and Sculpture*, National Gallery of Scotland, Edinburgh, 1957 ed., p. 15 (1677).
3 See Antonia Fraser, *Mary Queen of Scots*, London, 1969, pp. 250ff., for the most recent account of the celebrated murder.
4 James Emerson Phillips, *Images of a Queen. Mary Stuart in Sixteenth-Century Literature*, University of California Press, 1964.
5 Antonia Fraser, 'Mary Queen of Scots and the Historians', *Royal Stuart Society Papers*, VII, 1974.
6 See p. xx. The picture was engraved by Francis Legat and published by Boydell. Dr Johnson provided the inscription beneath: 'Mary, Queen of Scots, harassed, terrified and over-powered by insults, menaces and clamours of her rebellious subjects, sets her hand, with tears and confusion, to a resignation of the kingdom' (J. T. Smith, *Nollekens and His Times*, London, 1829, II, pp. 284–5).
7 John Jope Rogers, *Opie and His Works*, London, 1878, pp. 191–3; Ada Earland, *John Opie and His Circle*, London, 1911, pp. 333–4.
8 On Scott and Mary see Avram Fleishman, *The English Historical Novel. Walter Scott to Virginia Woolf*, Johns Hopkins U.P., 1971, pp. 61–2.
9 George Chalmers, *The Life of Mary, Queen of Scots*, London, 1822, I, preface.
10 Carola Oman, *The Wizard of the North. The Life of Sir Walter Scott*, London, 1973, p. 256.
11 *The Waverley Novels*, Edinburgh, 1895 ed., XXI, *The Monastery*, pp. 5–6. Scott actually did not privately subscribe to the cult of the Queen, and refused to write a biography of her: 'and that I decidedly would not do, because my opinion, in point of fact, is contrary both to the popular feeling and my own' (Oman, *op. cit.*, p. 333).
12 See list, pp. 162–3.
13 *Paintings and Drawings by Sir David Wilkie, R.A., 1785–1841*, National Gallery of Scotland and Royal Academy, 1958 (catalogue and introduction by John Woodward), p. 46 (105).
14 *Ibid.*, p. 43 (90–91).
15 W. P. Frith, *My Autobiography and Reminiscences*, London, 1887, I, p. 110.
16 *Ford Madox Brown, 1821–1893*, Walker Art Gallery, Liverpool, etc.,

1964–5 (catalogue with introduction by Mary Bennett), p. 11. (3). The finished picture is lost.
17 This account of the Victorian concepts of the lady and of womanhood is based on: Robert Palfrey Utter and Gwendolyn Bridges Needham, *Pamela's Daughters*, London, 1937; Patricia Thomson, *The Victorian Heroine. A Changing Ideal*, London, 1956; Kate Millett, 'The Debate over Women: Ruskin versus Mill', *Victorian Studies*, XIV, 1970, pp. 63–71; *Suffer and Be Still. Women in the Victorian Age*, ed. Martha Vicinus, Indiana U.P., 1973.
18 Agnes Strickland, *Lives of the Queens of Scotland &c.*, Edinburgh and London, 1852, III, p. 223.

Cavaliers and Roundheads

1 M. H. Stephen-Smith, *Art and Anecdotes: Recollections of William Yeames*, London, 1927.
2 *Ibid.*, pp. 171–4.
3 See pp. 32–3.
4 David Hume, *The History of England*, Edinburgh, 1818 ed., VI, p. 465.
5 See *The History of Great Britain. The Reigns of James I and Charles I*, ed. Duncan Forbes, Harmondsworth, 1970, introduction.
6 Hume, *op. cit.*, VI, pp. 468–9.
7 On Scott and the Cavaliers see Avram Fleishman, *The English Historical Novel. Walter Scott to Virginia Woolf*, Johns Hopkins U.P., 1971, pp. 64ff.
8 *The Waverley Novels*, Edinburgh, 1879 ed., XXXIX, *Woodstock*, II, pp. 83–4.
9 *Daniel Maclise, 1806–1870*, Arts Council Exhibition, National Portrait Gallery, London and National Gallery of Ireland, Dublin, 1972 (catalogue and introduction by Richard Ormond), pp. 62–3 (68).
10 Roy Strong, *Van Dyck. Charles I on Horseback*, London, 1972, pp. 36ff.
11 F. Guizot, *History of the English Revolution of 1640*, transl. William Hazlitt, London, 1845, pp. xvi–xvii.
12 See R. J. B. Walker, *A Catalogue of paintings, drawings, sculpture and engravings in the Palace of Westminster*, 1962 (typescript), part IV, pp. 17ff., appendix IV, p. 167.
13 Henry Hallam, *The Constitutional History of England*, London, Everyman ed., 1913, II, p. 126.
14 Henry Hallam, *View of the State of Europe during the Middle Ages*, London, 1878 ed., II, p. 269.
15 *Victorian Engravings*, Victoria & Albert Museum, London, 1973 (catalogue and introduction by Hilary Beck), p. 65 (45).
16 Stephen-Smith, *op. cit.*, pp. 173–4.

Oliver Cromwell

1 Ford M. Hueffer, *Ford Madox Brown: A Record of his Life and Work*, London, 1896; *Ford Madox Brown, 1821–1893*, Walker Art Gallery, Liverpool, etc., 1964–5 (catalogue with introduction by Mary Bennett).
2 Bennett, *op. cit.*, p. 26 (42); *Catalogue of the Lady Lever Gallery, Port Sunlight*, 1928, p. 87 (21).
3 Hueffer, *op. cit.*, pp. 290–92.
4 *Ibid.*, p. 315.
5 *Ibid.*, p. 311.
6 On the historiography of Oliver Cromwell see Wilbur Cortez Abbott, 'The Fame of Oliver Cromwell' in *Conflicts with Oblivion*, London, 1935, pp. 151–80; Maurice Ashley, *The Greatness of Oliver Cromwell*, London, 1957, pp. 12–22; *Great Lives Observed, Cromwell*, ed. Maurice Ashley, Englewood Cliffs, N. J., 1969.
7 Ashley, *Great Lives, op. cit.*, p. 127.
8 *The Waverley Novels*, Edinburgh, 1879 ed., XXXIX, *Woodstock*, I, pp. 202–4.
9 Thomas Carlyle, *Oliver Cromwell's Letters and Speeches*, London, 1887 ed., I, p. 4.
10 See T. W. Mason, 'Nineteenth-Century Cromwell', *Past and Present*, 40, 1968, pp. 187–9; J. P. D. Dunbabin, 'Oliver Cromwell's Popular Image in Nineteenth-Century England' in *Britain and the Netherlands*, ed. J. S. Bromley and E. H. Kossman, V, The Hague, 1976, pp. 140–63.
11 Hueffer, *op. cit.*, p. 401.
12 W. J. Linton, *Memories*, London, 1895, p. 29.
13 J. H. Merle d'Aubigné, *The Protector: A Vindication*, Edinburgh, 1847, p. 134.

Epilogue: The Victorian Image

1 J. M. Kemble, *The Saxons in England*, London, 1849, I, p. v.
2 Spenser, *Faerie Queene*, I, introduction, iv.
3 Tennyson, 'On the Jubilee of Queen Victoria'.
4 Tennyson, 'A Welcome to Alexandra'.
5 Jerome Hamilton Buckley, *The Triumph of Time. A Study of the Victorian Concepts of Time, History, Progress, and Decadence*, Harvard U.P., 1967, p. 16.

Index

The index is to the main text of the book; the Appendix is not included. Page numbers in **bold type** refer to illustrations.